BUT WILL IT GET A LAUGH?

The Life of Doris Hare in Three Acts

Kate Crehan

Society for Theatre Research
London
2022

First published in 2022
by the Society for Theatre Research
Savile House, 4 Mansfield Road, Oxford, OX1 3TA

General Editor of STR Publications: Marion O'Connor
Volume Editors: Ann Featherstone and David Pattie

ISBN 978-0-85430-086-0

Typeset in Garamond Classic FS 12pt/14.3pt
by Leigh Forbes, Blot Publishing
www.blot.co.uk

Printed and bound by
Henry Ling Ltd., The Dorset Press, Dorchester DT1 1HD
www.henryling.co.uk

To the memory of Kate Tansley, theatrical matriarch

Theatre at its best is generous: actors give to audiences, and audiences respond. There's no more generous performer than Doris Hare. She makes you feel it's a pleasure to be alive and in the theatre.

Peter Hall
(Hall's tribute to Doris, 1977,
included in the programme for
her one-woman show, *Hare!*)

CONTENTS

ACKNOWLEDGEMENTS

Many people and institutions have contributed to the long process of writing this book. I am immensely grateful for their generosity and help. My sister, Susan Griffith, provided crucial help with the oral family history, filling in gaps in my own memory. Together we made a number of memorable trips to sites of Doris's youth. Others who provided significant facts about her career and allowed me to gain a richer understanding of her life as a performer, and what she meant to her audiences, include Vivyan Ellacott, Robert Ashby, Stephen Fry, Tony Warren, Anna Karen, Ray Cooney, John Hyslop, Craig Walker, Jo Stanley, Dafydd O'Connor, and Warrick Bell. I have benefitted from the knowledge and generosity of archivists at various libraries and archives: Steve Kings at Bargoed Library, Louise North and Trish Hayes at the BBC Written Archives, Jill Sullivan and the other archivists at the Bristol Theatre Archive, Liza Penn-Thomas and Susan Thomas at the Richard Burton Archives, Swansea University, Francis Younson at the Gwent Archives, Kathleen Dickson at the BFI, and the Sound archivists at the British Library. The support and encouragement of Shirley Lindenbaum and Roslyn Berstein, who read and commented on many drafts of the manuscript, was invaluable. The Biographers' Society provided further welcome encouragement by awarding me the Tony Lothian Prize in 2020. The Society for Theatre Research provided Doris's story with an ideal home. I thank Sophie Nield for suggesting them. At the Press, Marion O'Connor, Ann Featherstone, David Pattie and Trevor Griffiths helped refine my manuscript. I am also grateful to Kelsey Brewer and Leigh Forbes for their work on the illustrations.

NOTE ON SOURCES

My sister Sue and I grew up listening to our mother, Doris Hare, and her siblings' stories. They told us of our grandparents' portable theatre and their later lives as performers. This oral history was the starting point for this book. Some of the shorter quotations from my grandmother Kate Tansley (she also used my grandfather's stage name Breamer) and from Doris come from this family lore. Towards the end of her life, Doris lived in Wales with my sister. Her sisters Winnie and Betty would come for visits. During these years Sue tape-recorded a number of conversations with Doris, and a few with the three sisters. Unless otherwise indicated, the longer passages quoting them come from these tapes.

I learned a lot about Doris from Tony Warren. I first met him when he was trying to persuade her to accept a role in his new series *Coronation Street*. I quote from an interview that my sister and I recorded with him shortly before he died in 2016. I also quote from interviews with two of those with whom Doris worked, Anna Karen and Ray Cooney.

For much of the twentieth century Britain had innumerable local newspapers that published reviews of live entertainment, and later radio and television reviews. The British Newspaper Archive has now made many of these papers' archives available online. These have been invaluable, allowing me to trace the trajectory of Doris's career, and check her memory and the family lore against the documentary record. Citations for individual quotations are given in the notes. The BBC written and sound archives have been another important resource, as have the Richard Burton Archives at Swansea University and the University of Bristol Theatre Collection.

Doris was never much of a letter writer. She was acutely self-conscious about her rather ungainly handwriting, and writing was never a form of expression with which she felt completely comfortable, although she did keep a diary while she was living in America for a few months. But if she left little in the way of letters, she did leave a mass of photographs, documents and mementoes covering the Hare family's history and her own career. From quite early in her career, she kept scrapbooks into which she pasted anything that mentioned her. For many years she also subscribed to a newspaper cuttings service, but she let her subscription lapse in the 1950s, around the time the scrapbooks peter out. While these scrapbooks are a wonderful resource, they can be frustrating since she often fails to note dates and sometimes publication details. Also useful were the family scrapbooks kept by her sister Winnie. The sister Doris was closest to, Betty, seems not to have kept scrapbooks, or if she did, they do not survive. After Doris's death, however, my sister discovered among her papers an exercise book in which, late in life, Betty had begun to record some recollections of her parents' portable theatre. Chapter 1 draws on this account.

As Doris' ninetieth birthday approached, my sister contacted a wide range of people Doris had worked with and asked them for a remembrance, which we then compiled into a Ninetieth Birthday Book. I have quoted from some of these remembrances.

To get a better sense of the appeal *On the Buses* has for its fans, in 2017 my sister and I attended a two-day reunion to celebrate the forty-fifth anniversary of the shooting of the third spinoff film, *Holiday on the Buses*. Organised by *Buses* fans, Craig Wright and Richard Coghill, it was held at the Pontins Holiday Camp (now Prestatyn Sands Holiday Park) in Prestatyn, where the location shots were filmed. Talking to the 100 or so assembled fans, and participating in the various events, helped illuminate something of the programme's enduring appeal.

In telling Doris's story I have been guided by the work of theatre historians and other scholars. Another significant resource has been theatrical biographies and memoirs. All sources are listed in the notes.

ILLUSTRATIONS

Where no copyright holder is named and acknowledged for an illustration, the image has been understood to be not in copyright. For material identified as Doris's personal possession, reproduction right in the originals is held by the author, Kate Crehan, and her sister, Susan Griffith.

Fig. 22 – An actress sings 'Three White Feathers' to her future husband as she waits to be presented at Court, *Words and Music*, 1932
Photographer Unknown. Reproduced from Doris's copy of *The Play Pictorial*, November 1932.

Fig. 23 – Doris broadcasting for NBC, 1937
Photographer Unknown.

Fig. 24 – Bertie Hare in pantomime
Credit: University of Bristol Theatre Collection/ArenaPAL.

Fig. 25 – Bertie Hare as a soldier, c.1945.
Credit: University of Bristol Theatre Collection/ArenaPAL.

Fig. 26 – Doris as a reluctant evacuee in *Lights Up!*, 1940
Reproduced by permission of Punch Cartoon Library / TopFoto

Fig. 27 – Doris at the Merchant Navy Club, 1943
© BBC Archive.

Fig. 28 – Norman Mansbridge cartoon showing the response of some officers to Doris's signature opening to *Shipmates Ashore*, c.1943
Reproduced, from original in the British Cartoon Archive, Templeman Library, University of Kent, by permission of the Estate of Norman Mansbridge.

Fig. 29 – Doris's NUS membership card issued in 1942
Doris's personal possession.

Fig. 30 – The *On the Buses* Core Cast, 1969
Credit: © Keystone Press / Alamy Stock Photo.

Fig. 31 – Donald McGill postcard, 'Astonishing the Natives', 1933
Copyright © Donald McGill Archive www.donaldmcgill.co.uk.

Fig. 32 – Doris and Wilfred Bramble in *Holiday on the Buses*, 1973
Copyright © Mary Evans / STUDIOCANAL FILMS LTD / Alamy Stock Photo.

Fig. 33 – Lenare Studio portrait of Doris at home in 1947, with her husband, John Fraser Roberts, elder daughter, Susan, and the author.
Lenare Studio, photographer unknown.

Fig. 34 – Doris and Leslie Henson as the Common Man and his Wife in *1066 and All That*, 1947
Photographer Unknown. Reproduced from Doris's copy of *Theatre World*, June 1947.

Fig. 35 – Doris as Granny Tooke in *Valmouth* in the original 1958 production
Copyright© David Sim Estate /Arena PAL.

Fig. 36 – BBC2's *Old Boys Network* line-up, 1981
Copyright© PA Images / Alamy Stock Photo.

Fig. 37 – Doris and Patrick Magee in the Royal Shakespeare Company's 1964 production of David Rudkin's *Afore Night Come*
Photographer Zoë Dominic. Copyright © ZOË DOMINIC / Catherine Ashmore.

Fig. 38 – *A Horse! A Horse!* (1954) with Doris, Hugh Wakefield, and (working the horse's head) Harold Pinter
Photographer Unknown. Print owned by Doris.

Fig. 39 – Doris and Bryan Pringle in the Royal Shakespeare Company's production of Harold Pinter's *The Birthday Party*, 1964
Copyright © David Sim Estate/ ArenaPAL.

Fig. 40 – John Gielgud's note to Doris congratulating her on her performance in *The Birthday Party*, 29 June 1964
Copyright © the Sir John Gielgud Charitable Trust. Reproduced by permission of the trustees.

Fig. 41 – Doris the serious actress, 1977
Polaroid taken by unknown photographer in the course of filming *Shooting the Chandelier*.

Fig. 42 – Doris opening the cinema at Springbok Training Centre for Merchant Seamen in 1949
Photographer Unknown. Print owned by Doris.

HARE FAMILY GENEALOGY

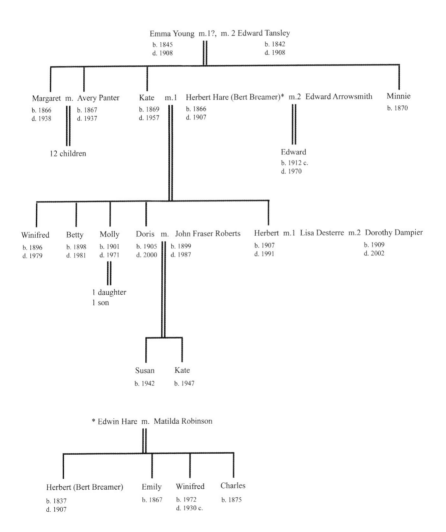

Emma Young m.1?, m. 2 Edward Tansley
b. 1845   b. 1842
d. 1908   d. 1908

Margaret m. Avery Panter   Kate   m.1   Herbert Hare (Bert Breamer)* m.2 Edward Arrowsmith   Minnie
b. 1866   b. 1867   b. 1869   b. 1866   b. 1870
d. 1938   d. 1937   d. 1957   d. 1907

12 children

Edward
b. 1912 c.
d. 1970

Winifred   Betty   Molly   Doris   m.   John Fraser Roberts   Herbert m.1 Lisa Desterre m.2 Dorothy Dampier
b. 1896   b. 1898   b. 1901   b. 1905   b. 1899   b. 1907   b. 1909
d. 1979   d. 1981   d. 1971   d. 2000   d. 1987   d. 1991   d. 2002

1 daughter
1 son

Susan   Kate
b. 1942   b. 1947

* Edwin Hare m. Matilda Robinson

Herbert (Bert Breamer)   Emily   Winifred   Charles
b. 1837   b. 1867   b. 1972   b. 1875
d. 1907   d. 1930 c.

ACT ONE:

MASTERING HER CRAFT

CHAPTER 1: A FAMILY BUSINESS

Doris was straight out of a prop basket,
shaken up, dusted down and ready to go on.
Tony Warren (creator of *Coronation Street*)

I was once in Sarajevo and needed a place to stay overnight. It was the early 1970s, before the breakup of Communist-run Yugoslavia, and all tourist accommodation was controlled by the state-run tourist agency. Through one of their offices I found a room in a private house. A local youth was deputised to take me there. Wordlessly – I had no Serbo-Croat, he no English – he showed me to a room in a dark and cluttered flat, and then departed. My hosts were nowhere to be seen. As I was settling in for the night my refuge was suddenly filled with the sound of a cockney woman's voice speaking English. It was my mother, Doris Hare, in her role of Mum in *On the Buses*. On the other side of the wall a Yugoslavian family was watching, presumably with subtitles, that most British of sitcoms. Early the next morning I left without ever seeing my hosts.

This book tells the story of the woman behind the wall in Sarajevo: the Doris Hare her audiences knew, not the private Doris. She may be best remembered today for *On the Buses*, but that was only one chapter of a career that spanned almost the entire twentieth century. It began with the Alexandra Theatre, a portable theatre run by her parents, Kate Tansley and Herbert Hare (known professionally as Bert Breamer), that travelled around the mining towns of South Wales. As a child in the early years of the twentieth

3

century Doris acted in the melodramas and farces that were the portables' stock in trade, first with her parents' theatre, then, after its demise around 1911, with various touring companies. A little later she moved on to variety, performing in the juvenile troupes popular during the inter-war years. From there she progressed to being a dancer, singer and impressionist in cabaret and variety, before finding a new level of success in the 1930s revues of Noël Coward and André Charlot. During World War II she hosted a popular, but now forgotten radio programme, *Shipmates Ashore*. Twenty years later she would find television fame with *On the Buses*. There were also forays into serious theatre, most notably three years with the Royal Shakespeare Company and the National Theatre in the early 1960s, a particularly exciting time in British theatre. She continued performing until a few years before her death in 2000. This lengthy career provides a particularly interesting vantage point from which to observe the shifting character of British popular entertainment over the course of the twentieth century. And because her speciality was always comedy, the story of her life also tells us a lot about gender and comedy, and the complicated relationship between popular entertainment and 'high' culture.

There is a long history of disdain for popular entertainment, sometimes even by its practitioners. In an essay entitled 'The Theatre and the Mob', Henry Arthur Jones, co-author of *The Silver King*, one of the most popular of all nineteenth-century melodramas, lamented the state of 'drama' in Britain. His earlier attempts at serious plays had been commercial and artistic failures. Part of the problem, as he saw it, was drama's unhealthy hybridity:

> The drama is an art, but it is also a competitor of music-halls, circuses, Madame Tussaud's, the Westminster Aquarium, and the Argyll Rooms. It is a hybrid, an unwieldy Siamese Twin, with two bodies, two heads, two minds, two dispositions, all of them, for the present, vitally connected. And one of these two bodies, dramatic art, is lean and pinched and starving, and has to drag about with it, wherever it goes, its fat, puffy, unwholesome, dropsical brother, popular amusement.[1]

In truth, popular culture has often revitalised highbrow drama. It was a vital ingredient of the mid-twentieth-century revolution in British theatre – a revolution that took Doris to those bastions of the highbrow, the Royal Shakespeare Company and the National Theatre, proving that 'dramatic art' and 'popular amusement' can come together in productive ways very different from the dysfunctional, warring relationship described by the despairing author of *The Silver King*.

Cheap Luxuries

To understand Doris as a performer we need to begin with the world into which she was born: the world of the portable theatres. Barely remembered today, this form of 'popular amusement' once brought live theatre to working-class audiences across the British Isles. Theatre historians who have written about these travelling theatres include Cecil Price, Josephine Harrop, and Ann Featherstone. Price provides the most detail about the Welsh portables. According to him, in the second half of the nineteenth century there were more than a dozen such companies in Wales.[2]

Portables were not the only travelling theatres. There were also fit-up companies. These would hire a local building, such as a barn, and fit it up as a theatre. Kate and Bert's Alexandra Theatre was a true portable, however, hauling its theatre, sets, props and costumes from one Welsh mining town to another on wagons. Once erected on a suitable site the theatre would then stay for several months putting on a different play each night. Kate and Bert's winter base was often a field in the town of Bargoed, beneath an imposing railway viaduct. It was here on 1 March 1905 that Doris was born.

Bargoed[3] made sense as a base. The development of deep mining technology at the end of the nineteenth century had allowed the exploitation of the area's previously inaccessible coal seams. By 1905 Bargoed was something of a boom town. In the previous five years its population had more than doubled, from 4,453 to over 10,000. The increasing numbers of English immigrants meant that English was replacing Welsh as the dominant language both at work and at home. While the miners may not have been paid lavish salaries, they had some disposable income, as did those working in

Fig. 1 – The field by Bargoed Viaduct in 2017. The Hare family's living vans were parked here when Doris was born on 1 March 1905.

Fig. 2 – Doris as a baby with her mother, Kate Tansley. Like all travelling actors Kate stored her possessions in a big, travelling basket. Professionally distinctive as well as capacious, such luggage had the disadvantage, as Kate's children remembered, that clothes always emerged from the basket creased: NB Kate's dress.

the service industries supported by the mines. This disposable income was available for what George Orwell referred to as the 'cheap luxuries which mitigate the surface of life'.[4] An evening at a theatre where the cheapest seat was 3d, and the most expensive ones 1s, was this kind of cheap luxury. By way of comparison, a pint of beer in 1901 cost 2d.[5] Acknowledging the potential of the coal towns, portable theatre owners travelling in Wales would tell each other to 'stick to the coal'.[6]

Doris was Kate and Bert's fourth child (see genealogy, p. xvi). Their first, Winifred Emma Kate (always known as Winnie), had been born in 1896, followed by Bessie Maud (later known as Betty) in 1898, and Molly in 1901. Their final child, a boy, was born in 1907, Herbert Edwin Hare (later known as Bertie). All five siblings would spend their life in the theatre.

The family was part of a tight-knit community of travelling players. Kate was the child of theatrical parents, Emma and Edward (Ted) Tansley, or at least this was what my sister Sue and I had always been told. It was only when I began the research for this book that we discovered – thanks to some careful detective work by theatre historian and blogger Vivyan Ellacot – that the story is more complicated. Kate was in fact born Kate Young. In 1871, according to that year's census, she, two siblings and her mother Emma Young were living as lodgers in the house of one John Holmes. The children were identified as Margaret, aged five, Kate, three, and Minnie, one. Emma was listed as a twenty-six-year-old 'play actor'. It seems that Emma, very likely a widow, married Edward Tansley at some point between the date of the census and 1874, when a Mr E. Tansley and a Mrs E. Tansley are listed in *The Era* as among the members of Mr T. Payne's company.[7] T. Payne was Tom Payne, proprietor of a well-thought-of portable. Emma's second marriage produced no further children.

Both Kate and Margaret (Maggie) acted with their parents as children. No one in the family ever mentioned the third sibling, Minnie, who may have died young. Maggie soon abandoned acting. When she was about twenty the family was appearing at Kettering. Here Avery Burditt Panter, a local man not in the theatre, wooed and won Maggie. They married, settled in Kettering, and had twelve children. In later years when times were hard, Kate and her children would sometimes find refuge with her sister, where Panter was in business as an ironmonger. Doris always spoke fondly of her Auntie Maggie, and had warm memories of a welcoming home where there was always plenty of food, not always the case in her childhood. Two of Maggie's children would join the Alexandra Theatre in its final years. One, Mr O. Panter, is listed as Business Manager on the bill shown in Fig. 3.

That Edward Tansley was Kate's stepfather rather than her biological father is revealed by Maggie's marriage certificate. While it names the groom as Avery Burditt Panter, the bride's name is given as Margaret Young. Presumably, although Emma's children had taken their stepfather's name, he had not formally adopted them. When Kate married Bert on 21 February 1892, she used the name Kate Tansley. Her real age was twenty-three, but she claimed to be nineteen, probably so that the date of her birth would postdate her mother's marriage to Tansley. For whatever reason, she was reluctant to use the name Young on her marriage certificate.

Doris's father Bert's background was not theatrical, but it was musical. Born in 1866, he was the eldest son of an army bandsman, Edwin Charles Frederick Hare (see genealogy, p.xvi). His younger sister Nellie Winifred (1872-1930) would become a successful singer and actress, using the name Winifred Hare. Kate and Bert's first child, Winifred Emma Kate, was named after her famous aunt and her grandmother.

Aunt Winifred was famous for her principal boy roles in pantomime, that longstanding British tradition featuring transvestism: pantomime dames played by men, principal boys by women. As Fig. 4 shows, the principal boy's costume was not intended to portray a convincing man. A major part of the attraction lay in the transgressive thrill of seeing shapely women's legs encased in form-hugging tights. Given their importance, the tights needed to be pristine; Winifred often passed on her slightly used tights to her sister-in-law.

The year Doris was born was a busy one for Winifred. She was in two pantomimes. At the Theatre Royal Sheffield early in the year she starred in *Cinderella,* a production presented by Fred Karno, the

Fig. 3 – Alexandra Theatre Bill from 1911, when Kate was running the theatre on her own after Bert Breamer's death. *The Anarchist King* is advertised with a series of dramatic moments, a format that would later become standard in film trailers. Also on the bill were: *The Factory Girl or All that Glitters is Not Gold* by John Maddison Morton, author of the farce *Box and Cox* (in which Doris would appear at the Royal Court in 1961 (see pp. 234–5), and the melodrama *The Woman in Red* (see pp. 66–8). The bill highlights that the theatre charges 'People's Prices'.

Fig. 4 – Winifred Hare in 1901 as Aladdin at the Coronet Theatre. The reviewer for *The Referee* (29 December 1901) declared, 'It would be difficult to imagine a more engaging Aladdin than that presented by Miss Winifred Hare, who combines grace, refinement, and vivacity with a fascinating personality.'

impresario responsible a few years later for bringing Charlie Chaplin to Hollywood. The *Era* review describes her as looking 'the very picture of the ideal Prince of pantomime'.[8] Then at the end of the year she was principal boy in *Robin Hood* in Liverpool.[9] She was also a popular music hall performer. In October 1905 she was a headliner at the Camberwell Palace of Varieties with one of the music hall giants, Little Tich.[10] Before that she could be seen for four months at Sir Oswald Stoll's magnificent, newly opened London Coliseum, designed to showcase spectacle and envisioned by its owner as a place where families could find respectable entertainment midway between serious theatre and music hall.

It remains a mystery as to why Bert chose to use the name Breamer rather than Hare. The family never talked about it, but one reason may have been to distinguish himself from his celebrated sister. A clear theatrical hierarchy stretched from the pinnacle of London's West End London theatres to the despised penny gaffs (entrance 1d) found in working-class districts. The portables occupied a niche a rung or two higher than the penny gaffs, but they were still considered a low form of theatre that pandered to the debased taste of working-class audiences. In general, West End theatres, music halls, portables, and penny gaffs were each seen as occupying separate spheres, even if in practice individual actors did sometimes move between them. Most commonly it was older actors who would drift down to the portables, although occasionally there were those who found fame after beginning their careers in the portables. Winifred, for instance, was on the bill at the Camberwell Palace of Varieties with Mark Melford, a well-known comedy actor and prolific author of farces, who late in life wrote a memoir that includes recollections of his early days as an actor in a portable theatre.

Until she married, Doris's mother Kate acted alongside her parents in whatever company they happened to be in. Within the world of the portables, she seems to have established herself as an actress quite early. In December 1888, when she was twenty, this ad appeared in the theatrical trade paper *The Stage*:

Musical Comedy Combination
WANTED, all applicants not yet answered to accept silence as respectful negative. Will Kate Tansley please write or wire at once? Vacancy for her.[11]

Interestingly, 'musical comedy combinations' were not portables. Was Kate being offered an opportunity to move up the theatrical ladder? If so, nothing came of it. Maybe she never saw the ad?

At the time Kate and her parents were probably part of a portable company run by Mr and Mrs Sinclair, where Kate was playing ingénues. She met Bert (calling himself Harry Breamer at this point) when he joined the company; they married in 1892. Kate would later tell her children that she and Bert learned a lot about acting from the Sinclairs. This was an era before drama schools when the craft of acting tended to be a skill passed on from one generation to the next primarily through a system of informal apprenticeship.

According to Doris's older sisters Winnie and Betty, a major reason Kate married Bert was to get away from her parents. For a young single woman at this time, even one capable of earning her living as an actress, marriage was one of the few respectable ways of leaving the family home. The couple posted an announcement of their marriage in the *Yorkshire Gazette*: 'On the 21st [February] at Normanton Parish Church, by the Rev. H. P. Thornton, vicar, Herbert Edwin Hare professionally known as Harry Breamer to Kate Tansley, both of Frank Payne's company.'[12] After her marriage, Kate would sometimes use the name Breamer (sometimes spelt Breamar), sometimes Tansley and sometimes Hare. Her oldest daughter, Winnie, was the only one of the siblings who would adopt Breamer (later Braemar) as her stage name, possibly to avoid confusion with her famous aunt.

By the summer of 1894 Kate and Bert (still working under the name of Harry Breamer) had moved on to another portable, the Prince of Wales Theatre, based at Briton Ferry, near Neath, run by the Johnsons, a family with a long history running travelling theatres, and much respected in the portable world. Fifty years later, *The Stage's* obituary of one Jack Johnson would describe him as 'the last of the Welsh travelling-theatre proprietors'.[13] When Kate and Bert joined them, the company was headed by John Johnson and his wife. Jack Johnson presumably belonged to the next generation, perhaps a son? Doris's sister Betty remembered the family being striking-looking; their dark good looks suggested to her that they had Roma blood:

They were a handsome family of gypsies really, the Johnsons. John Johnson couldn't read but he was so handsome. He used to play all the leading parts. His wife used to read them to him and he would memorise them. ... His star role was Macbeth. ... He had a wonderful set of kilts, you know, modern kilts with the shawl and everything and he used to come on and play Macbeth in this thing. He looked like a drum major.

Macbeth was not the only Shakespeare play they staged. Shakespeare was an important part of the portable theatres' repertory. Doris, who idolised her mother, always remembered Kate's delivery of Portia's 'The quality of mercy is not strained' speech: 'I never heard the speech spoken more beautifully.' While she was with the Johnsons Kate played Juliet in *Romeo and Juliet*, and later in life she recalled doubling Ophelia and Osric. Cross-gender casting in the classics was quite common in nineteenth-century theatre.

Kate and Bert stayed with the Johnsons for about a year. Kate was often mentioned in reviews. *The Era* praised her 'good work' as Juliet.[14] When she played the eponymous heroine in the Welsh melodrama, *The Maid of Cefn Ydfa*, *The Stage* also lauded her performance: 'Miss Kate Tansley as Annie Thomas was excellent.'[15] Harry Breamer is less often mentioned although his work as 'scenic artist' is noted: 'The scenery was very nicely arranged and appropriate, and reflected much credit upon the scenic artist, Mr Harry Breemer [*sic*].'[16]

By August 1895 Kate and Bert had again changed employers, moving to the Haggar company, headed by William Haggar, and one of the largest and most successful of the Welsh portables. Their family history is recorded in a 1953 article by Walter Haggar, one of Williams's sons, and in a 2007 family memoir by Peter Yorke, Williams's great-grandson. These family accounts provide an invaluable source of information about the world of the portables.

Around 1890 the Haggar theatre was doing so well that William decided to open another portable, the Castle Theatre, to be run by his son, William Haggar junior. It was this theatre that Kate and Bert joined. In 1897 Kate appeared in their pantomime, *Ali Baba and the Forty Thieves*, as the Captain of the Thieves 'charmingly dressed', according to *The Stage*. Was she wearing a cast-off pair of her sister-in-law Winifred Hare's tights? The review also noted that 'her singing and dancing are all that can be desired'.[17] Bert was responsible for the pantomime's new scenery. The reviewer's account gives a sense of the elaborate effects portables were capable of staging:

> the grand transformation is well worked out. First comes the expedition to the North Pole, and we see ships frozen in, the Aurora Borealis, and the sledge crossing the ice &c. Then comes a change to the Soldier's Dream of Home; next an episode of Dr. Jim's ride in the Transvaal, and a change to the full set, showing the silver lake in the fairies' home. Mr Bert Breamer has excelled himself in some of the new scenes.

Kate also performed serious roles. In his memoir, written when memories of Doris's wartime radio show *Shipmates Ashore* were still fresh, Walter Haggar remembers Kate's success in the title role of *Trilby*, although he gets her name a little wrong: 'The part of Trilby was played by Kate Townsley (Mrs Bremmer), mother of Doris Hare, the now famous radio compere. There was a packed house and the audience were enthralled by the performance.'[18] *Trilby* would be one of the Alexandra Theatre's regular attractions.

The play is a dramatization of the novel by George Du Maurier, first performed at London's Haymarket Theatre in 1895. In this case the Haggars were performing a recent London success. Whether or not they paid a royalty is unclear. At the Haymarket it had starred Herbert Beerbohm Tree as the villainous Svengali who through his hypnotic powers controls the bohemian artist's model Trilby. Normally Trilby has no singing voice, but when mesmerised by Svengali – and only then – she can sing divinely and becomes a world-famous opera singer. The free-spirited Trilby, who smokes cigarettes and goes about barefoot, titillated 1890s audiences. This was supposedly the first time an actress had acted on a London stage with bare feet. The part was a good fit for Kate, who had certain bohemian traits herself. Her children remembered that they always knew when she was going to play Trilby because she had to wash her feet.

All Kate's children remained devoted to her until her death in her late eighties in 1957. But while she was a very loving mother, her style of parenting could be somewhat casual. Some years after the demise of the Alexandra Theatre, Doris's sister Betty recalled in one taped interview Kate's dismissive response when Doris and Molly were sent home from school because they had nits. 'Nits? They sent them home because they had a few nits?', Kate scoffed. It was left to Betty to deal with the problem. The extent of Doris's formal education is something of a mystery. She always claimed that her schooling amounted to three weeks attending Cwmfelinfach's primary school when she was about six. The story of the nits calls this into question. It seems likely that she and her siblings attended local schools intermittently wherever the theatre happened to be playing.

Further evidence of Kate's mothering style is again provided by Betty. Kate apparently did not believe in washing children before they went to bed, even if they had been playing outside all day. Betty remembered being dragged out of bed one evening when she was about six, dirt and all, to play the small part of little Isobel in *East Lynne*, one of the most popular of all nineteenth-century melodramas. In the version played by the Alexandra Theatre, at the dramatic conclusion to Act I, Isobel comes on stage with her governess and embraces her father, Sir Archibald Carlyle, throwing her arms around his neck and delivering the line: 'Papa, papa, where is mamma?'. Mamma, Lady Isobel, has in fact just eloped with her villainous seducer. In a fury Sir Archibald orders the governess to take the child back to the nursery. 'Come, Isobel,' says the governess, whereupon Sir Archibald utters the act's closing lines: 'No, no. Never let that name be mentioned within the walls of East Lynne. Isobel no longer, from now on let her be known as Lucy,' whereupon the curtain slowly descends. As it did so the actor playing Sir Archibald exclaimed, as Betty recalls, 'Good God Almighty, who let that kid come on in that state?'

The convention-defying Trilby, who shocked London audiences, must have been even more shocking to provincial Welsh audiences. Although portables had to be careful not to offend local moral arbiters, a degree of titillation was a reliable way to bring in audiences. Another play that would also become a staple of the

Alexandra Theatre's repertory was *Peeping Tom*, based on the legend of the medieval Lady Godiva's naked ride through Coventry to win relief from taxation for her husband's tenants, her modesty only preserved by her long hair. When business was bad, the play could be relied upon to draw an audience. Peeping Tom, played by Bert, the only person who disregards the injunction to stay inside and avert his eyes from the spectacle, is punished for his voyeurism by being struck blind. Kate was Lady Godiva. A local horse was hired, and Kate would ride across the stage wearing a long wig, dressed in fleshings (something like a body stocking) and a pair of Aunt Winifred's second-hand tights.

In the Spring of 1897 Kate and Bert placed an ad in *The Stage* that 'Breamer, Mr and Mrs Bert, (Kate Tansley), Comedy, Old Men, Lead' were 'Concluding two years' most successful engagement with W. Haggar Esq. All communications, Castle Theatre, Tony Pandy.'[19] This suggests they were thinking of moving on. Around this time the Haggars decided to sell the Castle Theatre, possibly because they were planning to build a new, more substantial theatre, or because William Senior was becoming increasingly interested in the very latest novelty in popular entertainment: the bioscope, which showed moving pictures. In the event, Kate and Bert bought or leased the existing Castle Theatre. In 1905 they announced in their ads: 'The original Alexandra Theatre. Established over 15 years.'[20]

This dates the theatre's origin to the establishment of the Haggars' first Castle Theatre.

Exactly when Kate and Bert bought or leased the theatre is not clear, but their timing was terrible. In April 1898, just as they were preparing to open the theatre under their management, the Welsh coalfields went on strike, a dispute that would turn into a bitter six-month lockout. By this point it seems that Emma and Ted Tansley had again joined forces with their daughter and son-in-law. At this moment of crisis, the theatre was packed up and left in their care. Fortunately, Kate and Bert had many contacts in the travelling theatre community, and they found employment with a Scottish portable company run by John Fyffe. Kate, Bert, and their two small children would relocate to Scotland for the duration of the strike.

Once the coal strike ended the family returned to Wales and by November the theatre, still at this point called the Castle Theatre, was up and running under Bert's management. But almost immediately there was another setback, as reported in the *Cardiff Times*: 'On Wednesday [23 November 1898] the Castle Theatre stationed at Ton (Ton Pentre) was smashed by the weight of snow that lodged upon it during the night. The proprietor, Mr Bert Breamer, and his company have sustained heavy loss.'[21] Undaunted, Kate and Bert continued on. The name of the theatre was soon changed to the Alexandra Theatre, probably in honour of Princess Alexandra, wife of the Prince of Wales. This may have been to avoid confusion with the new Castle Theatre that the Haggars had opened in 1897.[22] For the next twelve years the Alexandra Theatre would tour a circuit of Welsh mining towns, often enduring hard times when audiences were thin, and Kate and Bert struggled to pay their bills.

The Alexandra Theatre's Later Years

The Alexandra Theatre's later years were particularly tough. On 20 September 1907 Kate gave birth, once again in Bargoed, to her fifth child and first boy, Herbert Edwin. In early November the baby developed a fever. As soon as he had finished his performance, the anxious father, still hot and sweaty, rushed out into the chilly night in search of a doctor with, according to family lore, 'a stick of greasepaint still in his hand'. The baby soon recovered but Bert became seriously ill with a throat abscess. A few days later he was dead, dying as he was being carried to a local pub for surgery it was hoped might save him. He was just forty-one years old. He was buried in Bargoed's Bedwellty Church. The account of his funeral in the local newspaper notes it was attended by 'a large gathering of the theatrical profession, as well as the general public'.[23] The list of mourners included most of the major portable theatre proprietors of the day. Kate's finances, however, did not run to a headstone and the grave remained unmarked. When I was writing this book my sister and I visited Bargoed for the first time. We searched the graveyard but were unable to locate Bert's grave, or those of the two actors beside whom he was reportedly buried.

One person who did not attend was Bert's sister Winifred. According to the newspaper report, she was 'unfortunately bound to an engagement at the Metropolitan Theatre'. Winfred may have been far more successful than her brother but she was childless and in the wake of his death she was eager to adopt the new baby. Kate rejected this out of hand, but she did accept her sister-in-law's offer to pay for her namesake's education, and the young Winifred, aged eleven, was sent to a convent for a few years.

Ironically, the very week of his death, Bert, an expert handyman and constructor of scenery, had placed this advertisement in *The Stage*:

Wanted, Bioscope, for Sunday Concerts.
Up-to-date Films, Song Slides. Open to hire or purchase. Also 2 Brins, Cylinders, with Regulators. Full Particulars,
BERT BREAMER
Alexandra Theatre, Bargoed.[24]

What might have become of the Alexandra Theatre had Bert lived is a tantalising but unanswerable question. As it was, Kate was left to run the theatre with five children, the oldest, eleven, the youngest, a baby of less than three weeks. For the moment, investing in bioscope equipment was out of the question; simply keeping the theatre running was a challenge.

Kate and Bert were founder members of the Travelling Theatres Managers' Association, founded in 1907 shortly before Bert's death. Their theatre bills would now include the line 'Member of the T.T.M.A.' (see Fig. 3). A report of the Association's 1908 Annual General Meeting (published in *The Stage*) alludes to the financial problems Kate faced after Bert's death, noting that 'a member [clearly Kate] was in difficulties through her husband's death'. Even before his death it seems Bert had fallen behind on his 5s monthly subscription, but given the circumstances, 'it was decided to present her with a clean book and remit the husband's arrears of subscriptions.'[25]

Bert's death was not the only loss Kate faced. Within a year both her parents died; her mother Emma Tansley, aged seventy-one, on 22 March 1908; and in June her stepfather Ted Tansley, seventy-six.

Kate, however, remained committed to her theatre, and even though times were often difficult she managed to keep it running for another four years. Widows taking full control of portables after their husbands' death was not unusual, as Ann Featherstone notes.[26]

The end came in the autumn of 1911 in Cwmfelinfach. Throughout the year Kate had been regularly advertising in *The Stage*, early in the year for 'variety people in all lines', and even in *The Stage*, in the 'Wanted Bioscopes, Operators, Etc.' column, for 'Good Operator with own machine' (May 18). This may have been something of a desperate last throw. By this time moving pictures were rapidly gaining ground, and portable owners were increasingly embracing the new technology. None of Kate's children ever mentioned the Alexandra Theatre including bioscope performances in their shows and it seems unlikely that her ad for a bioscope operator ever came to anything. The ad she placed in the July 20th *Stage* was for 'Entire Company (with exceptions)'. It seems that after experimenting with a programme of variety turns, she was going back to performing plays.

She placed her last wanted ad, for 'good responsible people, capable of Line and Turn' and also 'good property man', in *The Stage* for November 2nd. But tragedy struck, bringing the story of the Alexandra Theatre to an end. After the evening performance it was crucial that all the doors were securely fastened before the theatre was closed up for the night. If there was a wind and a door had been left unfastened, the wind could get under the canvas tilt roof and lift it off. According to family lore, one night, after a performance of *Firematch the Trooper* to a particularly thin house there was a terrible storm. As the winds howled, Kate sat down to her customary post-show supper of an onion, a piece of cheese, and a Guinness. Suddenly she heard a terrible crash. Realising what had happened, she cried: 'My God, someone's left one of the doors open!'. Rushing outside she saw that the canvas tilt had been blown off. The next morning, when the storm had subsided, she found the tattered remains in a nearby field. It was the final blow. She admitted defeat, declaring – as she surveyed the wreckage of the theatre to which she had devoted so many years of her life – 'Let the bugger lie there.'

Kate sold what was left of the theatre for a few pounds, but there was still the waggon in which the family was living, probably just one waggon now her parents were dead. By early 1912 she managed to have the waggon transported from Wales to her sister in Kettering. An ad she placed in *The Stage*, 7 March 1912, provides the end of the story: 'Wanted to sell, Good Pullman Living Waggon, Cheap for immediate cash. Good cooking stove. Road or Rail. BREAMER, 206 Bath Road, Kettering.'

CHAPTER 2:

THE WORLD OF THE PORTABLES

Our line is not bricks and mortar, but rags and sticks.
Edward Ebley (portable theatre proprietor)[27]

Portable theatres were the product of a particular historical moment. The Theatres Act of 1843 abolished the long-standing restriction of so-called 'legitimate' drama (understood as the traditional genres of tragedy and comedy) to the London Patent Theatres, Drury Lane, Covent Garden and the Haymarket. The Act also established a separation between theatres that performed plays but were not allowed to sell food or drink, and places of entertainment that were licensed by local magistrates to stage music and dancing, but not plays. These places of entertainment permitted smoking and were allowed to sell food and drink in the auditorium. The Act led both to the expansion of theatres staging plays, and from the 1850s the development of music hall, where, as with modern cinemas, the sale of food and drink was a key money maker. The 1843 law, however, only applied to permanent theatres. Travelling players had long been a standard feature of fairs, setting up booths in which they performed short plays and other entertainments. Dickens gives us a vivid picture of the entertainment provided by such booths in 'Greenwich Fair', one of his 1835 newspaper articles later published as *Sketches by Boz*. The booth Dickens describes was run by John Richardson (1766-1836), a famous early-nineteenth-century fairground theatre proprietor.

> This immense booth, with the large stage in front, so brightly illu-
> minated with variegated lamps, and pots of burning fat, is

'Richardson's', where you have a melo-drama (with three murders and a ghost), a pantomime, a comic song, an overture, and some incidental music, all done in five-and-twenty minutes.[28]

Doris always claimed that her grandparents Ted and Emma Tansley had performed in these kinds of booth theatres, and stories of their exploits were handed down in the family. But perhaps it was Doris's great-grandparents, Ted Tansley's parents, who were the booth performers? Ted Tansley was born in 1832, just over ten years before the 1843 Theatre Act and the gradual transformation of the old booth theatres into portable theatres, independent of the fairs. He seems a little young to have made his career as a booth actor. The 1874 reference in *The Era* to Mr E. Tansley and Mrs E. Tansley, cited on p. 7, has them as members of Mr T. Payne's company appearing at The Theatre, Northwich in 'high class plays' that included *Hamlet*, *King Richard III*, and various melodramas, such as Dion Boucicault's *The Colleen Bawn*; a programme that seems several steps up from that provided by the booths. Payne's theatre was one of the portables that proliferated after the 1843 Act. The Tansley family may well have had a history as booth performers, but perhaps, as sometimes happens with oral reminiscences, over time generations were collapsed?

The framers of the 1843 law were careful to exempt fairground performances, including this clause:

> nothing herein contained shall be construed to apply to any theatrical representation in any booth or show, which by the Justices of the Peace, or other persons having authority on their behalf, shall be allowed in any lawful fair, feast, or customary meeting of the like kind.[29]

It was out of the fairground booth theatres that the portables emerged. Fairground troupes that had a good reputation in the eyes of the local authorities would often be allowed to go on playing for weeks after the fair had ended.[30] As the years went on, portables became increasingly detached from the fairs. An important factor in their spread and increasingly independent existence was the improvement of roads in the later nineteenth century, and the

Fig. 5 – Alexandra Theatre Bill from before Bert Breamer's death in 1907. Trilby was one of Kate's roster of starring roles (see p. 14). This performance of *Trilby* was a benefit performance for the Pontlottyn Drum and Fife Band, 'under most distinguished patronage'. *One Woman's Wickedness*, 'a great moral lesson and warning to all', features 'Miss Kate Tansley in her finest dual role'.

coming of the railways, both of which greatly facilitated the transportation of theatre and actors from place to place.

The Theatre by Day and Night

Some portable theatres were large, impressive structures accommodating as many as two thousand spectators, capable of staging elaborate spectacles that rivalled those of the smaller permanent theatres.[31] Kate and Bert's Alexandra Theatre was a more modest affair. It did promise, however, that those who came to see *Rogues of the Turf* would see 'the horses race past in full view of the audience' (see Fig. 5). The core of the company, in common with most portables, was the family, with three generations, parents, grandparents and children all performing or contributing in different ways. Family members were supplemented by a shifting group of hired actors and musicians. Many years later Doris's older sister, Betty, began writing down some of her memories of the portables in a notebook my sister discovered long after her death in 1980. Her account of being dragged out of bed to play little Isobel in *East Lynne* comes from this notebook.

The notebook also describes the family theatre. It was built up on six waggons. Two of these would become the stage. On each side of this stage was a waggon with dressing rooms. Presumably, although Betty does not mention this, one side would be for the men, and one for the women. Two waggons formed the seating area. On the smaller of these were the more expensive seats. Closest to the stage were three rows of benches with the luxury of a baize covering. Seats on these cost 1s. Behind these were another twenty-four or so rows of bare benches. These cost 6d. On the second, larger and higher waggon, was erected the gallery with stadium seating. At 3d these were the cheapest seats. Stage and seating area were enclosed by wooden shutters, or possibly canvas walls. Betty does not provide details, but it was crucial to the finances of the theatre that only paying customers have access. The only entrance to the theatre was via a single set of steps at the top of which was the pay box. Betty remembers her grandmother, Emma Tansley, as being in charge of this. In addition to the waggons that made up the theatre, there were the living waggons or vans in which members of the company lived: three, as Betty recalls: one for Kate and Bert, one for the children, and another for Kate's parents. Other members of the company would take local lodgings.

Seat prices were cheap. The 1s, 6d and 3d ticket prices seem to have been standard in the portable world and they remained unchanged during the lifetime of the Alexandra Theatre. Affordability was crucial. A number of the theatre bills and newspaper ads stress that while they are offering magnificent spectacle, the prices are 'popular prices' or 'people's prices' (see Fig. 3).

Actors in a portable company were expected to do more than act. When the theatre's sojourn in one place came to an end there would be a 'hammer call' when the theatre would be dismantled, and another hammer call when they arrived at their next stop to reassemble it. In the Theatre Collection in the Richard Burton Archives at Swansea University there is a 'List of Rules to be observed by members of Mrs Latimer's Mammoth Theatre' (a portable). The first rule is: 'To assist in building and pulling down the Theatre'.[32] All the male members of a portable company were expected to travel with their own hammer. The women, too, had their responsibilities. The theatre's roof consisted of a circus-like canvas known as the tilt, supported by wooden rafters. Mrs Latimer's final rule notes that the company's women were expected to keep the tilt in good repair: 'All the Ladies to assist in mending the tilt etc.'. Dismantling the theatre took up to a week, putting it up again would take rather longer. Everything was packed up on the waggons and the company would make its way to the next location, sometimes by road, sometimes by rail, and the theatre reassembled on its new site. If by road, horses were hired to haul the waggons. After a stay of several months the waggons would often have sunk deep into the mud and the horses would struggle to get them free. Betty recalls being a small child watching in horror her father, who had quite a temper, cursing the horses as they strained to shift the waggons, 'Come on you buggers, you bloody buggers,' words that were considered far more shocking in those days. Fearful for her father's soul, she would offer up a silent prayer, 'Please God, forgive him, don't let him swear.'

Once the theatre was re-erected on its new site there would be a play every night except Sunday, usually a different play each night. The core of the repertoire was melodrama; some old chestnuts such as *Maria Marten, or the Red Barn*, an anonymous dramatization of a notorious 1827 murder, some taken from recent London successes, such as *Trilby*. Audiences were given a full evening's entertainment. The main drama would normally be followed by a brief comedy, always described as a 'laughable farce'. During scene changes, members of the company would perform a 'turn': a song, a recitation, a comedy skit or some such. Advertisements for portable actors in *The Stage* would frequently include the line 'must be able to do a turn'. One spectator remembering the portables of his youth recalled, 'We had three hours entertainment for three-pence.'[33]

Running a portable theatre was a precarious way of life: audiences were fickle, periods of prosperity were interspersed with times when audiences, for whatever reasons, stayed away and money was short. And then there was always the threat of opposition to their 'godless entertainment' from local clerics and other upholders of moral order. Even when they were regarded more favourably, they saw themselves, and were seen by locals as visitors from an alien world. To many of their potential audiences these temporary sojourners in their midst embodied an otherworldly magic, the magic of theatre, removed from the mundane reality of their day-to-day lives. The actors were often seen as dangerously seductive figures, likely to lure away suggestible young women, a stereotype found almost everywhere there were travelling theatres. During a trip to Taganrog, the provincial Russian town where he had grown up, Anton Chekhov included some local gossip in a letter to his family. 'Last season,' he wrote, 'Manya', the wife of a friend – described rather cruelly by Chekhov as 'a plump, well-cooked piece of Polish meat' – had

> all but ran off with an actor, after going as far as to sell her rings, earrings and such. ... Generally I get the impression that it is the height of Taganrog fashion to run off with an actor. Quite a lot of men wake up to discover their wives and daughters have gone missing.[34]

Whether in Russia or Britain, it is easy to imagine the appeal of these exotic outsiders in small provincial towns and villages, and the mingled fascination and fear they aroused.

One of Kate's favourite fictional portrayals of actors was the Crummles family in Charles Dickens's *Nicholas Nickleby*. Dickens was a great lover of the theatre. He regularly attended performances at both popular and more elite theatres, and was an enthusiastic organiser of amateur performances in which he himself performed. Early in his life he had even briefly considered becoming an actor.[35] The self-important patriarch, Mr Crummles, his daughter, the Infant Prodigy, eternally ten years old, and the rest of the company were all characters Kate recognised, as were the theatrical conventions to which they adhered. In the novel Dickens captures the two contrasting faces of the theatre, one facing outwards to its audience, one inward to the workaday world of the producers of magical illusion.

Nicholas and the simple-minded Smike have just joined the Crummles' company and are making their initial visit to the theatre where they are to appear. Although it is daytime, little light penetrates the theatre.

> Nicholas found himself close to the first entrance on the prompter's side, among bare walls, dusty scenes, mildewed clouds, heavily daubed draperies, and dirty floors. He looked about him: ceiling, pit, boxes, gallery, orchestra, fittings and decorations of every kind – all looked coarse, cold, gloomy, and wretched.
>
> "Is this a theatre?" whispered Smike, in amazement; "I thought it was blaze of light and finery."
>
> "Why so it is," replied Nicholas ... "but not by day, Smike – not by day."[36]

For actors the theatre is the place where they produce magic, magic that if done right is capable of seducing audiences and transporting them to another reality. The 'bare walls, dusty scenes and dirty floors' are the base materials they transmute through their alchemical skills. Their possession of these skills binds them together with other initiates of the theatrical mysteries. Actors often refer to themselves as 'pros', that is professionals, seeing themselves as something like members of a guild. This was certainly true of Doris, who for her entire life defined herself as above all a 'pro'.

The Last of the Strolling Players?

There is a temptation to see these long-vanished players hauling their theatres along the roads of Britain as the last dying embers of a tradition stretching back to the time of Shakespeare. This is how Cecil Price sees them: 'the portable theatres were conservative by habit. They clung to outworn traditions and customs; they were always old fashioned. They belonged to "the profession" and they cherished all its more ancient usages.'[37] But how accurate a picture is this? It is true that the bulk of their repertoire tended to be tried and true melodramas, and that viewed from the vantage point of the higher echelons of the theatrical establishment, their acting style seemed old fashioned. But the owners of the portables were also entrepreneurs, always on the lookout for new economic opportunities.

In this precarious business the fickleness of audiences was an ongoing anxiety, one Doris imbibed from her earliest childhood. After asking God's blessing on all the family members, her nightly prayers as a small child would always end: 'And, please God, give us a good house on Saturday night.' In this uncertain business, as Walter Haggar records, portable owners were always ready to experiment, indeed even to the extent of dispensing with live actors altogether. In the late 1880s the Haggar enterprise was going through hard times. Walter's father, William Haggar, decided on a radical change:

> the entire company was dismissed. We then changed from a theatre to a Marionette Show. My father invented and carved each Marionette figure with his own hands. I once heard him say to a Police Sergeant who was watching this work in progress, "I can put these actors away and take them out when I want them. They will get no pay and they will always be sober," (as I regret to say the latter was not always the case among live actors!)[38]

The experiment was not a success and the Haggars soon reverted to live theatre, but there was no sentimentality about maintaining a tradition. One feels that Haggar would have agreed with the nineteenth-century West End theatre entrepreneur John Hollingshead, who remarked that, even if this should only be admitted in private, 'no particular training in literature and art is necessary for the good government of a theatre, but precisely those qualities that make a good cheesemonger.'[39] The important thing was to run a successful business and be willing to adapt to changing circumstances. Early in his theatrical career, finding it hard to support his growing family, William Haggar even opened a shooting gallery. Initially quite successful, this venture, too, failed. Within a couple of years the family went back to running a portable theatre,

The marionettes may not have been successful, but a few years later a new way of replacing live actors emerged, one that would ultimately transform popular entertainment: the bioscope, which would develop into the modern cinema. The age of cinema began in Britain with performances of 'living pictures' by the French Cinématographie-Lumière at the Empire Theatre of Varieties in Leicester Square in 1896. Other music halls were quick to adopt their own 'living pictures'. Within a year they were being featured as a novelty item in practically every major music hall in the country.[40] The technology spread rapidly to fairgrounds and travelling theatres, and some of the earliest and most enthusiastic adopters of the new technology, most commonly termed the bioscope, were portable theatre owners. William Haggar was one of these early adopters. His great-grandson, Peter Yorke, tells the story of his conversion.

Fascinated by the new invention as soon as he heard about it in late 1887, and undaunted by a total lack of experience with the technology, he invested the sizeable amount of £80 in 'a Cinematograph and Triunal Lantern, including the gas cylinders, regulators, gauges, lantern slides, films, etc.'[41] – all the paraphernalia needed for this new form of entertainment. After careful reading of the instruction manual, and some fairly hair-raising experiments, he and his sons managed to master the equipment. A select audience, including the local doctor and vicar, were invited to the inaugural performance. The performance was judged a success. While other members of the Haggar family would continue in the portable business for some years, William decided to switch from live theatre to the new technology. It was around this time that the Haggars' Castle Theatre was sold to Kate and Bert. For the next ten years the Haggar bioscope toured the local fairs as a show that combined live and bioscope performances. Initially there were very few films available so in 1901

William invested in a camera and began making his own films. These included what were termed 'actualities', the filmed scenes of real life that were the standard fare of early bioscope shows, but he also began making fiction films based on the portables' repertory of melodramas and farces, utilizing sets and costumes from the remaining Haggar theatres. By 1910, however, travelling with a bioscope had become harder. One new obstacle was the 1910 Cinematograph Act. This mandated that there be a fireproof barrier between the audience and the projectors and the highly flammable films. Previously a simple canvas screen had been deemed sufficient. Seeing cinema as the future, William, this businessman who never clung to tradition for its own sake, started building up a chain of permanent cinemas, becoming one of the pioneer cinema entrepreneurs in Wales.

The Morality Wars

As Ann Featherstone has written, 'Portable theatres struggled with the law throughout their existence.'[42] The legal minefield portables had to navigate became even more challenging after the adoption of the 1888 Local Government Act, which made the granting of licenses the responsibility of local justices. Those wanting to erect a portable theatre had to apply to the local magistrates for a licence allowing them to erect a theatre and stage plays, usually for three or six months. There was always a long list of Rules and Regulations to which they had to adhere, and adding to the challenge, the demands were different in different regions. A major concern shared by all the licensing authorities was safety; fire was an ever-present hazard. Applications would normally also include drawings of the proposed building. Another concern was morality. The Alexandra Theatre would usually apply for a licence in what is now the county of Gwent. Rule 13 of the Gwent licence specified: 'No profanity or impropriety of language to be permitted on the stage'. Rule 14 stated: 'No indecency of dress, dance, or gesture, to be permitted on the stage.'[43] One of the surviving Alexandra Theatre bills includes the admonition: 'Strictest Order Maintained. All Disorderly Persons Expelled' (see Fig. 5).

The morality of the theatre and its effects on working-class audiences were the subject of impassioned debates. As usual, there was little concern as to its effects on richer patrons. Suspicion of theatre's potentially corrupting effects was particularly strong in Wales where Methodism had a powerful hold. Opposition to the portables was often spearheaded by church leaders. In 1904, the year before Doris was born, 'the Free Churches of Gilfach Goch petitioned the Council to refuse licences for portable theatres and thus "aid the church of God in improving the moral tone of the district".'[44] Four years earlier Neath Rural District Council had refused Bert a licence to erect a portable theatre at Skewen at the request of 'a deputation from Skewen', who 'strongly opposed the application on "moral" grounds'.[45] Some Chapels threatened their members with excommunication if they attended the theatre, and, according to Price, even carried out this threat.[46]

Theatre owners mounted a spirited defence, insisting on the positive moral effects of their dramas. Edward Ebley's playbill included this statement:

> Mr Ebley wishes to impress upon his patrons, that every play which he produces has been personally supervised by him, and that anyone visiting the Theatre, even for the first time, will find that every feature of vulgarity has been eliminated from the text which would be calculated to displease the most fastidious mind. His only wish is to place before the public Plays which not only appeal to men's hearts, but will leave a lasting impression upon them, and if he only succeeds in making one *bad man think*, he will then be worthy to join the ranks of those inspired apostles who, by their purity teaching, help to keep the universe together.[47]

The fear of a sudden religious revival and increased opposition to the 'Theatre' was a one reason for Ebley's distrust of permanent structures (quoted in this chapter's epigraph). Unlike a permanent theatre, a portable could quickly cut its losses and move on if local opposition became too strong.

The portables, however, also had their supporters among local notables, including those who sat on the councils charged with granting or denying them licences to erect their theatres. There was a vocal contingent that saw portables, which were not allowed to sell alcohol or permit it on their premises, as helping to keep their working-class audiences from drink. This was very much a concern for mine owners and other employers, although their interest was efficiency rather than morality: they wanted a sober workforce. In 1897 a colliery manager testified in a case brought against Mrs Hannah Orton's portable company for playing without a licence in Abertillery. 'Before he came to Abertillery', he reported,

> he lived at a place where there were about 2,000 workmen at the colliery, and from his own experience of the little theatre in that town there was less drunkenness among the workmen, who attended work more regularly; he thought all were the better for that little theatre.[48]

An earlier case in 1870 reported in *The Era* also illustrates this positive view of the theatre. It was undeniable that the defendant, Edward Wildman, proprietor of the Prince of Wales Theatre (a portable erected on Hounslow's fair-field), had 'present[ed] a stage play in a building not specially licensed for that purpose', but 'The Bench were not at all anxious to convict in this case, more especially as they heard such a good character of the Theatre, and because they believed that a poor man's evenings would be better spent, perhaps, in such a Theatre, than in a beer house.'[49] The Magistrates did convict, but imposed only a nominal fine of 1s.

It was crucial for the portables to maintain good relations with local authorities and moral arbiters, and to demonstrate the uplifting character of their dramas. Benefit performances that gave the profits of one night's performance to an individual actor were a long-established tradition in the theatre at all levels, from the prestigious 'legitimate' theatre to the cheap popular theatres. They were an expected element of an actor's income. Travelling theatres also staged benefit performances for local charities. When the Johnsons' Prince of Wales Theatre applied for a renewal of its licence in 1894, a report in *The Era* noted that several members of the Briton Ferry local board 'referred to Mr Johnson's kindness in having recently given two performances for the local fire brigade, and for the sufferers of the Albion Colliery disaster, which produced very substantial amounts'.[50]

Fig. 6 – An undated publicity photo of Bert Breamer in *Charley's Auntie* [*Charley's Aunt* by Brandon Thomas]. Kate always claimed that her husband Bert was a very funny comedian. An early review of Bert in the pantomime *Ali Baba and the Forty Thieves*, agreed: 'Mr H. Breamer as Cassim proves himself a clever pantomimist, keeping the fun rolling merrily with unflagging spirit and humour.' (*The Stage*, 7 January 1897)

The Alexandra Theatre also gave benefit performances for local charities. In July 1905 it announced in the *Monmouthshire Beacon* that there would be a 'Grand Hospital Night' when 'the famous farcical comedy, *Charley's Aunty*', would be performed as a benefit for the Monmouth Hospital. The comedy was 'to be followed by a Variety Entertainment, and [the] whole concluding with a Laughable Farce entitled "CAPTAIN THINGAMY" or "THE DEAF WAITER"'.[51] *Charley's Aunty* would have been a performance of Brandon Thomas's enormously successful farce, *Charley's Aunt*, first produced in London in 1892. By modifying titles travelling theatres avoided copyright fees: the royalty for a new play at this time was around three guineas a performance,[52] unaffordable for a portable selling seats at 'popular prices'. The announcement drew attention to the local dignitaries supporting 'The Grand Hospital Night'. The performance would be 'Under the most distinguished Patronage of His Worship the Mayor of Monmouth (G. R. Edwards Esq.); Lord Raglan (officer commanding), and officers of the Royal Monmouthshire Royal Engineer Militia; Hamilton T. Bailie Esq. Etc. Etc.'.

In 1909 the theatre announced a benefit performance for a different kind of charity: the Monmouth cricket club.[53] A month or so earlier the men of the company had assembled a team to play the club. Only a few of the actors seem to have been competent crick-eters and they were soundly beaten.[54] The real point was probably to foster a sense of connection to the local community. At one point the Haggar family also had a cricket team that played local teams. As Walter Haggar stressed, 'Whether we won or lost matters not: there was a good gate which was given to some charity.'[55] Kate employed another strategy aimed at local families. The 'splendid Burlesque Pantomime Robinson Crusoe' would feature 'New Scenery! New Dresses! New Music, Songs and Dances! And local children taught and trained by Mrs Bert Breamer'.[56] Presumably, the local children would have ensured a good attendance by their relatives. This strategy of recruiting local children with a view to boosting audi-ences was likely common among portables.

One challenge portable theatres faced in their efforts to present themselves as a force for good was portable actors' well attested fondness for alcohol. The temperance melodramas they regularly staged, such as *The Bottle*, *The Drunkard*, and *Ten Nights in a Bar Room*, may have dramatized the dangers of the demon drink, but actors, particularly in the lower echelons of the profession, were notorious for their intemperance. One aspiring actor, Louis Bradfield, later a musical comedy star, made his debut in the provinces in 1885. Writing to his brother, he voiced his disgust at what he was seeing: 'the profession I do like immensely, but the professionals I do not like. Really I never in all my life saw such dissipation. All last week and this there has been somebody drunk.'[57] A powerful trope in accounts of the portables is the once successful actor who due to his or her fatal weakness has been reduced to acting in portables. Mark Melford, who had shared the same music hall bill as Doris's aunt Winifred Hare in 1905, encountered one such old actor in his sojourn with a portable in his youth. In his memoir Melford describes this actor, to whom he gave the name 'Mr Mountarney', as 'a great actor, an intense and thrilling actor, who on occasion rose to the highest pitch of tragic power' reduced to acting in a portable due to what we would now call his alcoholism. Recognising Melford's talent, one day Mountarney took him aside and delivered a fervent plea to him:

> 'Mr Melford, I've seen enough of you already to note you are out of place here – I am a bonded slave and can never rise again, but don't you be content with this degrading life. For God's sake don't be content to resign yourself to this – make your determination to go out into the world where there is a future for you.'
>
> 'But you, sir – what of you?' I asked.
>
> 'I have no future – but this,' said he. 'I was once juvenile man at Drury Lane, and drink is the secret of my presence here – I've neither the will nor the chance to remount the downward path I've trodden. This is my destination, and here I end.'[58]

That the stereotype of the drunken portable actor had a degree of truth to it is evident in the emphasis on the importance of sobriety in the wanted ads for actors in the trade papers. In the issue of *The Stage* for 13 April 1888 John Johnson and Mrs H. Sinclair, two of the portable owners with whom Kate and Bert worked before running their own theatre, placed wanted ads for actors. Johnson's read: 'WANTED for good Portable, Juvenile Gent, Salary low but sure. Join at once. Sobriety and attentive to business'; Mrs Sinclair's 'WANTED, Company with few exceptions, for good Portable wood roof. Must be sober and respectable'. An ad in *The Era* the same year was blunt: 'Thirsty Men need not waste stamps.'[59]

It is perhaps understandable that alcoholism was an occupational hazard in a profession based on live performance in front of often rowdy audiences that the actors had to win over and control. It is not surprising that so many used drink to unwind after the tension of performing. And it is probably true that a disproportionate number of those who came to rely on drink rather than simply using alcohol to relax, or to build a sense of community with local audiences by drinking with them, drifted down to working in the portables. It certainly made running a portable a challenge. When Doris's father Bert died so unexpectedly in 1907, her ever-resilient mother Kate was left, as Doris put it, 'to run the theatre with a lot of drunken actors'.

The Decline of the Portables

The portables' general outsider status, their continual tussles with local councils that had the power to grant or withhold licences, and with those who disapproved of theatres in general on moral grounds, helped to create a sense of solidarity. Nonetheless there were limits to this. In 1905 Edward Ebley published this announcement in *The Stage*:

WANTED, PORTABLE THEATRE MANAGERS TO KNOW
that the appeal case 'Blaina District Council v. Ebley's Portable Theatre,' was decided in the High Court of Justice, London against the 'Blaina District Council'

———

Mr Ebley wants to Thank most heartily Mr. W. Haggar jun., and Mr Bert Breamer for their substantial support, and to express his regret that other portable managers in the district did persistently withhold their aid in a matter which closely affected their interests and threatened them with extinction.

———

Edward Ebley
Olympic Theatre
Senghenydd[60]

The case had involved Ebley's challenge to the Blaina Council's refusal of a licence for him to erect his portable theatre in Blaina. Ebley insisted that under the law his building, a wooden structure covered with canvas, was deemed to be a 'booth' and a 'temporary' construction and therefore not subject to standard building requirements. Blaina was adamant and the case went to the High Court, which to Ebley's great satisfaction, decided in his favour, allowing his season in Blaina to go ahead.[61]

Given the obstacles they faced, portable theatre managers began arguing in letters to *The Stage* that they needed their own organisation to defend their interests against hostile councils and other threats, and generally provide mutual support for the benefit of all travelling theatres. This was the context for the creation in 1907 of the 'Travelling Theatre Managers' Association' (T.T.M.A.), of which Kate and Bert were founder members. The association provided members with a regular free newsletter, *The Portable Times*, which reported on the latest struggles over licencing and other issues affecting travelling theatres, as well as providing actors with a place where they could advertise their availability. The Association also negotiated with plays' copyright holders to authorise performances by portables at affordable rates. A year after their founding they announced in *The Stage* : 'The Travelling Theatres Managers' Association has secured the acting rights of more than one hundred copyright plays.'[62] According to the June 1909 *Portable Times*, 'T.T.M.A. Members have paid in royalty fees since October, 1907, to March, 1909, the sum of £233. 5s 0d.' That they were able to negotiate affordable royalties on the grounds that their members only played in smaller towns is suggested by the note that 'Members in districts that do not touch the outskirts of large towns can arrange with our Agents to play "The Tyrant"'.

The T.T.M.A. survived for about ten years until declaring bankruptcy in 1916.[63] Very few copies of *The Portable Times* have survived. I was able to track down only three issues, from 1909, in the Theatre Collection, Richard Burton Archives at Swansea University.[64] The scarcity of issues in the archives suggests that the Association's membership was never very extensive. Its very founding is evidence perhaps of the struggle for survival of a form of theatre whose heyday had passed, and that was already in decline by the early twentieth century.

As popular entertainment the portables had always had competition. They developed around the same time as the music halls which offered entertainment plus alcohol. The portables of the later nineteenth century erected their temporary theatres in towns too small to attract the new touring companies, or to support a music hall. In the later nineteenth century more serious competition came from the new travelling pleasure fairs with their huge steam organs that blared out music. These were rather different from the old, traditional fairs. At a time when there were few retail outlets, the regular seasonal fairs had provided markets for everything from livestock, household goods, and labour. Those seeking employment, and those looking for labourers or servants would use the fairs to find each other. Over time the old seasonal fairs gradually evolved into the pleasure fairs that used the new technologies, such as electric light, to provide novel, more exciting entertainment. Even the most stirring of melodramas could seem a bit staid and old fashioned compared to their delights. The ultimate cause of the demise of the portables, however, was most likely the new technology of moving pictures, first the bioscope and then the cinema, which would transform popular entertainment. Moving pictures were proving not to be a passing fad as so many had predicted, but something like the young cuckoo that heaves the competing fledglings out of the nest. An item in the gossip column of one local paper in September 1911 is revealing:

> Some people wonder why the Picture Palace, Bargoed, remains so popular and that the attendance does not diminish as time goes on. The answer is to be found by the fact that the pictures are always new and the very latest productions. There you can get comfort and pleasure as well as instruction for a few coppers and the maximum of laughter for the minimum of expenditure.[65]

Those prescient portable owners, such as William Haggar, who saw the shape of the future, and adopted the bioscope, survived; those unable to make the switch for the most part did not. World War I, which led to the call up of so many men, including actors, was a final blow. By the end of the war there were only a handful of portables left, their place in popular entertainment taken by cinema and the new variety that developed out of the old music halls.

CHAPTER 3

DORIS, THE CHILD ACTRESS

Theatrical folk did not imagine that their children could do anything but follow their parents' professions.

Ellen Terry[66]

When the storm that destroyed the Alexandra Theatre in 1911 ended her mother's career as a theatre manager, Doris was six and already a performer. The family claimed that her first stage appearance was when she was carried on as Eliza's baby in *Uncle Tom's Cabin*. She would repeat this story in interviews throughout her life. Growing up I have to admit I had my doubts. It was certainly a good story, but could *Uncle Tom's Cabin* really have been a crowd pleaser in small Welsh towns where most people had probably never seen a Black person? As I began looking into it, however, I discovered that *Uncle Tom's Cabin* had caused a sensation on its publication in Britain and was rapidly adapted for the stage. The country, it was said, succumbed to 'Tom Mania'. By December 1852 there were eleven different dramatizations on London stages alone. Many of these were only loosely based on Harriet Beecher Stowe's original novel. 'In one London version, Tom is a dashing hero "who performs acrobatic feats and daredevil horseback rides" and is able to escape from the Legree plantation "on a race horse."'[67] *Uncle Tom's Cabin* was a travelling theatre staple well into the twentieth century. I further discovered that in 1905 from 22 June to 26 August, the Alexandra Theatre played a ten-week season in Monmouth, performing 48 different plays.[68] On Monday, 24 July, when Doris would have been about four months old, the play to be performed was *Uncle Tom's Cabin, or the Death of Little Eva*.

Music was always an important element of the entertainment provided. Included in the Alexandra Theatre's announcement of *Uncle Tom's Cabin* was the line 'Introducing all the Negro songs and dances. A treat for all.'[69] The version of the play performed by the Alexandra Theatre may well have been their own improvised one. By this time *Uncle Tom's Cabin* was so familiar to travelling theatre performers that they could dispense with a formal script. The reference to 'all the Negro songs and dances' indicates that they were drawing on a blackface tradition, already well established in British popular entertainment. Again it was only when I began exploring the different worlds of popular culture through which Doris moved that I realised the prominence of blackface in British as well as American popular culture. Originating in caricature and mockery of African Americans in a slave-holding society, by the time Welsh working-class audiences were enjoying what they imagined to be 'Negro songs and dances' in the early twentieth century, blackface in Britain had become a recognised form of entertainment. Those watching did not need any familiarity with actual Black people. Rather they would have recognised these fantasy 'Negroes' from other blackface performances. Blackface continued to be a staple of British popular entertainment for much of the twentieth century. The BBC's *Black and White Minstrel Show*, featuring white singers and dancers performing in blackface, continued until 1978.

The portable repertory offered a wealth of children's roles, and all Kate and Bert's children began performing at an early age. Doris was given her first speaking role at the age of three or four – she always claimed three. For the rest of her life she remembered the title of the play, *Current Cash*, and a line she had to say: 'My father never told you to say that.' Maybe this was when the Alexandra Theatre performed *Current Cash* on 11 August as part of their 1909 Monmouth season[70]? If so, Doris would have been four. I'll come back to *Current Cash* in the next chapter.

A Gendered Profession

Nowadays female performers are increasingly referred to as actors rather than actresses. The term 'actress' is seen by many as outmoded, a historical relic on a par with 'authoress'. When I

40

started writing this book, I wrestled with the question of how to refer to Doris. I decided on 'actress' rather than 'actor' partly because that was how she would have described herself, but primarily because in the years she was performing, 'actress' was the accepted term for female performers. Over the course of the twentieth century gendered terminology in most professions either disappeared, or was never adopted – a development lamented by H. W. Fowler, author of one of the most popular reference books of the twentieth century, *Fowler's Modern English Usage*, first published in 1926 and still in print in a revised version:

> [F]eminines for vocation-words are a special need of the future; everyone knows the inconvenience of being uncertain whether a doctor is a man or a woman; hesitation in establishing the word *doctress* is amazing in a people regarded as nothing if not practical.[71]

But no linguistic arbiter could hold back the trend towards gender-neutral nomenclature. 'Actress', however, remained a stubborn exception. Only relatively recently have things begun to change. One reason for the long persistence of 'actress' may be the role of gender in the acting profession.

When Doris made her first appearances with the Alexandra Theatre, acting was one of the few professions with a long history of offering women the possibility of making at least a semi-respectable living. Women had been regularly appearing on English professional stages for centuries. Until the 1642 Parliamentary ban on 'public stage plays', female roles had almost always been played there by boys dressed as women. After the collapse of the Commonwealth and the return of Charles II in 1660, playing companies reformed under royal patronage, and with a difference: actresses. Restoration theatre owners and managers rapidly realised the drawing power of young, attractive women, especially if dressed in revealing clothing. Hereafter, female roles would be played by women, male ones by men. This meant that women performers, such as Doris and the other women of the Hare clan, were not directly competing with men; they had their own separate domain, the domain of the actress. It is this structural reality, I would argue, that lies behind the persistence of the term 'actress' – a reality that makes the lives of actresses especially interesting for feminists. Women performers had their own defined space within which they could exercise considerable power, while at the same time they had to make their way in a world that, like the wider society, was dominated by men.

These women may not have defined themselves as feminists. Doris herself certainly did not: she tended to be dismissive of isms in general. Nonetheless, to me (someone who does define herself as a feminist) the way she lived her professional life reflects a feminist outlook, and the story of her career reveals both the opportunities available to her as a woman performer, and the limitations she faced – particularly as a female comedian who specialised in 'low' comedy.

Historically, their profession offered actresses the possibility of an economic independence rarely available to other women who had to work for a living. At the same time, actresses could never completely escape the prevailing norms defining a woman's 'proper' place in society, and how she should comport herself. They might sometimes flout these norms, but they could not ignore them completely.

At the beginning of the twentieth century the actress was still viewed by many as morally dubious. Overall the status of the acting profession might have risen, particularly in the case of those occupying its higher reaches, with a few of the most celebrated male actors, such as Henry Irving, even being awarded knighthoods, but the achievement of respectability was much slower for women. In later life the actress Maud Gill, born in 1888, described the mixed emotions aroused by the 'actress' in her youth: 'If you saw a rather conspicuously attractive woman in the street you gently squeezed your companion's arm and said: "Look! I think she must be an actress," with a mixture of awe, envy, and disapproval.'[72] Actresses, after all, not only lived, or seemed to live, independent lives, free of male control, they displayed themselves on public stages in front of anyone prepared to pay the price of admission. The world of the Hare family, however, was the world of their fellow performers, and they rather relished the romance of actors as, in the words of the old Elizabethan statutes, 'rogues and vagabonds', while at the same time seeing themselves as hard-working, respectable professionals.

Moving on From the Portables

After the demise of the Alexandra Theatre in 1911, Doris's mother Kate, left virtually destitute, departed for Devon. Through her links among the tight-knit portable community she had found a job with one of the last portables. Doris, now six years old, was left behind in the care of a landlady in Cwmfelinfach, a dark, bleak time she remembered all her life. She was expected to do chores to help pay for her keep: 'God, it was awful, it was so cold .... I used to get up in the morning and light the fire and make the tea.' Why she was left behind is a mystery, as are the exact whereabouts of the other siblings. Kate certainly took her young brother, the four-year-old Bertie, with her, and probably her sister Molly, now ten. The oldest sibling, the fifteen-year-old Winnie, may have already reunited with the family after her time at the convent, or was about to. The next oldest, the thirteen-year-old Betty, was possibly acting with another portable: there are family stories of her periodically being lent out to other companies. After a few months, likely a seeming eternity to a six-year-old child, Doris was rescued by Betty and rejoined Kate and her siblings. Betty, Doris claimed, was always the most organised of the family, and this seems to have been true even when she was no more than twelve or thirteen.

I have not been able to track down precise details of the family's history for the next few years, except for some scattered facts. It was when they were in Devon that Doris and Molly were sent home from school because they had nits. Molly remains an elusive figure. In this large, close-knit family she was the outsider, the one who distanced herself. Perhaps this accounts for her relative absence from the family narrative.

At some point Kate married again and had another child, Edward, always known as Teddy. This second marriage was relatively brief: within a few years her husband, Edward Arrowsmith, was dead of tuberculosis. Doris seems to have had no memories of him. Teddy, born when Kate was in her forties, was always, in the language of the day, a little slow. He too would spend much of his life in the theatre, but as a stagehand, not an actor. He would occasionally visit us when I was a child; one Christmas he built an elaborate puppet theatre for my sister and me. I seem to remember Doris

Fig. 7 – 'Fun in the Kitchen', c.1912. A sketch devised by Doris's mother after the demise of the Alexandra Theatre. Remembered by Betty as 'a terrible turn', the sketch featured Kate and her two oldest daughters: Winnie, the pert chamber maid; Betty, the saucy Boots; Kate as the disciplining cook.

sending him cheques from time to time, and my father passing on some of his older, custom-made suits, but he remains a shadowy figure, about whom I have not been able to discover much.

Soon after arriving in Devon, Kate, now reunited with Winnie and Betty, devised a comic turn, 'Fun in the Kitchen'. Betty remembered it as 'a terrible turn', and it appears to have been short-lived. By late 1912, again through one of Kate's many contacts, Winnie had joined a touring company run by Mr and Mrs F. G. Kimberley. She seems to have stayed for about a year. The company's plays were written by Mrs Kimberley, a prolific author who wrote over forty melodramas. Reflecting perhaps the dominance of women in so much popular theatre at this time, the Kimberleys' company is

Fig. 8 – Betty Hare, 1920. In the Hare family it was agreed that Betty was the 'beauty', just as Doris was acknowledged as the 'funniest' of the siblings.

most often referred to as Mrs Kimberley's company, and I have followed this convention. From October 1912 Winnie is mentioned in reviews of Mrs Kimberley's *The Wild Girl of the Forest*, and the following year she is one of the cast of *Her Path of Sorrow*.[73]

By late 1913 the two oldest Hare sisters, Winnie and Betty, were performing a sister act in variety bills accompanying cinema programmes. In May 1914 one of the Picture Palace Polesworth's weekly programmes included the pictures *The Rattlesnake*, *Madonna of the Storm*, and *Heart of an Outlaw*, and the 'Starring Engagement of *Sisters Hare*, Refined Duettists and Burlesque [in England, parodies of plays, not striptease]. Artistes, including Betty Hare, the lovelight girl'.[74] This latter referred to a song sung by Alice Lloyd (sister of the great music-hall star Marie Lloyd) 'on her second successful American tour', as the sheet music boasts.[75] The popularity of the song probably owed a lot to Lloyd's stage business.

While singing she would hold a hand mirror deflecting a spotlight onto individual men in the audience as she sang pleadingly:

You are the boy that I would die for.
You are the boy that I adore

...

Wouldn't you like to win this prize?
Don't be angry, there's a darling,
Can't you see I'm only looking for the love light in your eyes?

Betty, by now a very pretty sixteen-year-old, used the same stage business with a mirror. She had great success with it in the early months of World War I when the family was earning a little money entertaining the troops in the Portsmouth barracks. They were paid 15s for their performance, which culminated in a tap dance from the nine-year-old Doris. In her seventies Doris still remembered the words of the 'Lovelight' song. She also had vivid memories of Kate, with Teddy in a pushchair, Betty and herself, making the long walk to the barracks from the last tram stop 'with our sheets of music and our props in our hand'.

Meanwhile by December 1914 Winnie was once again with Mrs Kimberley, this time in a play entitled *Australian Nell*.[76] A year later Betty is listed in this production,[77] possibly replacing Winnie, who had left to join the pantomime *Dick Whittington*, another of Mrs Kimberley's productions.

In 1915 Doris, now ten, was about to embark on her own career, joining Mrs Grace Warner's company.[78] Warner was a former West End actress from a distinguished theatrical family now running her own touring company. There is no mention of other members of the Hare family in the cast; it seems Kate sent her youngest daughter off on her own. She would be billed as Little Doris Hare. For the next few years, in order to evade the licensing regulations, she travelled with the birth certificate of one of Kate's sister Maggie's children, a slightly older cousin. Should any sceptical official question her age, it would be explained that she was a midget.

Doris had warm memories of her time with Warner. She often talked about how much she learnt from this early mentor, including how to use her hands on stage. As an adult Doris was an attractive woman but never a beauty; she did, however, have lovely hands with long tapering fingers. She credited Warner with teaching her how to use them. Drawing from the gestural repertoire of melodrama, Warner explained that to draw an audience towards you, always keep your palms facing you, palms facing outwards pushes the audience away. These were lessons she never forgot. Decades later Doris was in 'What a Sweet Little Room', an episode of a 1960s television detective series, *Randall and Hopkirk (deceased)*, playing a fraudulent medium (still available on You Tube). The elegant use of her hands is evidence of the lasting effect of Warner's teaching. C.B. Cochran, one of the dominant impresarios of the first half of the twentieth century (Doris would appear in several of his revues) agreed that proper use of the hands was crucial for an actress. In one of his auto-biographies he describes how he selected women for his famous showgirls: 'I notice, too, how the applicant stands in repose and how she holds her hands. There are women with beautifully shaped hands who nullify their beauty by hanging them clumsily or making restless, ungraceful use of them.'[79] I think we can assume that Cochran did not apply the same criterion to male actors. Acting offered women more opportunities than most professions, but they still needed to conform to the expected gender norms.

Doris's first play with Mrs Warner's company seems to have been *Midnight London* in 1915 in which she played Kitty.[80] In July 1915, she appeared in the cast of *Lady Audley's Secret*, a melodrama which was much performed, although perhaps not often, as in this production, as a musical-comedy drama. The *Arbroath Herald and Advertiser* wrote of Doris's performance: 'The musical numbers are a big treat ... wee Doris Hare and Miss Wayne sang a rollicking duet and joined in a clever Dutch song.' *Lady Audley's Secret*, in the reviewer's opinion, was an improvement over the previous night's play, *Till Kingdom Come*, being 'even richer in acting, and certainly more musical and funnier'.[81] It was *Till Kingdom Come*, however, that Doris remembered best.

Till Kingdom Come by Roy Rhind, is set, like a number of melo-dramas during this period, in the American West. Licensed by the Lord Chamberlain in 1913, its plot is a wonderful collection of melo-dramatic tropes. The heroine Kate Meredith (played by Warner) is a

Fig. 9 – Doris in 'Dutch' costume. 'Dutch' costumes were popular for child performers. Doris would have worn something like this when she and Miss Wayne sang their 'clever Dutch song' in *Lady Audley's Secret* in 1915 (see p. 47).

much put-upon woman. She exemplifies melodrama's figure of inno-cence, continually beset by villainy but, through the working of destiny rather than her own agency, ultimately triumphant. Her child has been kidnapped by Indians, her husband killed by the villain for his gold claim. She herself is falsely imprisoned, then vindicated, but not before she is struck blind when the prison catches fire. As she searches for her lost child, a young Indian boy, White Hawk, is her faithful guide and protector. She also befriends a little Indian girl, Blue Moon – this is the role Doris played – who falls sick and is nursed back to health by the grieving mother. As thanks, the child gives her a locket with the initials B. M.: 'That's why they call me Blue Moon', she explains. The blind mother feels the locket with her hands and immediately recognises it, exclaiming: 'Not Blue Moon, but Brenda Meredith, my own lost child!' – the shock simultaneously restoring her sight. Warner would then clasp her recovered child to her ample, corseted bosom; Doris had vivid memories of crashing into the rigid whalebone stays. Meanwhile White Hawk has finished off the villain with a well-aimed shot and all ends happily.

Doris's time with Mrs Warner's company seems to have come to an end towards the end of 1915. I have been unable to pin down exactly where she went after leaving Grace Warner's company, but it seems likely that for a few months she joined The Seven Leroys, billed in *The Era* as 'The Greatest and Cleverest Juvenile Novelty Act in Vaudeville'.[82] 'Juvenile troupes', child performers who sang, danced, and did little sketches, were extremely popular at the time. Doris sometimes talked about her time with this troupe. There are scattered references to it in *The Era*, *The Stage*, and various provincial newspapers, the earliest 17 February 1914 and the latest 20 December 1917. If these were the years the troupe was active, then sometime between late 1915 and the autumn of 1916 is the only possible period that Doris could have been with them. None of these references mentions Doris by name, but in 1951 the manager of the troupe, Scott Sanders (stage name Roy Le Roy), reminisced in *The Stage* about those who had been members of The Seven Leroys at one time or another, and the first name he mentions is 'Doris Hare'.[83] The Seven Leroys was not the only juvenile troupe with whom Doris performed: a few years later she would be a member of the Five Bing Kids.

A family photograph of 'Little Doris Hare' may well date from her time with The Seven Leroys. Notice her wrinkled cotton socks in the photograph. This was deliberate. From a very early age she insisted that she was 'a realist actress' and rejected certain stylised conventions of stage performance. The ordinary children she saw in the streets, and represented on stage, did not have neatly gartered socks, and neither would she. Her world may have been the world of the theatre, but all her life she was a close observer of how those outside that world lived their lives and would draw on these observations in her performances.

Fig. 10 – Little Doris Hare, the 'realist' actress, c.1915. Winnie cut this image of her little sister out of a larger photo, sticking it in one of her family scrapbooks.

Porcelain Visions

Doris and her siblings never made a conscious choice to be actors. From their earliest age that was what they were. None of them ever attended drama school. They learnt their craft by watching other performers and performing themselves. For these children born into the trade, the theatre could be magical, but it was not remote. Their introduction to live performance was very different from that of the Welsh actor and playwright Emlyn Williams, whose life in later years would repeatedly intersect with that of the Hare family, a connection that would begin early. Born in November 1905, a few months after Doris, Williams' working-class family had no ties to the world of theatre. The first live performers he saw appeared to him as other-worldly beings. He recalls this transformative moment in his autobiography, *George*. When he was about twelve his family moved from a small village to Connah's Quay, a town with a cinema. For several years the highlight of his week was a visit to this palace of wonders.[84] The evening's entertainment would include live performances by comedians, singers, and other variety acts. And at Connah's Quay Williams encountered and was entranced by the juvenile troupes, including one he remembered as the Eight Bing Babies:

I was left cold by the comics ... But I feasted on the occasional troupes: The Eight Bing Babies, in their dazzling Song and Dance Scena "Babes in Toyland", were ladies of seventeen dressed as flaxen-haired toddlers in tiny frills over biscuit-coloured tights, holding parasols and tap-dancing in graceful time to the tinny piano. They were radiant beings never to be identified with the furtive hooded creatures who had slipped down the aisle into the little door and must perforce lodge in the Quay. After the final number – high kicks in rhythm with the spinning parasols. "There's a Girl ... for Every *Sole*-jah!" – I was startled to see two of them pirouette down into the audience and squeak "Postcards of the Babes, one penny each!" That they should move among us was somehow an offence, and to stop the porcelain visions cracking into painted masks, I shut my eyes.[85]

Fig. 11 – The Bing Kids, c.1919. Doris has labelled this photo 'The Five Bing Kids', although it shows six 'kids'. Doris is sitting on the piano, fourth from the left. Mamie Souter, the star of the troupe, is on the far right.

The Bing Babies, or more accurately, the Bing Babes, were one of a number of juvenile troupes managed by Lal Edwards. They first appear in ads in *The Stage* in 1917, and with some modification of the name they continue to feature in ads in various newspapers until at least 1937. The name Bing probably came from the 1916 show *The Bing Boys are Here*, one of the most popular musicals of the war years. They were more often billed as 'The Bing Kids', some- times 'The Five Bing Kids', or 'The Six Bing Kids', but although their number occasionally rises to seven, I could not locate any reference to 'The Eight Bing Babes'. It is understandable that Williams, writing his autobiography more than forty years later, confuses the name and the number a little. Over the years indi- vidual members of the troupe would come and go. Doris joined Edwards's troupe – always in her memory 'The Five Bing Kids' – a couple of years after Williams' encounter with 'The Bing Babes'. This was probably in 1919 around the time she turned fourteen. Child performers under fourteen were required to be licensed by the local magistrate and managers preferred not to have to jump through this bureaucratic hoop – although Scott Sanders seems not to have worried about this when putting together his Seven Leroys. Edwards's ads often solicited bookings for his juvenile troupes with the inducement 'no licences required'.[86] Children would be recruited through ads in *The Stage*. Perhaps Kate had responded to this one in 1919?

> Wanted, Children for Vaudeville Act, smart Juveniles, between 14 and 16. Must be good Buck and Schott dancers. Also good Juvenile Speciality Girl, capable of Comedy and Character. To open Feb, 17. Six months' contract to right girls – send full pars [particulars], age, height, and photo, Lal Edwards. [87]

A 'live-in' contract provided lodging in the different towns where the troupe performed, and a matron to supervise the girls.

Child performers have a long history in British theatre. They were extremely popular in the nineteenth century. In the twentieth century juvenile troupes, like the Bing Kids, were a staple item of variety shows at least up to World War II. Fourteen may have been the age of legal employment, but it is not clear how strictly this was enforced. According to Noël Coward (born 1899), who began his career as a child actor very young, licences were granted as a matter of course.[88] Still, someone like Edwards in the business of managing juvenile troupes probably had to be careful. At the same time the girls had to pass as being actual children. A number of Edwards's ads specify that the girls need to be 'small'. Doris remembered the bourgeoning breasts of Bing Kids' star, Mamie Souter, being strapped down before performances to maintain the illusion of childhood. The erotic frisson should not be too blatant. As Graham Greene observed in his notorious review of a 1937 Shirley Temple film (a child performer very much in the mould of these juvenile troupes) in the magazine *Night and Day*,

> Adult emotions of love and grief glissade across the mask of childhood, a childhood skin-deep. ... Her admirers ... respond to her dubious coquetry, to the sight of her well-shaped and desirable little body, packed with enormous vitality, only because the safety curtain of story and dialogue drops between their intelligence and their desire. "Why are you making my Mummy cry?" – what could be purer than that?[89]

Pointing out this truth was hazardous. Greene's acuity resulted in a successful libel suit by Twentieth Century Fox (Shirley Temple's studio) against *Night and Day* with hefty damages that led to the demise of the magazine, and the suppression of the review for decades. There are some things that are not to be spoken. But even if they chose to deny it, theatre world insiders had always recognised the erotic undercurrent of child performers. Ever the realist, Doris's mother knew from her years of experience what audiences wanted. When the nine-year-old Doris was dancing for the troops in Portsmouth, she remembered being told to flip her skirt at the end of a number: 'Show 'em your drawers,' Kate would say.

Touring with a juvenile troupe meant not only hard work but, as Doris remembered, freezing cold theatrical digs and never enough food. Once, probably when she was with The Seven Leroys, she ran away back to Kate. Anxious to have her back, the troupe's managers entered into negotiations. All her life Doris loved cheese, and eventually she agreed to return on condition that every night she would be given Welsh Rarebit for supper.

Touring with the Family

Life was not easy for Kate during these years. After the demise of the Alexandra Theatre she had rejected her sister-in-law's offer to adopt Bertie, but in 1916, when he was nine, she made the difficult decision that it would be best for him to go to the Actors Orphanage.[90] The orphanage took not just orphans but children with one living parent who was finding it hard to manage. According to Doris, it was Betty who was responsible for arranging her brother's admittance. In 1916 the Orphanage's October minutes record 'the application for admis-

Fig. 12 – Doris's brother Bertie. The photograph may have been taken around the time he was admitted to the Actors' Orphanage in 1916.

sion [of] Herbert Edwin Hare, aged 9, son of the late Herbert Edwin Hare (professional name Bert Breamer), actor, and Kate Hare, Actress'.[91] Five recommenders were listed, one of whom was Grace Warner, and another Alfred Denville, an old friend of Kate and Bert's from the Travelling Theatre Managers' Association. One reason for sending Bertie to the orphanage may have been his health. The November minutes record the admittance of Herbert Hare, who was 'suffering from tonsils and adenoids, and has been operated on by Dr Wood, and is now quite well'.[92]

There is no record of when Bertie left the orphanage but a review in a local paper of the orphanage's annual pantomime in January 1925, notes his performance in a drag role: 'Bertie Hare, whose make up as the lady, Cogia, was excellent, as also was his vivacious acting, especially in that funny song, "Father bob your whiskers ere the robins nest again".'[93] Bertie would then have been seventeen. Presumably he would have left the orphanage soon after. He spent his life in the theatre, nearly always employed, although never achieving great success.

In September 1916 Mrs Kimberley was once again embarking on a long tour of the provinces with one of her own plays, *Just a Little Pair of Shoes*, described by her as 'a story with a moral told by a woman for women'.[94] Winnie, Kate, and Doris were all engaged; perhaps this was a factor in the decision to send Bertie to the orphanage? The play was certainly not to the taste of the male Lord Chamberlain official who read it for licensing, although he did not go so far as to ban it: 'A forcible-feeble domestic drama ... Amateurish and crude in its technicality, but otherwise inoffensive, and Recommended for Licence'.[95]

The theme of this play 'told by a woman for women' was the potentially disastrous effects of jealousy, here a jealous wife who suspects her husband of interest in another woman. Doris played Little Sweetie, a pair of her baby shoes giving the play its title. Winnie and Kate were the two maids, Sulky Jane and Smiling Liz, whose tussles over the affections of the servant, Bobbie, provide comic relief. The eleven-year-old Doris was noticed by reviewers. For *The Era*, 'Little Doris, a child actress of remarkable intelligence, scored a distinct success as "Sweetie".'[96] The *Gloucester Journal* wrote,

'Sweetie is very prettily played by Little Doris Hare ... Some of the prettiest scenes are those in which this little actress takes part.'[97]

Mrs Kimberley's tour included: Bargoed, where Doris was born; Ton Pentre, where Kate and Bert's newly launched theatre was severely damaged in a snowstorm; and other small towns in the Rhondda valley that had been part of the Alexandra Theatre's circuit. The itinerary is evidence that the demise of the portables was due not only to the competition from the new 'moving pictures', but also to the increasing reach of touring companies like those of Mrs Kimberly and Mrs Warner. These companies were now visiting even the small towns they had previously left to the portables, offering a similar repertory of melodrama but one more lavishly staged in more comfortable venues.

Most likely it was after Mrs Kimberley's tour ended in 1918 that Doris joined the Five (or Six) Bing Kids (Fig. 11). She was already a versatile performer. All actors in the lower echelons of the theatrical hierarchy were expected not only to act but also to sing and dance. Doris's 'rollicking duet' and 'clever Dutch song' with Miss Wayne, when she was with Mrs Warner, suggest that she developed these skills early. They stood her in good stead as the popularity of melodrama declined in the years after World War I, and audiences deserted it for variety (replacing the old music halls), and the new medium of film. During her time with the Bing Kids Doris further honed her song and dance skills. She and Mamie Souter performed a duet, 'Little Mr Baggie Britches' (another 'Dutch' song), where she was Mr Baggie Britches, one of the first of a series of urchin roles she performed over the years.

From her earliest years Doris was totally committed to her profession and determined to learn as much as she could. Neither she nor Kate ever considered drama school. All her life she remained sceptical of academic training for actors, a scepticism shared by Noël Coward, later to be a key figure in her career. A line in his song discouraging over-eager stage mothers, 'Don't Put Your Daughter on the Stage Mrs Worthington' goes, 'Though they said at the school of acting she was lovely as Peer Gynt',[98] a joke that reflects Doris and Coward's belief that drama school teaching had little to do with the realities of the commercial stage. For these two performers, both of whom started as child actors, you learnt the craft of acting by watching others performing in front of live audiences. One of Coward's first roles was with Charles Hawtrey's company. As Sheridan Morley tells the story, 'Coward, astute eleven-year-old child that he was, realized that here was a man [Hawtrey] from whom he could learn – by what he taught and, more important, by the way he acted on stage.'[99] Morley describes how 'Coward would stand nightly in the wings watching and learning'.[100] And that, too, was how Doris learned. In a 1987 edition of the Radio 2 programme *It's a Funny Business*, she reminisced about her time in juvenile troupes:

> In Variety it was wonderful because you could stand on the side of the stage and watch all these wonderful people, all the greats, and watch them do their numbers. Like Ella Shields, she was this enchanting woman with hardly any voice. ... And there was another lovely one called Dainty Daisy Dormer. So seeing all these stars I absorbed everything standing on the side of the stage. ... And, of course, if there was ever a dancer on the bill, I'd stand there doing my walloping [Doris's term for her energetic dancing], pinching all the steps. ... The moment the theatre was open, we were all in there, learning to dance better.

That, for Doris, was how you learnt your craft.

Comedy was at the heart of Doris's persona as a performer, and her training in comedy began early. All the Hare women knew how to play comedy. For the *Leigh Chronicle* reviewer of *Just a Little Pair of Shoes*, 'The scrap between "Sulky Jane" (Miss Kate Braemar) and "Smiling Liz" (Miss Winnie Braemar) is one of the funniest scenes imaginable.'[101] Kate was Doris's first teacher. Family lore has it that Doris's father, too, was a great comedy actor, one of his roles with the Alexandra Theatre having been the lead in *Charley's Auntie* (Fig. 6). He died too early, however, for Doris to have known him as a performer.

Ireland

I have not been able to track down where Kate went after the end of the tour of *Just a Little Pair of Shoes*, but by September 1919 she was in Dublin with Roberto Lena's All-Irish Dramatic Company in *The Link that Binds*, a romantic drama by Gladys Hastings-Walton. Perhaps she responded to this ad that Lena placed in *The Era* on 25 June 1919: 'WANTED, good useful Lady and Gent. for Repertoire Co., Ireland; long comfortable tour; state if do turn.' Lena may have promised 'a long comfortable tour' but this was a time of unrest and violence in Ireland. Three years after the failed Easter Uprising in 1916, and three years before the creation of the Irish Free State in 1922, the Irish Republican Army (IRA) was waging a guerrilla war that was met by fierce reprisals by the British Army.

The Link that Binds played at the Queen's Theatre in Dublin. The Queen's was, in the words of its historian Séamus de Búrca, 'a people's theatre'[102] rather different from the more famous Abbey Theatre founded by W. B. Yeats and Lady Augusta Gregory in 1904 to 'bring upon the stage the deeper emotions of Ireland'.[103] Melodramas like *The Link that Binds* constituted the staple fare of the Queen's. The *Irish Independent* described the 1919 production as 'Melodrama of a comparatively tame character, it embodies many moral maxims and homely truths'. The villain, 'one of the most dissipated lords in London', attempts to work his villainy on a 'group of honest fisherfolk'. The leading roles of the hero, 'a breezy sailor lad', and 'the flashy young lady of unsavoury repute' were played by Lena and Kate (now fifty-one), 'very successfully', according to the reviewer.[104]

Winnie and Doris either accompanied Kate to Ireland or soon joined her there. After Kate's engagement with Lena, the three of them did go on a long tour, though it was not with Lena, and it was not always comfortable. Kate always travelled with a large tin of Keating's insect powder, which promised that 'a small quantity placed in the crevices of a bedstead will destroy bugs; a little sprinkled upon the pillow and sheets at bedtime will prevent persons being bitten by these or other offensive insects'.[105] Despite Kate's precautions, 'in some of those places', Doris remembered, 'we were eaten alive with bugs.' The travelling theatre they joined was run by Breffni O'Rourke (1889-1946) and his wife Alice Cole. This was not a portable, but a fit-up company, as was Lena's probably. Fit-ups would hire a local barn or other suitable space and fit it up as a theatre. Like portables, they played a different play each night, and the entertainment they offered was much the same, melodramas supplemented by short comic pieces and variety turns. But while portables would stay in a town for several months, fit-ups stayed for far shorter periods; O'Rouke's company seems to have moved every week.[106]

Also in the company was Alice's son, Cyril Cusack, who would grow up to become one of Ireland's leading actors. His father, James Cusack, was a South African policeman, whom Alice, a former chorus girl in London, had divorced when her son was six. The two of them then moved to Ireland where she met O'Rourke. Cusack spent six or seven years travelling with his mother and his stepfather's company. In 1971 when he was a guest on the *This is Your Life* that featured Doris, he recalled his ten-year-old self having something of a crush on her. His time with the fit-up would leave Cusack with a love and respect for the melodramas they played, particularly those of the Irish playwright Dion Boucicault (1820-1890). 'The melodrama most emphatically has a place in the theatre', he wrote in the 1970s, 'It is good theatre: theatre theatrical, not theatre of the intellect.'[107] Doris had less fond memories of some of the plays they did and the songs she sang, many seemingly from the blackface repertory: 'What was it I used to sing? It was always about Dixie or Carolina, a song of Carolina, all those songs. God they were terrible.' By now Doris was a rather gangling fifteen-year-old adolescent and moving on to adult roles. In one unnamed play she was a villainess, wearing a blonde wig and high-heeled shoes, which she remembered only just about managing. She also had a cigarette holder that she managed rather better: 'I did all this very high-class stuff, [saying] "Cora Cornell I will get this man", with a cigarette. No smoke ever came out of it but I did all the gestures. It was the most terrible play.' In melodrama, as Jerome K. Jerome noted, 'A cigarette on the stage is always the badge of infamy. ... behind the cigarette on the stage lurks ever black-hearted villainy and abandoned womanhood.'[108]

The political 'Troubles' were a constant background to the family's time in Ireland. Doris had memories of the company being told by the local IRA to vacate at least one barn in which they were performing because 'We're going to blow the place up.' O'Rourke himself was a Irish nationalist, which probably gave them some protection. Doris remembers him singing Irish rebel songs in the concert part of the bill. After leaving O'Rourke's company in December 1920, Kate, Winnie, and Doris were booked to appear in the Gilbert O'Mara Repertory Company's Christmas pantomime, *Shaun and the Golden Apples*, at the Theatre Royal, Waterford,[109] but it is likely they never appeared. Increasingly uneasy as violence escalated in late 1920, Kate and her children decided to return home.

By early 1921 they were back in England, where Molly, the elusive sibling, was on tour with a production of *The Better 'Ole*. This was an enormously successful musical comedy that a few years later was made into film starring Charlie Chaplin's brother Syd. It was inspired by a famous Bruce Bairnsfather World War I cartoon, featuring two British soldiers in a shell-hole, with shells exploding all around them. One is saying to the other 'Well, if you knows of a better 'ole, go to it.' The twenty-year-old Molly was playing the part of Victoire, a French woman who helps the hero Old Bill. This was one occasion on which Molly responded to the call for family solidarity, securing a part in the show for her younger sister. No longer Little Doris Hare, Doris was about to embark on her career as an adult performer. Before taking up that story, however, I want to look in a little more detail at melodrama and the performance style associated with it, since this was the milieu that first shaped Doris as an actress.

CHAPTER 4

OF MELODRAMA AND PERFORMANCE

Melodramas, however much they would seem to be offering a narrative distant from our daily lives, however much they might be labelled 'escapist', are always about something far more immediate, even if we fail to recognize what that something is.

David Mayer[110]

Born into a theatrical family, Doris had no ambivalence about her profession. From her earliest years she embraced her identity as an actress. A story from her childhood she liked to tell recalled one of the few periods she attended school. In general she had very little in the way of formal education; she and her siblings' real life was in the theatre, even if from time to time they might be sent to a local school for a few weeks or maybe months. During the bleak months when she was left alone in Cwmfelinfach after the collapse of the Alexandra Theatre in 1911, she remembered attending the local primary school. Even then, aged six, she saw herself as an actress: 'Always being an entertainer, I entertained the children, told them stories about my life in the theatre.' And she used her special status as 'the little actress' to secure a place by the only source of heat in the freezing cold school room, explaining, 'I get so cold and I have to watch my voice.' As a result, 'they sat me in the corner by the fire and I'd sit there and make faces at the kids. I was such a show off. I was getting laughs anyway.'

Doris's sense of herself as an actress and an independent woman was bolstered by her upbringing surrounded by strong women, all part of the theatre world. Her father had died when she was two, but she had her mother, Kate, to whom she remained devoted throughout her life. For Doris, Kate was a tower of strength, an unfailing source of comfort and down-to-earth wisdom. Then there were her two older actress sisters, Winnie, and especially Betty. And while the more prestigious theatre realms may have been dominated by male actor-managers, at the lower levels there were many women theatre managers, such as Mrs Warner, and Mrs Kimberley, two of Doris's earliest mentors (the previous chapter told the story of her time with them). Her early socialisation among strong women helped to give Doris self-confidence and a belief in herself as a performer that lasted her whole life. And there were times when she very much needed that belief.

The Truth of Melodrama

Doris was first schooled in the craft of acting through performing in melodramas, which constituted the core of both the portable theatre repertoire, and that of the plays toured by Mrs Warner and Mrs Kimberly. Of the four plays listed on the 1907 Alexandra Theatre Bill (Fig. 5), the three that are given legible descriptions are described as melodramas. To Alexandra Theatre audiences, melodrama was a familiar genre with its own well-known conventions. And this was true not only of the portables. Until the rise of realist drama in the twentieth century, melodrama was the dominant genre of popular drama in both Britain and America. Since its fall from favour, its long popularity is often seen as evidence of the naivety of nineteenth-century audiences, a good example of what E. P. Thompson termed 'the condescension of posterity'.[111]

It is true that judged by the standard of realism, nineteenth-century melodramas cannot be taken seriously. Their stock one-dimensional characters, impossibly pure, innocent heroines, utterly wicked villains with no redeeming features, absurd plots piling coincidence on coincidence, and stylised, unnaturalistic dialogue, offend too gravely against realist cannons. But perhaps this is not the appropriate standard to use? Perhaps melodrama should be seen not as failed realism, but as aiming at the portrayal of a different kind of truth? I am reminded of Anna Laetitia Barbauld's criticism of 'The Ancient Mariner' as recorded by Samuel Taylor Coleridge: 'Mrs Barbauld told me that the only faults she found with the Ancient Mariner were –

that it was improbable, and had no moral.'[112] The absurdity of judging 'The Ancient Mariner' against real life is obvious, and it is poor Mrs Barbauld who comes across as ridiculous, but maybe those who criticise melodrama for its lack of 'probability' are making a similar category mistake? More than forty years ago, Peter Brooks provided a stimulating new way of thinking about melodrama. While Brooks's primary focus was literary rather than theatrical, and more recent scholarship has complicated and enriched our understanding of melodrama in the theatre, his identification of the moral structure at the heart of the genre, and his clarity in delineating this, is still useful in helping the modern reader think their way into the now distant world of melodrama – the world that provided Doris with her earliest education in the nature of 'drama'.

Tracing its origins to the plays of Guilbert de Pixerécourt, written in France in the turbulent aftermath of the French Revolution, Brooks describes melodrama as

> the drama of morality: it strives to find, to articulate, to demonstrate, to "prove" the existence of a moral universe which, though put into question, masked by villainy and perversions of judgement, does exist and can be made to assert its presence and its categorical force among men.[113]

Pixerécourt himself was an educated and literate man who took his art seriously. Reportedly he said that he wrote plays for those who could not read.[114] The English melodramas performed by the portables in the later nineteenth century by contrast tended to be the work of hack playwrights, often unacknowledged translations of French melodramas churned out in a matter of days. Dickens's account of Mr Crummles's instructions to Nicholas Nickleby when he enlists him not only as an actor, but also a playwright, is probably not far removed from the reality of the authorial process. To Nicholas's dismay Mr Crummles announces to the assembled company that his new recruit will provide them with a new play in a few days. Nicholas protests: 'But really I can't ... My invention is not accustomed to these demands.' To which Mr Crummles responds with impatience:

"Invention! what the devil's that got to do with it?" cried the manager hastily.

"Everything my dear sir."

"Nothing, my dear sir," retorted the manager, with evident impatience. "Do you understand French?"

"Perfectly well."

"Very good," said the manager, opening the table drawer, and giving a roll of paper from it to Nicholas. "There! Just turn this into English, and put your name on the title-page."[115]

The appropriation of French plays without acknowledgement or any royalty payment was standard. As the theatre historian Michael Booth writes,

From the manager's point of view it was much quicker and much cheaper to pay an author a few pounds to translate and adapt a French piece than to get him to write something new. ... All through the century French fiction and drama were fruitful sources of ideas, and many of the best melodramas were originally French.[116]

In the years the Alexandra Theatre was operating there were hundreds of such plays available to them.

Current Cash

The play in which Doris made her acting debut at around age four, *Current Cash*, is a good example of the melodramas so central to the Alexandra Theatre's repertory. I had difficulty tracking down a copy of the play, written in 1886 by C. A. Clarke. No print copy seems to survive but I did manage to locate a typescript in the Charles Morton Agency Collection of American Popular Drama at the University of Chicago Library.[117] No author is credited; the typescript may well be a pirated copy.

Doris played Sophie, who appears in the prologue as a child. This prologue features the 'villainy' that sets the play's plot in motion. Villainy, as David Mayer notes, is the central propelling force in melodrama: 'The villain, for reasons which are personal to him and altogether reprehensible, must instigate an action which destabilizes the hero and heroine'[118] threatening them with ruin and misfortune. As with many popular melodramas of the time, Empire is part of the play's backdrop. The prologue is set in a British fort in Afghanistan, ten years before the events of the subsequent three acts. The hero, Mark Milton, a British officer, unjustly condemned of cowardice in battle, is about to be shot. His wife Grace and six-year-old daughter Sophie arrive. Grace brings news that Milton's uncle's will has finally been proved and that he now has an income of £10,000 a year. Villainy is represented by Gordon Challis, a fellow officer Milton asks to assist him in drawing up a will to ensure the future of his wife and child. Challis tricks Milton into signing a will that leaves everything to him, Challis. The child Sophie plays a vital role since she overhears Challis, as he writes the fraudulent will, gloating over his tricking of his supposed friend. She then utters a line Doris always remembered, if a little inaccurately: 'My papa never told you to say that.' The line as written in the typescript is: 'My Papa never told you to write that.' In Act I, set some years later, we learn that Grace challenged the will, but her daughter's account of the forgery was discounted. Thanks to Sophie, however, her mother knows the truth. The child's line is an important plot point. That Doris never forgot the line suggests how firmly its importance was impressed on her as a four-year-old child.

Current Cash, assembled from a number of the standard tropes, exemplifies melodrama's moral landscape and the kind of truth to which it aspires: the falsely accused hero (Milton), who is apparently killed early in the play, only to return in disguise; the forged will that robs his wife and their child of their inheritance; the villain and his comic henchman; the mismatched lovers whose constant bickering provides additional comic relief; the original will that is finally discovered; the hero's pardon that arrives in the nick of time; and the happy ending in which virtue is rewarded and villainy punished. Good and evil are unambiguous; the hero, his wife and child are purely virtuous, the villain purely villainous. The plot would doubtless not meet Anna Laetitia Barbauld's criterion of probability, but she could not have claimed that 'it had no moral'. Morality it supplies in spades, laying out in the clearest terms, as Brooks puts it, 'a moral universe which, though put into question, masked by villainy and perversions of judgement, does exist'.[119]

Performing Melodrama

Unlike Emlyn Williams, Doris and her siblings never encountered the theatre as an enchanted realm remote from everyday reality. But their familiarity with the drab reality of the theatre by day, did not mean that they were immune to the magic of performance and the power of melodrama. This was theatre in which actors were paramount; indeed, actors in more recent times have sometimes looked back with nostalgia to their lost centrality. Donald Sinden, who starred in a 1970 Royal Shakespeare Company production of Dion Boucicault's *London Assurance* (first produced in 1841), reflected on his fondness for nineteenth-century plays in a Foreword he wrote for a biography of Boucicault: 'The reason why I like nineteenth-century drama so much is that plays then were written for actors.'[120] Part of what this means is that performed by skilful actors, words that seem clichéd and flat on the page are transmuted into powerful emotional truth.

In the recollections she wrote many decades later in the notebook discovered by my sister, Betty recalled her vivid memories of watching her mother act Rudiga in *The Woman in Red*, part of the Alexandra Theatre's core repertoire (see Fig. 3).

Rudiga is a grieving Jewish mother, whose daughter has been stolen from her. Betty never forgot the play's great emotional climax:

> Rudiga is alone on the stage, broken hearted – she has lost her mind – and has a great dramatic speech going back over her life and her search for her lost child. Weeping she cries "Go to thy grave poor mother, you have been digging it for years." ... If I could only sneak in to see this play, I was in heaven, and could hardly bear to hear "Go to thy grave poor mother."

The Woman in Red is a translation of the 1859 French play, *La Tireuse de Cartes*, by Victor Séjour. There were numerous English versions. The one I found is by J. Stirling Coyne and was first performed in 1864.[121] It may well have been the one Kate performed. In its stylised language and the twists and turns of its plot, *The Woman in Red* follows the conventions of melodrama. Its main protagonist, however, Rudiga (the woman in red), is not a simple embodiment of good or evil. She has a moral ambiguity unusual in the protagonists of melodrama. Betty's memory of her mother's great dramatic speech is not entirely accurate, however. Rudiga has not 'lost her mind'; like Lady Macbeth, she is sleepwalking. The wording of her cry of despair as she goes back over her life and her search for her lost child is also a little different: 'Poor mother! To your grave, to your grave. They have been digging it for sixteen years; now 'tis ready to receive you. To your grave where this poor broken heart will be at rest.' What stayed with Betty was Kate's embodiment as an actress of maternal suffering, and her own intense identification with those sufferings as a member of the audience.

The moral dilemma at the heart of the play is one that remains relevant: the competing claims of adoptive and birth mothers. Rudiga is Jewish but her child Francesca has been kidnapped and brought up by Constanza, a Christian woman who has lost her own child. The play recognises both mothers' genuine love for Francesca, and how it makes each woman act cruelly to the other. At least as regards Rudiga and Constanza, the play's moral world is not simply black and while. In the year Doris was born, 1905, Britain had passed the Aliens Act, an Act, as Neal Ascherson explains, designed to control immigration, and in particular that of 'undesirable' and 'diseased Jews'.[122] At a time when anti-Semitic stereotypes were rife in popular entertainment, the play's empathy with the plight of the Jewish mother is notable, as is its enduring popularity with melodrama's working-class audiences. The Alexandra Theatre was still presenting *The Woman in Red* as late as 1911, almost half a century after the initial London production of Coyne's adaptation.

The kidnapping takes place in the Prologue. The story is taken up again in Act I, sixteen years later. Rudiga has spent those years desperately seeking her lost child, while Constanza and Francesca have formed a deep bond. After many trials and tribulations, in line with melodrama's fondness for happy endings, all is resolved. The villain who orchestrated the kidnapping is dispatched; and after witnessing the sleepwalking scene in which Rudiga recounts her anguished search for her lost child, Francesca and Constanza recognise the depth of the birth mother's love for her child. Rudiga for her part recognises the deep bond between Francesca and her adoptive mother and relinquishes her hatred for Constanza, who in turn asks Rudiga's forgiveness. In the last line of the play the latter addresses the audience:

> RUDIGA: And you who have pitied the sufferings, and felt for the wrongs of the poor Jewess, rejoice with her now, for she has subdued all, suffered all, and gained all by the powerful magic of a Mother's Love.

This celebration of the power of motherhood, and its eventual triumph over the villainy that assails it, whatever the trials and tribulations to which it is subjected, is in line with Brooks' definition of the essence of melodrama as the demonstration that even though assailed by 'villainy and perversions of judgement', nonetheless, there is 'a moral universe' which will ultimately assert itself.[123]

Like Betty, Doris remembered the power of her mother's performances. Kate also starred in *Jane Shore* by W. G. Wells: this highly fictionalised dramatization of the penance inflicted on the real-life Jane Shore, mistress of Edward IV, was another staple of the Alexandra Theatre's repertory. As in *The Woman in Red*, the play tells the story of a woman subjected to many trials and tribulations. Doris, like Betty, seems to have been particularly moved by their mother's powerful evocation of a suffering, humiliated woman, cruelly abused by those around her. Doris remembered how, subject to the scorn of the mob, Jane Shore's vulnerability and powerlessness was portrayed through the popular trope in melodrama in which a helpless woman is hauled around the stage by her hair. In dramatizations of *Oliver Twist*, for instance, Bill Sykes, before murdering Nancy, seizes her by her hair. Kate's embodiment of female humiliation stayed with Doris: 'when Kate used to play Jane Shore, oh I used to cry and cry. She had a long blonde wig and used to be dragged on the stage by this.'

It is notable that both these performances, which lodged themselves so firmly in the memories of Kate's children, portrayed female suffering. At the same time, however transported by the emotional intensity of her performance, her children knew that they were watching their mother *acting*. And it was through watching her and the other actors that they began to learn their craft.

The Portable Theatre Actor

Those who operated in more prestigious theatrical spheres tended to look down on portables and their actors, seeing their crude melodramas and old-fashioned acting style as pandering to the debased tastes of the poor and the ignorant. Such first-hand accounts as there are of portables tend to be by actors who early in their careers spent a short time in a portable but then moved on to more respectable forms of theatre. One such is a memoir written in 1938 by Maud Gill, a forty-year-old, self-described 'comparatively unknown actress' who had nonetheless earned a living acting 'from her eighteenth birthday to the present time'.[124] Gill came from a middle-class background with no theatrical links. Early in her career, sometime before World War I, she responded to an ad in *The Stage* for what she thought was a touring company. It turned out to be a portable company, a species of theatre until then completely unknown to her. Once she realises what she has got herself into, her attitude, tinged with condescension, has something of the fascination of an anthropologist observing a strange new tribe:

> The people themselves were the dearest, kindest crowd that could be imagined. Terribly poor and shabby, but full of good feeling and cheerfulness. I shared rooms with the comedian and his wife. He was very proud of being always "well turned out." He wore a stiff white collar; most of the men wore mufflers. On entering the house he used to remove his collar and cuffs, wrap them in a silk handkerchief and put them on again when he went out. This care made them last a week or longer and economized with the laundry.[125]

The importance of being 'well turned out' was something Doris imbibed from her earliest years, and it stayed with her throughout her life. 'An actress', she would declare, 'must look like an actress.' Whether she was on stage or off, her public must see an *actress*. In later life she was deeply disapproving of those who could be seen leaving the theatre after the show in a pair of scruffy old jeans, and no makeup. For Doris the theatre was about the creation of illusion and magic. Actors are guardians of the mysteries that produce the magic; they have an obligation to preserve the illusion.

The brotherhood and sisterhood of the theatre, as Gill's reference to 'the dearest kindest crowd that could be imagined' suggests, was essentially equalitarian. There is a fond, and less condescending account of this equalitarianism, in the humourist Jerome K. Jerome's *On the Stage - and Off* (first published in 1885), in which he recalls the time he spent as an aspiring actor in the 1870s:

> Among players there are none of those caste distinctions such as put an insurmountable barrier between the man who sells coal by the ton and the man who sells it by the hundredweight. "The Profession" is a Republic. Lead and Utility walk about arm-in-arm, and the Star and the Singing Chambermaid drink out of the same pewter, we were all as friendly and sociable together as brothers and sisters – perhaps even more so – and the evening spent in those bare dressing rooms was the pleasantest part of the day.[126]

Doris would have recognised this picture of actors, all actors, as members of one community: the community of 'pros'.

Portable theatres had their own way of working, quite different from that with which Gill was familiar. They would generally perform a different play every night, a necessity given the limited size of their potential audience in a small town; there was no time for extended rehearsals. At the first rehearsal her ignorance was revealed:

> The play in rehearsal was *The Mariners of England*, or *The Death of Nelson*. I asked for my part and caused consternation. I was the only one unused to Portable work. All the others had a good idea of the plots and scenes of the usual repertoires and worked without parts at all. The Manager told them what the scene was about; if he had a copy of the play he would read it to them; then they just "gagged." They went on and said lines which seemed appropriate to them and when one of them stopped another began. Of course,

the scenes were rehearsed several times, and if an unimportant character showed too much volubility he was checked.

I felt absolutely hopeless. Anyhow, everybody was very kind to me. The women of the company got together and with a penny exercise book and a stump of lead pencil and wrote down an outline of my part, and at the second rehearsal I talked with the best of them. The amazing thing is that after a show or two the scenes fixed themselves and hardly varied by a word. If anyone remembered a good line that he had heard years ago in some other play, he would warn the others and put it in. Our serious scenes were positively grim; our comedy scenes were mostly knock-about business.[127]

This was only possible because the core of their repertoire consisted of plays, primarily melodramas, known to all experienced portable actors. Walter Haggar explains:

There was a series of what were known as 'stock plays', such as *East Lynne, Uncle Tom's Cabin, Maria Marten, Sweeney Todd, Temptation*, and many others. Any one of these plays could be put on at a moment's notice and, when it was, would proceed with no undue hitches, stage waits or gagging, and with very little prompting[128].

The ability to 'gag' was an indispensable skill acquired by all actors in portables. Haggar again:

The players were never stuck for words. If they forgot their lines, they would indulge in this process known as "gagging." This meant that they made up their own words and it did not really matter what they said as long as it fitted in with the play, although this was frowned on by the management. The words "Stick to the script" were often heard at rehearsals.[129]

Improvisation was certainly a skill that Doris prized: 'I've never been cue-struck' she would declare – a skill that came in handy many years later when she was playing Mistress Quickly in a Royal Shakespeare Company production of *The Merry Wives of Windsor*. The cast included Timothy West. In a tribute to her on her ninetieth birthday he reminded her of how 'when you weren't absolutely sure of Mrs Quickly's next line, you would put your hands on your hips and say firmly: "I warrant you!" It seemed to work.' Doris was indeed sometimes a little disdainful of actors who could *only* stick to the script. For her theatre acting was a living art rooted in the relationship between actor and audience in the moment.

Gill may have liked her fellow portable actors, but she certainly did not like their technique or the plays they performed. She marvelled that they took the plays so seriously:

> None of them seemed to think that our efforts were ludicrous and pathetic except myself. Their robust technique, which luckily for my future I was never able to acquire and found difficult to simulate, made their ridiculous plays still more ridiculous.[130]

For his part, Mark Melford was happy to leave the portables for more elevated forms of theatre, nonetheless he stressed the potential value of the training they provided, even if there were some things that should not be learnt:

> if some of the ambitious students of the Thespian Art that I have met could be fortunate enough to participate in six months' downright hard work in a portable theatre, the tuition would be most valuable to them. It would teach them self-reliance – self-possession – readiness for emergencies – indifference that begets ease and spontaneity when handicapped by innumerable inconveniences ... There is no need to acquire the errors of these establishments, judgement and common-sense with true dramatic instinct should teach the novice what to profit by and what to leave behind.[131]

'A touring manager' was more critical in an article on melodrama written for *The Stage* in 1919:

> Are the higher ranks of the profession recruited from the lowest? No; emphatically no. And why, after serving a humble apprenticeship, can the actor not look for advancement? ... Because that very apprenticeship has spoilt what chance he may ever have had. Broadly speaking it is fatal to begin one's career in melodrama.[132]

We should not forget that the realities of performing in an age without microphones or sophisticated lighting systems imposed their own constraints. Actors needed to ensure that they could be heard and that audiences could follow a play's action. Late in life, the Edwardian actress Ellaline Terris, who died at age 100 in 1971, observed a little tartly, 'If more actors and actresses were schooled in melodrama today perhaps we should hear more in the theatre and suffer less from the mumbling and faulty articulation which modern audiences so often have to endure.'[133]

Something that made the constant change of plays and the lack of rehearsal easier was that every actor specialised in a particular type of role. These were the stock characters of melodrama and farce. In August 1909 several members of the Alexandra Theatre listed their roles in the 'Artistes Cards' section of *The Portable Times*. Mr Colin Foster (one of the Alexandra Theatre cricket team that were so soundly beaten) lists himself as 'Juv. [juvenile] and light comedy', while Mr John Copeland, plays 'Heavies [that is, villains]'.[134] The 'touring manager' saw this practice as one of the reasons for the decline in the popularity of melodrama: 'A step in the right direction [if melodrama is to become popular again] would be the elimination of those horrible terms which players attach to themselves like tradesmen's labels: "heavy lead," "juvenile lead," "chambermaid, and so on ad nauseam".'

Earlier, however, even actors in first-class stock companies in major theatres defined themselves by the stock types they played. Dion Boucicault, one of the most successful actor-managers and dramatists of the nineteenth century, listed a total of eighteen different types that a first-class company should have. It is notable that each type had both a male and a female representative. There was a leading man and a leading woman, a leading juvenile man and a leading juvenile woman, a low comedian and a chambermaid, a heavy man and a heavy woman, and so on.[135] Few portables could afford to maintain a company as large as eighteen. More commonly, according to Walter Haggar, a portable would have around twelve actors. A photograph taken on the occasion of the christening of Kate and Bert's son, shortly before Bert's sudden death, shows a slightly larger company of fourteen with, as in Boucicault's list, an

Fig. 13 – The Alexandra Theatre Company celebrating the christening of Doris's brother Bertie in 1907. Middle row: Bert, Kate holding Doris, Kate's mother (Emma Tansley) and stepfather (Ted Tansley). Centre, front row, is Duke the dog.

equal number of men and women. Once melodrama fell out of fashion there was far less equality as regards men and women's representation on stage. Many melodramas, such as *The Woman in Red* and *Jane Shore*, were essentially star vehicles for the leading woman.

Musicians were also indispensable to melodrama. In the same way that a film soundtrack underlines and reinforces its narrative, telling us what we are seeing, melodramas had a musical accompaniment that heightened and reinforced the drama. The two Alexandra Theatre bills both credit musicians: the pianists Mr E. King and Mr Frederick, and the cornetist Mr F. Loader (see Figs. 3 and 5).

There were also non-human actors. Prominent in the centre of the front row of the christening photograph is the dog Duke. Performing animals were a regular attraction in Victorian Theatre and Duke, a mastiff, was a valued member of the Alexandra Theatre company, appearing in a number of plays. Although on occasion he could disgrace himself, as when, just before a performance of Hamlet, he ate Yorick's skull, carefully fashioned by Bert from a stale loaf of bread. He had a starring role in a least one drama: Gelert in *Gelert or the Faithful Hound*. This was one of the Welsh-themed plays Kate and Bert staged in the hopes that they would attract local audiences. Based on a popular legend (in fact a Victorian invention), Gelert is the favourite hunting dog of the thirteenth-century Prince Llywelyn. One day the dog is left alone to guard the prince's baby. On his return Llywelyn discovers the baby missing, the nursery a shambles, and Gelert's muzzle covered with blood. In a fury he kills the dog, only to hear the child crying, but unharmed under the overturned cot. Only then does he see the body of a wolf killed by the faithful hound while protecting the baby. Duke was the faithful hound, Bert, dressed in a wolf skin, the wolf. He and Duke would stage a magnificent fight, which likely used the well-known trick of secreting a piece of raw meat, concealed in a handkerchief, next to the actor's neck. As the dog extracted the meat, it appeared as if it were worrying the actor's throat.[136] The fight ended with the wolf dead and Duke bloodied. The returning Llywelyn would then 'kill' the dog, who would play dead, probably reducing not a few in the audience to tears. This was one melodrama that did not end happily.

Acting Emotion

It is easy to ridicule the style of acting practised by the portables. As Brooks writes,

> Acting style was predicated on the plastic figurability of emotion, its shaping as a visible and almost tactile entity. We know something of the repertory of devices called upon to this end: the striking of dramatic postures, the exaggeration of facial grimace (including eye rolling and teeth gnashing), the use of an artificial diction to support a bombastic rhetoric. ... Such a non-naturalistic, irreal style of acting allowed the actor to call upon moments of direct communication with the audience, face to face confidences and asides.[137]

Dickens was fascinated by the relationship between actor and audience, and the audience response to what they saw on stage. In an article he wrote for his weekly magazine, *Household Words*, he gives us a view of melodrama from the vantage point of its popular audience. The article is based on a performance at an actual theatre that termed itself 'The People's Theatre', but includes an invented cockney character, Joe Whelks, through whom the drama is viewed. While, as in *Nicholas Nickleby*, Dickens ridicules the clichés of the plot and pokes fun at Whelks's unsophisticated appreciation, he is by no means wholly negative, and at the end of the article he makes an interesting comparison that reinforces the importance of music in melodrama:

> It is but fair to Mr Whelks to remark on one curious fact in this entertainment. When the situations were very strong indeed, they were very like what some favourite situations in the Italian Opera would be to a profoundly deaf spectator. The despair and madness at the end of the first act, the business of the long hair, and the struggle in the bridal chamber, were as like the conventional passion of the Italian singers, as the orchestra was unlike the opera band, or its "hurries" unlike the music of the great composers. So do extremes meet: and so is there some hopeful congeniality between what will excite Mr Whelks, and what will rouse a Duchess.[138]

To an opera aficionado, someone who laughs at a well-upholstered soprano in a performance of *La Traviata* lustily singing her heart out as she expires from consumption is likely to be dismissed as a philistine. To opera lovers *La Traviata* in its bringing together of human voice and orchestra speaks to a truth beyond banal realism. The appeal of melodrama lay not only in its non-stop action, the suspense as the innocent victims of villainy were subjected to ever greater peril, its interludes of comic relief, but, as Brooks argues, in its affirmation of a fundamental morality that always, ultimately defeats villainy. In another article Dickens describes the audience's response to the performance of a melodrama at 'a cheap theatre' that suggest how such live performances evoked and reinforced what we might call common sense moral truths:

> Throughout the evening I was pleased to observe Virtue quite as triumphant as she usually is out of doors, and indeed I thought

rather more so. We all agreed (for the time) that honesty was the best policy, and we were as hard as iron upon Vice, and we wouldn't hear of Villainy getting on in the World – no, not for any consideration whatever.[139]

Nowadays it is still often taken for granted that good acting is naturalistic, but melodrama demanded its own style of acting. Emotions were expressed through a conventional language of costume and gesture, well known to the audience, and expected by them. For instance, Mr Lenville, the heavy man in Mr Crummles's company, is described as

> taking an upward look at Nicholas, beginning at his boots and ending at the crown of his head, and then a downward one, begin-ning at the crown of his head, and ending at his boots – which two looks, as everybody knows, express defiance on the stage.[140]

And when coaching Smike for his role as the apothecary in *Romeo and Juliet*, Nicholas

> showed him how he must come in with both hands spread out on his stomach, and how he must occasionally rub it, in compliance with the established form by which people on the stage always denote that they want something to eat.[141]

Hair was an important signifier. Villains had black hair. 'In the 1880s', apparently, 'one English provincial actor attempted to perform villains with flaxen hair, but outraged audiences forced him to return to a black wig.'[142] For women, at a time when all respectable adult women wore their hair up, the recognised sign of anguish, loss of control, madness, was for a woman's hair to come tumbling down. The expression 'to let one's hair down' is evidence of this image. The long blonde wig that Kate wore when she played Jane Shore, and by which she was dragged on stage on her knees, embodied for the audience her humiliation and shame. Evidence that this sign was recognised by audiences is provided by Gill's account of the competition one company ran to boost audiences:

All over the towns we issued handbills on which was printed the long dramatic speech of our "heavy lead" actress, when she was arrested, during which ... she shook down her glorious hair. People were invited to learn this speech and to recite it on the stage in the longest interval on Friday nights. The competition was judged by a committee "of fellow townsmen". ... We would crowd into the wings to watch the competitors. Never did we find one who showed dramatic ability ... They were usually inaudible, often their memories failed them, their accents were marked, they sometimes appeared on the point of collapse, but the one thing that they always remembered to do was to shake down their hair![143]

The Decline of Melodrama

By the second decade of the twentieth century melodrama was falling out of fashion. In the eyes of the 'touring manager', whose lament in *The Stage* for the genre's declining popularity I have already quoted, a major problem was increasing competition:

Some years ago we had what was then the astonishing spectacle of musical comedy companies visiting theatres in minor towns. Previously the appearance of aught save melodrama and pantomime was unheard of; today melodrama is all but banished from these towns, and comedy by our best writers is almost as welcome as musical comedy or revue.[144]

In truth the landscape of popular entertainment was shifting. As the 1920s turned into the 1930s Mrs Kimberley herself was facing increasingly hard times. In 1934, by which time her (and Kate's) world of melodrama was seen as hopelessly old fashioned, she would send the novelist and playwright Compton Mackenzie a manuscript with this poignant appeal:

I am an old PRO and you may have heard my name as I have possessed many Theatres in my time and toured many Cos [companies]. I wrote my own plays for years and some ran years. With the advent of TALKIES came ruin. ... I must earn a living and I cant [*sic*] live on dreams. I WANT YOU TO READ THE MS and tell me if you think it any use or hopeless to go on. I know my name is known to the popular public. ... After so many years of management &c and affluence I feel my position deeply.[145]

It was not only melodrama that was suffering. Music hall, which had dominated popular entertainment in the second half of the nineteenth century in all the larger urban centres, was evolving into a new form of entertainment, variety. Music hall is often enveloped in a sentimental haze. Safely ensconced in the past, it glows as a genuine embodiment of working-class culture, one which may have been at times vulgar, and by modern standards even offensive, but that carries with it the aura of authenticity. Here, according to the myth, we see the soul of the working class in all its raw vigour. And this myth has been powerful. As Richard Hoggart wrote in *The Uses of Literacy*, 'Even a writer as astringent and seemingly unromantic as George Orwell never quite lost the habit of seeing the working-classes through the cosy fug of an Edwardian music-hall.'[146] In place of music hall's supposed authenticity, the variety that succeeded it tended to be seen as embodying crass commercialism, entertainment *for* the masses, not *of* the masses.

In reality, however, nineteenth-century music halls were commercial enterprises just like other forms of popular entertainment Doris participated in during her long career. The primary aim of the travelling theatres, Mrs Warner and Mrs Kimberley's tours, the venues that hired juvenile troupes and other variety acts, the impresarios who put on West End revues, film and commercial television companies, was always to generate a profit. They were capitalist enterprises, even if, as with the Alexandra Theatre, on a very small scale. Inherent in any capitalist enterprise, for good and ill, is a dynamic of change. The purveyors of popular entertainment have to run very fast to keep up with the ever-shifting taste of their paying customers. As profit-seeking enterprises, they are shaped by the demands and desires of their audiences, demands and desires that they in turn shape. The one partial exception, and an important part of Doris's story, is the BBC, envisioned as a public service. I explore something of the difference this made in Chapter 6.

Both music hall and variety were based on a succession of turns or acts by performers brought together in a single 'bill'. A successful bill provided a diverse range of acts – singers, comedians, animal acts, acrobats and many others – that would keep the audience entertained over the course of the show. There was no attempt to provide an integrated whole. Something they shared was performance based on a direct relationship with the audience. There was no pretence that those on stage were in their own world on which the audience was simply eavesdropping. The performers were always aware of those watching, and in conversation with them. The poet and classics scholar Tony Harrison, brought up in a working-class environment and a fierce defender of the popular, has never forgotten the shock of encountering the fourth wall for the first time:

> At the same time as I was studying, say, the *Alcestis* of Euripides ... I was going to the theatre and seeing more music-hall comedians and pantomimes than so-called serious theatre. The important thing about this kind of theatre is that it is all out front, it continually acknowledges the presence of the audience. ... When I saw my first proscenium play in a drawing room I was horrified that no one on stage seemed aware of me and the rest of the audience.[147]

Doris was shaped as a performer both by her early experience of acting in melodramas, and her time in juvenile troupes in variety, both entertainment genres in which the performer performs *to* an audience who is present in the same space. With the new media technologies of radio, television and cinema came new forms of the performer/audience relationship. Doris mastered these new media, but for her the ultimate model of performance was the comedian playing to actual people in real time. As she told the comedy writer and producer Mike Craig when she was in her eighties: 'The greatest joy in my life is a full house. To go on and hear them laugh, *know* you have got them in the hollow of your hand and can do *what* you like with them. It's a wonderful feeling.'[148]

CHAPTER 5

FROM CONCERT PARTY
TO CABARET AND REVUE

One of the secrets of [vaudeville] theatricality,
still preserved in the popular forms, is that the audience
is there to be addressed, not to be eavesdroppers on
some private happening.

Tony Harrison[149]

After the family's Irish adventures Kate retreated for a time to her sister Maggie in Kettering, advertising her availability in *The Stage*. In January 1921 she placed this ad: 'KATE BRAEMER – Dis[engaged], Heavies, Com[edy], Char[acter], Pathos',[150] giving a Kettering address. She soon returned to London, however, living for the rest of her life in a series of rented flats, usually in the Covent Garden area. When they were not on tour, or performing outside London, her daughters would with live with her. Doris only moved out permanently in the 1930s, occupying a series of modest flats in the same area until her marriage in 1941. As a child I have many memories of visiting Kate, Winnie and Betty in their top floor flat (no lift) at 118 Long Acre, and Bertie and his wife in their flat, also on Long Acre. Molly by then had her own small place (with an outside lavatory) in nearby Mercer Street, above Joe Pegg's Eel Shop. This was a very different Covent Garden from the gentri-fied, tourist trap of today. The wholesale fruit and vegetable market still occupied the old market hall, and the surrounding streets were littered with the decaying remains of the early-morning trading, but rents were cheap, and you were in the heart of the theatre district.

By the 1920s Kate was in the sunset of her career. The landscape of popular entertainment was shifting, and it was harder for Kate than her daughters to adapt. She was by now in her early fifties, although claiming to be in her mid-forties, and her style of acting was falling out of fashion. She did occasionally find work. In 1923 *The Stage* notes her appearance in a touring production of the 'farcical comedy' *How Like a Man!*, although it seems she only had a small supporting role.[151] A few months later their old employer Mrs Kimberley was putting together another touring company and placed an ad for various 'Dramatic Artists' that included the following appeal, 'Will Kate Braemer wire if disengaged.'[152] I do not know if anything came of this. Subsequently she more or less disappears from the record; it seems that by the mid-1920s she had effectively retired. In hopes of making a little money, from time to time the family tried to rent out a room. I found an ad she placed in *The Stage* for a bed-sitting room in 1926.[153] But these endeavours were never very successful, and her children remembered at least one occasion when they simply decamped from one flat, trusting that the landlord would not pursue them for the unpaid rent. Her obituary in *The Stage* when she died in 1957 refers to her as having retired about thirty years previously.

The Emergence of a Comic

As Kate's career declined the careers of her children began to take off. We left Doris at the end of Chapter 3 returning to Britain and about to join (thanks to her sister Molly) the tour of *The Better 'Ole*. This tour did not last long. On 17 February 1921 both Doris and Molly announced their availability in *The Stage*: Molly, then nineteen, inviting offers for 'Soubrette or juvs', the fifteen-year-old Doris, for 'Flappers or Boys'. By the summer, thanks to her favourite sister Betty, Doris had found work in a concert party. Concert parties, particularly associated with seaside resorts, were an increasingly popular form of entertainment in the interwar decades.

As workers increasingly won the right to annual paid holidays, and the spread of the rail network in the second half of the nine-teenth century made coastal towns more accessible, summer holiday makers began to attract entrepreneurs eager to make money entertaining them. Pierrot troupes, consisting of six to eight performers who sang, danced, juggled, and told funny stories, began appearing in seaside resorts at the end of the nineteenth century. Their name came from the costume they wore, a simplified version of the Pierrot costume with its roots in the venerable Commedia Dell'Arte tradition. Over time these troupes developed into the concert party, more sophisticated and professional but again based on a small group of performers, often wearing some form of Pierrot costumes. A major difference between concert parties and music hall and variety was that the concert party was a collective endeavour: members of the troupe had their own solo turns, but they also performed sketches together. Music-hall and variety bills by contrast consisted of separate, unrelated 'acts'.

Occasionally concert parties achieved success beyond their seaside audiences. Two that made it to the West End and enjoyed lasting fame were the *Pélissier Follies* in the years before World War I, and in the 1920s, the *Co-optimists*. For the most part, however, concert parties were regarded by the cultural elite as 'low' entertainment. The general attitude of condescension is captured in this comment by social reformer and chronicler of British poverty, B. Seebohm Rowntree, and G. R. Lavers in their 1951 study of English life and leisure:

> whereas, naturally enough, none of the concert parties makes any significant contribution to the nation's cultural life, few of them include turns that are objectionable. If, as we believe, their main function is to provide harmless relaxation at holiday time for people, mostly of the working- and lower middle-classes, who have worked hard all the rest of the year, they can reasonably be said to achieve this quite useful end.[154]

Providing this 'harmless relaxation' demanded a lot from performers, who had to capture – and keep – the attention of an audience not confined within a bricks and mortar theatre. In the words of the biographer of Max Miller, a comedian who started his career in concert parties, 'The essence of the appeal of concert party entertainment was the bond between the player and the audience.'[155] Doris's sister Betty seems to have been able to create this kind of bond from when she was very young, as when she enchanted the troops in the Portsmouth barracks with her *Lovelight* song, and she soon established herself as an accomplished concert party artist. In 1917 she was a member of *The Cubists*, in which she was described as a 'chic comedienne';[156] in 1918 in *The Qualities*, she was said to be 'a smart and sprightly comedienne';[157] a year later *The Folkestone Herald* declared that in *The Topics*, 'Miss Betty Hare, soubrette, acquits herself in a manner that charmed the audience.'[158] Evidence of how early she mastered this genre is this ad, which appeared in *The Stage* on 29 November 1917, when she would have been nineteen:

Wanted, First-class Concert Party Artists in All Lines, including Pianist-Entertainer. Miss Betty Hare, please write.

Prior to her career as a 'Concert Party Artist', Betty had also enjoyed success in pantomime as principal girl. In 1917 she played Alice in Mrs Kimberley's pantomime *Dick Whittington* for the second time. A typical review lauds her as 'a sweet and charming Alice'.[159] It seems she was a popular member of the company. At the end of the run she put this prominent announcement in *The Stage*:

BETTY HARE

Concluded Saturday 2nd successful engagement with Mr and Mrs F. G. Kimberley's "*Dick Whittington*," Principal Girl. Thanks Mrs Kimberley for handsome pendant and chain, Miss Ruby Kimberley [Mrs Kimberley's daughter] for bag, Miss Doris Evans for manicure set, Five Westmans for silver tray, and Miss Nellie Stuart for silver jar.

Now on tour with *Cubists' Concert Party*.[160]

Another 1917 show that included Betty provides yet more evidence of the tight-knit world in which the Hare family moved. This was *Watch the Box*, produced by Doris's early mentor Mrs Warner. Warner was now putting on shows in collaboration with the actor George Gordon, earlier a cast member of her production of *Till Kingdom Come*, the melodrama in which the ten-year-old Doris played Blue Moon/Brenda Meredith. Warner and Gordon, seemingly trying to cover all the bases in a shifting entertainment landscape, termed *Watch the Box* in their ads as a 'Merry Musical Farcical Comedy Revuette'.[161]

In January 1921 Betty had just returned from a year-long tour of Canada and the USA. Doris remembered her sending the family moccasins and other Canadian artifacts. Once back in Britain she announced her availability in *The Stage*.[162] She did not have to wait long before finding work with a concert party, Frank Blythe's *Shrapnel*, 'The Success of Four Years Standing. Entirely New Production, Dresses, Repertoire, Etc.'[163] As well as performing, Blythe wrote most of their material and produced the show. Betty is listed as one of seven artists, four women and three men. It was this concert party in which Betty secured a place for her little sister. Soon the sisters were doing a double act in addition to their solo turns: 'The Misses Betty and Doris Hare quickly danced themselves into favour and won particular applause for their contribution of the "Jazz Babies."'[164] This comedy number, full title 'Canadian Jazz Babies', had the two sisters performing a 'jazz' song but with exaggerated English accents. Fifteen years later when they were both in New York, it would be their party piece at show business parties where everyone was expected to perform. At the end of 1921 both sisters were again employed by Mrs Kimberley, this time in the tour of her Christmas pantomime, *Dick Whittington*, Betty once again as principal girl, Doris in a small supporting role.

After the end of the run of *Dick Whittington*, Betty found bookings for their act in variety. She was essentially the 'straight man' while Doris was the disruptive, comic element. From her earliest years comedy was central to Doris's persona as a performer, primarily the 'low' comedy of the music hall tradition. She was a comedian, however, at a time when comedy, especially low comedy, was dominated by men, and tended to be seen as an exclusively male preserve. In a celebrated 1941 essay on the seaside postcards of Donald McGill, George Orwell, who championed this kind of humour, argued for the value of what he terms its 'Sancho Panza view of life'.[165] He was also clear that this was not something to be attempted by women. In a review of a show in which Doris appeared with the comedian Max Miller (discussed at length in Chapter 7), Orwell applauds Miller's vulgarity, but then notes that 'A woman cannot be low without being disgusting'.[166] Doris, as we shall see, managed to escape Orwell's strictures.

Doris's lifelong compulsion to make people laugh may have its roots in the privations and insecurities of her early childhood. She saw herself as having to prove her worth. In her mind this went back to an overheard comment. She was Kate and Bert's fourth child, and fourth daughter. Understandably they had hoped for a boy this time. When she was very small, she heard Winnie say, 'Of course, Doris was a disappointment to us.' She never forgot this remark, and was determined to prove to her family that she was not a 'disappointment'. Years later when she had begun to become successful, she would triumphantly announce to them, 'I'm not a disappointment any more.'

In her act with Betty, Doris never had a script. As so often throughout her career she relied on the presence of the audience and the adrenalin of the moment to give her comic inspiration. Mostly it seemed to have worked. The *Gloucester Journal* reviewer wrote: 'Betty and Doris Hare are two of the most pleasing and entertaining singers and dancers appearing at the Hippodrome for some time.'[167] But there were times when it did not. Etched into both sisters' memory was their dismal failure at the Palace Attercliffe, Sheffield in early April 1922. The week before they had triumphed in Leeds. Doris remembered 'a little Scots comedian' coming up to her and saying, 'You know what, Doris, you've got a Moss act there.' Moss Empires at that time was generally considered the premier variety circuit. Attercliffe thought otherwise. In Doris's words, 'we died the death of a dog.' After the first night the theatre manager insisted they cut their first number: 'What's that first number you do about the Broadway Blues? That's no bloody good, cut it out.' The second night was even worse: they were told their second number had to go. After performing their truncated act on the third night they were so demoralised that Betty rang the manager and told him they were quitting. Betty rapidly found work with Ballard Brown's Concert Party, *Jake-a-Loo* (sometimes *The Perennials*), promising her little sister that she would get her in too. This she did, prevailing on Brown to employ Doris as a dancer at a pound a week. Soon both sisters were getting noticed in the reviews:

> Miss Doris Hare is a comedienne who leaves nothing to be desired, and who by her singing and her wholesome humour is a great favourite. Miss Betty Hare is equally gifted as a soubrette. ... These two artistes also give a number of duets and dances which form an important part of the programme.[168]

Doris never stopped working on her dancing, singing and comedy routines. She spent hours standing on the side of the stage, learning new dance steps, how best to put a song across, the best way to get a laugh, and then endlessly practising. By March 1923, when she turned eighteen, she was ready to launch a solo career, and at this point the sisters' careers diverge. There seems to have been no falling out between the sisters: over the years Betty would continue to champion her little sister, and until her death in 1981 she was perhaps Doris's closest friend.

After *Jake-a-Loo* Betty went on to another concert party, *Supremacy*, and Doris joined the tour of *Snap*, a successful London revue. Revue was an increasingly popular new form of live show, described by one historian as a 'cross between Variety and musical comedy'.[169] The tour of *Snap*, advertising itself as '17 snaps of fun, melody and dance',[170] continued until some time in the summer of 1923 when Doris's career took a new turn.

Moody's Jazz Club
In the years after World War I a new kind of venue began springing up in London's West End: the nightclub. Catering to members of high society, artists, and bohemians of all stripes, as well as criminals (as long as they were well dressed), nightclubs offered opportunities to dance, and what was seen at the time as sophisticated and sometimes daring entertainment, not to mention the all-important benefit of after-hours drinking. During the war strict laws governing where and when alcohol could be sold had been intro-

duced with the aim of ensuring the productivity of factory and munitions workers. Nightclub owners, sometimes with the help of bribes to the local police, found ways round these laws, providing spaces, often elaborately decorated, where their patrons could relax, drink, and enjoy the latest dance crazes, such as the Charleston. One of these clubs was Moody's Club in Tottenham Court Road. And sometime in the summer of 1923 the eighteen-year-old Doris joined the club's chorus, the Moody's Club Follies – as chorus leader she always claimed.

At Moody's, according to a recent local historian, 'A future king [the Prince of Wales, very briefly Edward VIII] was a habitué, black jazz musicians, Chinese dope peddlers, "flapper" dancers, and good time girls all rubbed shoulders in a Jewish-owned Tottenham Court Road club.'[171] The club has a claim to fame in the history of jazz in Britain. Jazz arrived in Britain in the years after World War I, and was soon taken up by nightclubs. To some early listeners what they heard was not only novel but disturbing and threatening. To describe it they fell back on familiar tropes of primitive savagery. In June 1924, for instance, one horrified commentator, Miss Violet Quirk, recorded her impressions in a long piece for the *Sunday Chronicle* entitled 'Jazzing to Jeopardy'. 'The negro musicians', she wrote, 'knew well how to recapture the inflaming noises made by their far-back ancestors, and which are still enjoyed by cannibals during their most important ceremonies.' Where, one wonders, did Miss Quick get her first-hand knowledge of present-day cannibal ceremonies? As for its effects on women: 'These women cannot know how revolting they appear, as they shuffle round the room with striding legs too far apart, rigid bodies, and fixed staring eyes.'[172]

Moody's was one of the first nightclubs to have a dance band that played this daring new music, and to feature African-American musicians: Victor Vorzanger's Famous Broadway Band, who played at Moody's in the early 1920s. According to jazz historian Howard Rye, unlike in America at this time, 'in London the presence of the African-American musicians in Victor Vorzanger's band at Moody's Club in Tottenham Court Road was a selling point.'[173] Another jazz historian, Catherine Parsonage, sees Moody's as providing space for a less watered-down jazz: 'it is tempting to propose, for example, that the musicians in Vorzanger's band played popular dance music at the East Ham Palais for financial reasons, and then returned to Moody's to jam.'[174] Certainly Doris was an early enthusiast. She and her brother Bertie would eagerly seek out imported American jazz recordings once these became available in London record shops.

A silent film made in 1923, *Moody's Club Follies* (archived in the British Film Institute), provides a glimpse of the club as it was when Doris danced there. We see the club's interior, decorated in the orientalist, Moorish style so popular at the time; on a low raised platform next to the dance floor there is a band of eight musicians (not Victor Vorzanger's band). They play to patrons in evening dress, women in fashionable gowns, men in white tie and tails, sitting at tables surrounding the dance floor. White tablecloths cover the tables on which sit bottles of wine (?champagne) in ice buckets. Doris's audience was now a good few rungs higher on the social ladder.

The Follies perform six numbers in the film, with different costumes for each. Is Doris one of the chorus girls? Frustratingly, there is no information as to when in 1923 the film was shot, and there are no close-ups of the chorus girls. At the BFI I ran and reran the film several times; I *think* I can spot Doris, particularly in their final number, announced on the title card as 'a good old English tune, "John Peel"'. In line with this song celebrating a huntsman, six of the Follies emerge with feathered hats, and what to modern eyes look a little like old-fashioned bathing costumes, wearing reins, and pawing the ground. The seventh Folly, sporting a top hat, holds the reins. This, another title card informs us, is 'the Follies in their Pony Trot'. Doris I am pretty sure is the one holding the reins, which would fit with her being the chorus leader. Her hair matches the Louise Brooks bobbed hair she had around that time.

One of Doris's memories from her Moody days suggests her leadership role. The club's patrons would often send the chorus bottles of champagne. The dancers accepted that these offerings would never reach them, but they felt they deserved something, and Doris was deputised to ask the management that in lieu of the champagne, they be given a big bowl of chips. To the delight of the Follies - all very young women who were almost always hungry – the request was granted. Earlier when she was with the juvenile troupes, it was Doris who would be sent to beg the landlady for a bit of bread to toast in front of the meagre one-bar electric heaters provided in their bleak, and usually freezing-cold, lodgings.

In the same year that Doris began working at Moody's, a musician who would later play a significant part in her performing life, was asked by the Entertainment Director of the Savoy Hotel, William F. De Mornys, to head a new band, the Savoy Orpheans, so called because they 'played like gods – like Orpheus'.[175] The musician was Bill Debroy Somers, who had a fondness for putting together musical programmes that told a story. To mark the band's first anniversary in 1924 the Savoy Orpheans gave a concert entitled 'Revolution of Syncopated Music from ragtime to symphonised syncopation'. Somers was clear that this represented an advance, explaining in the concert's programme that the audience would have the opportunity 'to study syncopated music from its birth and origin, through its gradual phases and improvements, finishing with the modern symphonised music of today'.[176] Like other white musicians at the time, Somers took it for granted that the original 'syncopated music' needed improving, needed to move beyond its primitive origins and become more like western symphonic music.

The dangers posed by nightclubs were not only the potentially corrupting influence of jazz. They were also widely believed to be haunts of vice, where innocent young girls were lured into drugs and prostitution. The year before Doris started working at Moody's, Freda Kempton, a young dance hostess at another West End nightclub, had overdosed on cocaine. Her death, and her association with a notorious Chinese drug dealer, Brilliant Chang, were widely published and led to heightened anxiety about nightclubs and drugs. Parsonage found evidence in the Public Records Office 'that Moody's Club, known to feature black musicians was subject to an extensive series of detailed police observations soon after Kempton's highly publicised death'.[177]

Doris must have been aware of the reputation of Moody's, but by her own account, she was very innocent when she began working there. Kate had instilled a strong moral sense in her children, and moreover Doris was firmly focussed on her career, on becoming a success, and through this financially secure. She promised Kate that when she was a success, she would buy them a cottage with a garden. A promise she would keep ten years later. In addition to working on her dancing, Doris did, however, receive another kind of education at Moody's. As one might expect, the club was frequented by a number of 'ladies of the night'. Doris remembered two in particular, who were highly protective of young chorus girls like her, and would fend off customers who got the wrong idea about them. She also remembered these women teaching her about birth control, information not easy for young girls to come by in the early 1920s.

One night when Doris had been working at Moody's for about a year, a Frenchman, Henry de Bray, came with a party. He had recently scored a big success in C. B. Cochran's London production of George M. Cohan's musical comedy *Little Nellie Kelly* and was looking for a dancing partner to join him for a new act to be called 'Snitches and Snatches of Cabaret and Vaudeville', borrowing the title of the hit song, 'Snitches and Snatches' he sang in Cohan's musical. Impressed by Doris's dancing and her gift for comedy, de Bray invited her to become his partner. In the act, choreographed and directed by him, the two of them would burlesque various cabaret and vaudeville acts. Doris's audience might have become more upscale, but her strength was still comedy.

Entertaining 'your man home from the outskirts of Empire'
One of de Bray and Doris's earliest engagements was in the New Princes' Frivolities at the newly refurbished Princes' Restaurant, Piccadilly, where Percy Athos, an impresario who had begun his career as a fancy roller-skater, was to present 'a new edition' of the Princes' cabaret 'with a new stage and bandstand'.[178] We can get some idea of the ambience of Princes', and what 'cabaret' meant to its patrons, from a 1924 article 'The Cult of the Cabaret', by E.P Leigh-Bennett, published in the 9 July issue of the weekly magazine *The Bystander*[179]. The article and the magazine also provide an insight into the place of Empire in inter-war Britain. *The Bystander's* cover features a portrait of 'Mrs Dudley Coats, who with Lady

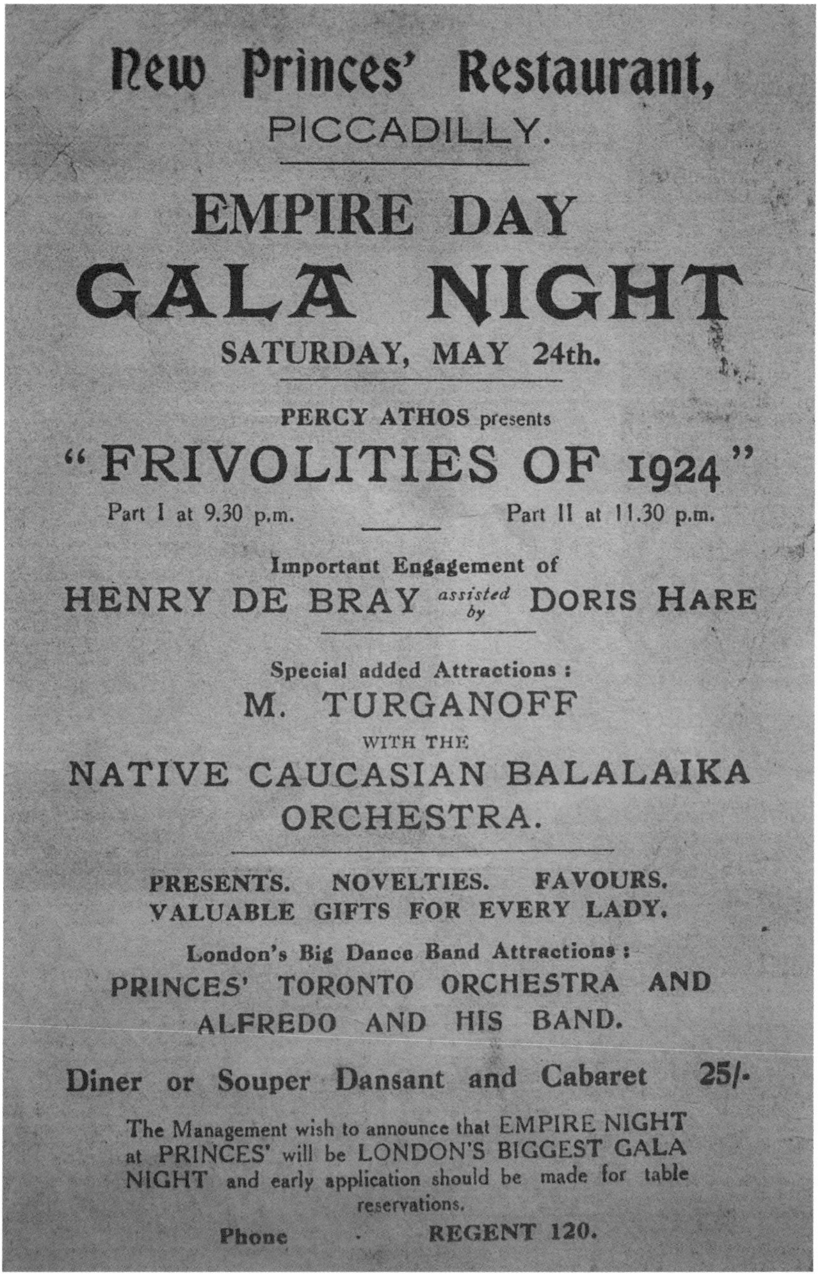

New Princes' Restaurant,
PICCADILLY.

EMPIRE DAY
GALA NIGHT
SATURDAY, MAY 24th.

PERCY ATHOS presents
"FRIVOLITIES OF 1924"
Part I at 9.30 p.m. Part II at 11.30 p.m.

Important Engagement of
HENRY DE BRAY *assisted by* DORIS HARE

Special added Attractions:
M. TURGANOFF
WITH THE
NATIVE CAUCASIAN BALALAIKA
ORCHESTRA.

PRESENTS. NOVELTIES. FAVOURS.
VALUABLE GIFTS FOR EVERY LADY.
London's Big Dance Band Attractions:
PRINCES' TORONTO ORCHESTRA AND
ALFREDO AND HIS BAND.

Diner or Souper Dansant and Cabaret 25/-
The Management wish to announce that EMPIRE NIGHT at PRINCES' will be LONDON'S BIGGEST GALA NIGHT and early application should be made for table reservations.
Phone - REGENT 120.

Fig. 14 – Empire Day Gala Night 1924 at the New Princes Restaurant, Piccadilly. This dates from early in De Bray and Doris's partnership when the billing was still 'Henry De Bray assisted by Doris Hare'.

Violet Benson, has arranged the Procession of England in a Pageant of the Heart of Empire Ball held at the Albert Hall today (Wednesday)'. As John Julius Norwich recalls, in his childhood in the 1930s, 'Empire was all around us, celebrated on our biscuit tins, chronicled on our cigarette cards, part of the fabric of our lives. We were all imperialists then.'[180] Doris, too, grew up in a world saturated with the glories of Empire. At the time of the South African War (then commonly termed the Boer War) two decades earlier, her Auntie Maggie had named her ninth child, born in 1902, Harold Kitchener Panter in honour of Lord Kitchener, chief of staff of the British forces in South Africa, and notorious in posterity's eyes for his scorched earth policy against the Boers.

The Empire was a crucial source of employment, particularly for middle and upper-class men. It is such men, likely with a connection to the colonies, that Leigh-Bennett assumes patronise Princes. He begins his article by contrasting the old and the new Princes':

> Princes' is associated in many people's minds with that private dance given by Estelle's people at her coming out [as a debutante, the rite of passage that signalled an upper-class young woman's arriving at a marriageable age] with the dance given by dear old What's-his-name when he made that unholy haul in the rubber boom ... Princes' is a landmark to Piccadilly people ...
>
> But what a metamorphosis had enveloped it now!
>
> Men just home from the outskirts of Empire and passing by the old familiar building on the top of a bus, see a hint of it through the windows and say, "Hullo what's happened in there?"

While for Leigh-Bennett the band is central to this kind of cabaret club, he does not see the club's patrons as jazz afficionados: 'few of us are really competent to judge of the fine distinctions between first-class jazz bands. Sufficient unto us is that they pulse and throb with just that momentum which claws us to our feet from dinner or supper table.' Returning to the man home from 'the outskirts of Empire', the article continues with an image that brings to mind Chekhov's provincials dreaming of Moscow or St Petersburg:

Observe with me for a moment the effect on your man home from the outskirts of Empire when Percy Athos prepares to present his Frivolities and his Beauties. The Man Who Went Home is sitting, resplendently replete, on the edge of an ebony black floor. ... Everywhere round and about is glass and glitter, and the sort of life he has dreamed about in the intervals from cursing mosquitos.

After rhapsodising over 'the Athos avalanche of nymphs' advancing on The Man Who Went Home, 'in wisps of clothing, across a waste of shining floor [who] come so mockingly close and as soon are so terribly far away,' Leigh-Bennett moves on to consider the principals:

There are certain bigoted people who affirm that we Britishers have not got the Cabaret sense, the elan of the French. How that opinion can stand after having seen Henry de Bray and Doris Hare is beyond me. De Bray's dance, called "Bright though Tight" – the title is tersely comprehensive – and the pair of them in an Apache scene called cryptically "Jewels" through which a most alluring melody thrums, shows clearly enough how futile such a statement is. Both are gems of cabaret artistry.

De Bray and Doris's 'Apache scene' in which Doris was 'murdered', burlesqued a dance popular at the time. According to the *Sunday Post*, in the summer of 1924 there was 'an epidemic of Apache dances in London'.[181] And not only in nightclubs and dance venues. In *The Rat*, a play that had recently opened in the West End, one of Britain's most popular performers, Ivor Novello, portrayed a Parisian Apache dancer. The dance originated in Paris in the years before World War I. Its name came from street gangs the media termed Apaches because of their ferocity (equated with the supposed ferocity of the Apache Indians of North America). Drawing on moves seen in bars frequented by gang members, the dance portrays a violent confrontation between a woman and a man, probably her pimp, in which the woman is thrown around the stage, often by her hair, and generally abused, sometimes fighting back, sometimes not. De Bray and Doris also performed their version of the dance in variety. At London's Oxford Theatre, their 'ludicrous caricature of an apache dance', according to *The Era* reviewer, 'almost reduced the audience to tears.'[182] It could be hard on Doris, however. They often had to dance on wood floors that were far from pristine, thrown by de Bray she would slide across the floor, and end up with splinters in her bottom. She long remembered the painful process of extracting them.

It was de Bray and Doris's comedy that impressed *The Era* reviewer: they 'scored heavily with their burlesques of vaudeville and cabaret'. In addition to their Apache dance, there was 'a screaming travesty of a cabaret waltz'. This was a hesitation waltz in which the partners kept missing each other. And then there was their 'burlesque

Fig. 15 – Doris and de Bray's Apache dance, c.1924. In their burlesque dances, Doris and de Bray did not merely dance, but portrayed distinct characters.

of a Yankee couple dancing the "blues"', which played on the same mismatch between the spirit of African American music and its white would-be appropriators, as had Betty and Doris's 'Canadian Jazz Babies'.[183] This was very much a double act in which Doris's comedic skills were central to its success, a fact reflected in the evolution of the act's billing. At first it was 'Henry de Bray' (in large type) 'assisted by Doris Hare' (in much smaller type), but soon it became Henry de Bray and Doris Hare with both names the same size.

Foreign Adventures

In the autumn of 1924 de Bray and Doris embarked on an extended tour of South Africa, playing Johannesburg, Durban and Cape Town, and Australia where they performed their act in Melbourne

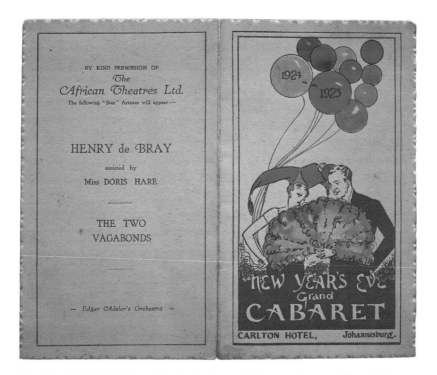

Fig. 16 – 1923/1924 New Year's Cabaret, Johannesburg. African Theatres Ltd (later African Consolidated Theatres) controlled almost all South African theatres and cinemas between 1920 and 1960. There were regular tours by visiting artists from Britain.

and Sydney. Judging by the reviews Doris pasted into one of her scrapbooks, the tour was a success, although she remembered the audiences in Sydney as being tough. There were many such tours by British variety artists at this time, arranged by managers who specialised in overseas engagements. The South Africa in which she and de Bray performed was a segregated society: they would have played to exclusively white audiences; but it would probably not have occurred to them that it could have been otherwise, so embedded were the existing racial hierarchies. For Doris the tour was simply a great adventure. She eagerly looked forward to visiting some of the exotic and romantic places that had figured in so many of the melodramas she had grown up with, and that she had read about since she was a child. Through her reading we can begin to understand the images such places are likely to have conjured up to a nineteen-year-old cabaret artist who had grown up in imperial Britain; images that shaped her experience of this 1924 tour.

Doris may have had little in the way of formal education but from an early age she read voraciously, and like so many others in Britain she read novels set in the Empire, or British Dominions like South Africa and Australia. One of her favourite books as a child was Rudyard Kipling's *Kim*, a huge best seller at the time. *Kim* tells the story of an orphan growing up on the streets of Lahore who becomes entangled in the Great Game, the long struggle between the British and the Russian Empires during the nineteenth century for control over 'the North-West Frontier' (modern-day Afghanistan) that was fought out though espionage and secret negotiations with local rulers.

It was only when I decided that I wanted to write a book about Doris's life that I actually sat down and read this Kipling story which meant so much to her. Growing up I accepted unquestioningly Orwell's characterisation of Kipling as 'morally insensitive and aesthetically disgusting', a 'jingo imperialist'.[184] This is Orwell in a 1942 essay, written in response to T. S. Eliot's defence of Kipling's poetry. Published when so many in Britain still believed, implicitly if not explicitly, in the imperial project, Orwell's condemnation is understandable. Reading *Kim* in our very different historical moment, I realised, like a number of more recent critics such as Edward Said,[185] that there is more to Kipling than crude jingoism; his attitude to Empire, particularly in novels such as *Kim*, is more nuanced than Orwell allows. Indeed, for Abdul JanMohamed, writing in 1985, in the novel 'we are introduced to a positive, detailed and non-stereotypical portrait of the colonized that is unique in colonialist literature.'[186]

Kipling is a wonderful storyteller. For Doris, a child growing up in cold, damp Britain, *Kim*'s evocation of exotic tropical locations peopled by unforgettable characters, opened a window onto an entrancing and quite 'other' world. And then there is Kim himself, a spunky young orphan – probably close in age to Doris herself when she first read the book – who has to make his own way in the world. Doris probably identified with this boy, 'a poor white of the very poorest'[187] but resilient and resourceful. *Kim* may be set in India, not South Africa or Australia, but it would have helped shape how she imagined the subjects of the British Empire living in other far-off lands.

Doris, who was always observing the particularities and quirks of different individuals, admittedly with a view to maybe using them in her performances, likely appreciated the way Kipling, like that other favourite author of hers, Dickens, brings his characters and their eccentricities to life. And as someone who had grown up with melodramas suffused with images of Empire, amidst imperialist popular culture, the adolescent Doris would have taken for granted the existing imperial hierarchies.

The book that specifically shaped her perception of rural Africa, *Jock of the Bushveld* by Percy Fitzpatrick, exemplifies a far cruder racism than *Kim*. First published in 1907, it rapidly established itself as a children's classic and is still in print. The Jock of the title is Fitzpatrick's hunting dog, and the book is an account of the dog and his master's adventures in the rip roaring 1880s in the goldfields of the Transvaal when Fitzpatrick was an ox-wagon transport rider. Unlike Kipling's sympathetic portraits of the colonized, Fitzpatrick's Black Africans are the ugliest racial stereotypes. But while the book's racism seems so obvious to modern readers, it is unlikely to have registered with a young girl whose only knowledge of Africa came from the imperialist and racist popular culture of early-twentieth-century Britain. For Doris the book was simply a wonderful evocation of a romantic, exotic landscape.

When the dancing partners set off on their tour there were those who were shocked that Kate was allowing her daughter, still only nineteen, to travel with a man in his mid-thirties with a reputation as something of a roué, but Kate had confidence in her daughter. Her reply, according to Doris, was simple: 'Doris'll be alright, Doris is a good girl.' And Kate's confidence was, it seems, justified. She was, she would say in later life,

> a good girl all the way there and all the way back. Well, you didn't think of anything like that. I mean, a) you would be terrified of getting pregnant; and b) you just didn't do it, and the man didn't expect you to do it.

Fired by her reading of *Jock of the Bushveld* she was, however, longing to see the veld. And after she enthused to one man: 'I've love to go out to the veld, it must be wonderful there,' he immediately offered to take her. They drove out together, and 'then, of course, [he] tried to put it across me in the middle of the veld.' Fortunately, the down-to-earth Kate, knowing the ways of the world however 'good' a girl might be, had given her daughters good advice about how to fend off over-eager men. Doris remembered Kate's wise words all her life: 'I thought of my mother's good advice, make 'em laugh, and I did, and he brought me back.' It was a tactic she used many years later when she was in her fifties and part of the cast of a serious play. One night after the show she was sitting in her dressing room unwinding with a drink when the door opened and one of her fellow actors appeared, his dressing gown open and with a gigantic erection. Advancing on her, he appealed to her, 'Touch it, go on Doris, touch it.' Never at a loss for a quip, she rapidly defused the situation, responding, 'Oh no, dear, I might break it.' Of course, she was by this time a mature, self-confident woman: the experience was in no way traumatic, it simply provided her with material for a funny anecdote that amused the play's director and other cast members.

As for de Bray all those years earlier in South Africa, Doris recalls him as interested in more mature women, and finding plenty of willing ones. One of Doris's roles was to extricate him from awkward situations: 'God, I used to get him out of scrapes with these women and I would say that I was his friend and do the big act, you see.' Another ploy was for Doris to come bounding up to him saying, 'Henry, we seem to have a problem with the laundry, and I need your help.'

Doris always valued her time with de Bray: 'Henry was a great influence on my life really because I'd learned so much from him.' She learned from him as a performer: 'he taught me how to stand still on the stage, how to use my hands.' He also helped Doris become more confident, instructing her on how to come into a room. De Bray told her:

> When you come looking for me [at the grand hotel where he would be staying], don't come in the door and cower in the corner. When you come in, make an entrance. Come in and look for me and if you don't see me, look for somebody else and say 'Ah, hello,' even if you don't know them, and it was marvellous advice for a young kid like me.

De Bray also gave Doris some lessons in French cooking, something for which I am very grateful. Unlike so many families in 1950s Britain, our salads did not consist of a few limp lettuce leaves, some slices of tomato and cucumber arranged around them, with a bottle of Heinz salad cream off to the side. Henry taught Doris to toss a salad in a proper vinaigrette, made with garlic, oil and vinegar.

Back to Variety and Revue

By August 1925, de Bray and Doris were back in England. For the next few months they travelled around the country, performing in variety. By November, however, they had decided, quite amicably it seems, to part ways, Doris announcing in the 12 November issue of *The Stage* that she was 'at liberty'. By March 1926 she was back at Princes as part of the *Frivolities* cabaret in a solo act, continuing there until the following September, when she put a large ad in *The Stage* inviting offers after 'concluding 6½ months with New Princes Cabaret'.[188] At Princes she was one of the principals, indeed for one reviewer, when the cabaret visited Liverpool for a special three-day engagement, 'Miss Doris Hare, the sauciest of mimics and the most infectious of dancers, was the star turn.'[189]

Early in the run of *Frivolities* Doris had an encounter with a rather different audience: the House of Commons, performing at the Parliamentary Press Gallery's Annual Dinner. In one of her scrapbooks she pasted an account of the occasion she gave to one newspaper a few months later, although as so often, she failed to identify the newspaper and the date of the article (all the quotations in this paragraph come from this article). A number of artists were supposed to perform but 'for one reason and another the only artist able to put in an appearance on the night was Miss Hare'. She was to follow a speech by Winston Churchill. This was many years before Churchill became Churchill-the-godlike-war-leader. In 1926 he was a very unpopular Chancellor of the Exchequer who had blundered in returning Britain to the gold standard. For Doris he was just a politician, who was going to make her late for her appearance at Princes. There she was, as she recalls, 'frightened to death through having to appear in these unusual surroundings and before all these famous people, shivering in a corner and waiting and waiting'. Churchill's speech

> was such a speech as I have never heard before. It went on and on and then as I began to think it was finished he took a deep breath and started again. I began to sympathise with the unfortunate M.P.s who spend half their lives listening to speeches with their own speeches in their pockets, and waiting for the other man to sit down.

This was far from the wartime speeches that would become such rhetorical icons.

When it was finally her turn, Doris found to her relief, as she explains, that

> Members of Parliament are not more difficult to amuse than other people, and if you ask me I think they are easier. Perhaps it is because they have had to suffer from so many bad jokes, in one debate, that they are usually more than pleased to hear once in a while a good one.

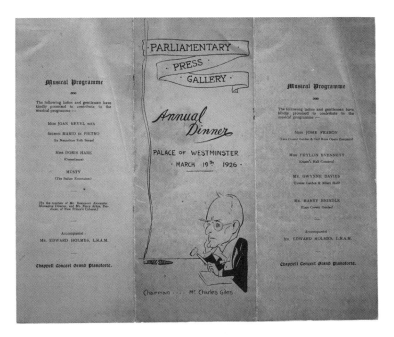

Fig. 17 – 1926 Parliamentary Press Gallery's Annual Dinner's Musical Programme. In the event Doris was the only one of the advertised performers who appeared.

After leaving Prince's Doris was snapped up for a new revue, *Miss 1926*, the latest production of the veteran producer T. Elder Hearn, billed as 'The Show of Novelties'. A review from December 1926 gives an idea of these kind of revues in which spectacle, leavened by comedy, was central:

> There is about 'Miss 1926' – T. Elder Hearn's latest revue – a brightness, a sparkle, a *joie de vivre* which renders the production every bit as attractive as the young lady from whom it takes its title, but the keynote of this finely-staged revue is surely its novelty. Whether one is gazing with wonder upon a crescent moon which floats about the auditorium, the waterfall scene on the banks of Minnetonka, the spinning and glittering balls from which emerge lady members of the company or other of the many skilfully contrived effects, one always has the feeling of novelty. By laying stress on this aspect we do not suggest that there is not abundant humour. Murray Leslie's

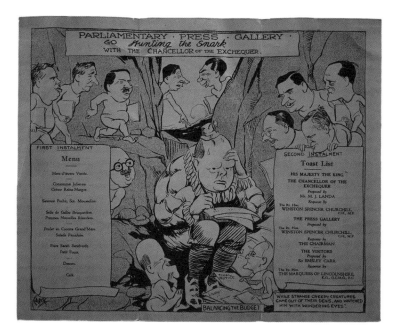

Fig. 18 – 1926 Parliamentary Press Gallery's Annual Dinner's Programme (verso of Fig. 17). The cartoon was printed on the back of the programme. Based on Lewis Carroll's *The Hunting of the Snark*, it shows another Winston Churchill than the revered wartime leader.

capacity for comic work is remarkable. Doris Hare is a leading lady whose grip of her art never relaxes whether she is being grave or gay. Her work in the cabaret scena 'The Lonesomest Girl on Earth' is proof of her talent for heavy acting.[190]

Doris stayed with the show as it morphed into *Miss 1927* and then *Miss 1928* until it ended in the Spring of 1928. After this she and Henry de Bray reunited, once again performing their 'Snitches and Snatches of Vaudeville and Cabaret', as 'the leading act' at London's West End 'Tricity Club's late night cabaret,[191] in variety around the provinces, and at London's Coliseum, where they were on the bill with the celebrated American gospel choir, the Fisk Jubilee Singers. That September they returned to South Africa where, according to the *Rand Daily Mail*, their act was 'as robustly successful as ever'.[192] By January 1929 they were back in Britain at

Fig. 19 – Doris as one of the stars of *Miss 1927 Revue*. Doris with her Louise Brooks haircut. The top right-hand corner shows her in the sailor's costume in which she danced a burlesque hornpipe.

the 'Tricity Club, but by March their career paths were diverging, and they decided to go their separate ways. Henry was by now almost forty, quite old for a dancer, and seems to have been increasingly focussing on his career as producer of floor shows for cabaret clubs.

Doris meanwhile continued to build her career as a solo performer, with her sister Winnie as her pianist. They did some cabaret but mainly variety. Winnie, who was presumably taught piano during her time in the convent, was far from an accomplished pianist. Doris always said she played with two fingers, but she seemed to have managed. For a few months in the summer of 1929 they toured with a variety bill. Topping the bill, somewhat improbably, was Sir Robert Peel, Bart. and his Staffordshire

Harmony Band. Great-great grandson of the Tory prime minister Robert Peel who created the Metropolitan Police Force (still colloquially known as 'bobbies'), this Robert Peel was a handsome but feckless man, who tried many things in his relatively short life, without much success at any of them. At this point he had taken up the saxophone and put together a competent if not outstanding band. Since 1920 Sir Robert had been married to Beatrice Lillie, one of the great funny women of the twentieth century, but the marriage too, was not a success and they were mostly living apart. Doris sometimes reminisced about the handsome baronet. Apparently, the two of them had some kind of flirtation. However far it went, it seems only to have lasted as long as they were touring together.

By November Doris had moved on to a new show, *Fools in Paradise*, described in *The Stage* as 'an entertainment of the revue type'.[193] There were a number of such shows, often essentially variety bills labelled revues to make them sound more sophisticated and up to date. *The Era* noted that 'Miss Doris Hare is a sheer delight. Her radiant personality shines in many ways, but in none with quite as much success as in that series of clever impersonations which she gives in the first half of the programme.'[194] This sounds closer to variety than revue. The star of the show was Max Miller, a performer very much in the music hall/variety tradition of low comedy in which acts directly addressed the audience. According to the variety historian Roger Wilmut, Miller's comedy only worked when he had a live audience: 'he needed the live audience to work to. Only when he could put ideas directly into an audience's head could he achieve the rapport with them that made him one of the top stars of the 1930s.'[195] The comedy in revues, by contrast, was based on sketches in which the audience was allowed to listen in on performers who were supposedly interacting with each other rather than with the audience.

After *Fools in Paradise* ended its tour in February 1930, Doris was given an opportunity to demonstrate her versatility and her ability to star in a show, taking over from the enormously popular Gracie Fields in *The Show's the Thing*, the latest of a series of revues Fields's then husband, Archie Pitt, had built around his wife. After running for eighteen months at London's Victoria Palace, it was to tour the provinces for a year with Doris in place of Fields; a considerable challenge given the devotion 'our Gracie' inspired.

The review of the London production by *The Tatler* – a publication catering to the upper-middle classes - lauds the show with a tinge of condescension:

> For those who think of revue in terms of [C. B.] Cochran, [Noël] Coward, [Jack] Hulbert, [Andre] Charlot and Co., it should be explained that *The Show's the Thing* holds out no sophisticated hand to the intelligentsia. It is just a provincial entertainment devised for low-brows by low-brows who know their business inside out.

Fields herself, according to this reviewer, 'is acclaimed the greatest music-hall comedienne of her day', one who 'belongs, heart and soul to the music-hall. In her sphere she is an electrical artist.'[196] For *The Bystander's* reviewer, 'it is Gracie Fields who carries this show on her shoulders, and she does it triumphantly.'[197]

Gracie was clearly a hard act to follow, but Doris seems to have managed. *The Era* declared: 'Miss Doris Hare has never been seen to better advantage than in this show. Her versatility and vivacity are amazing .... Her comedy powers are enormous. ... We have nothing but praise for Miss Hare's work throughout *The Show's the Thing*.'[198] When they played Northampton, one reviewer declared that she 'will one day be hailed as a second Gracie Fields – if she is not already'.[199] Interestingly, despite the long line of women comedy performers in music hall, a funny woman was still often regarded as an anomaly. 'Seldom,' the *Todmorden and District News* noted in its review, 'is such clever comedy work seen from a member of the fair sex.'[200]

The show did not consist only of comedy, singing and dancing. Archie Pitt had included a poignant playlet, 'Local Colour', featuring a working-class daughter whose parents have taken a middle-class playwright as a lodger. The playwright takes an interest in the girl. She falls for him, only to discover that he has cultivated her solely because he was in search of 'local colour' for a play he is writing. Doris's performance, in the eyes of the *Brighton and Hove Herald*, had the real inwardness of drama that underlies all true humour [as] shown by her appealing performance of the deluded little slum girl in 'Local Colour' - the best 'thing' in all 'the show'. Miss Hare lifts this little episode on to a high plane of intimate drama.[201]

Predictably, *The Tatler*'s response to the playlet in the original production had been less enthusiastic, condemning it for that sin of sins for the sophisticated, sentimentality: '"Local Colour" is of that ponderous, maudlin, sentimental quality which is not ashamed of mixing tear-drops with laughter. ... Sloppy and slow no doubt, but a slice of life immensely to the liking of nine-tenths of the audience.'[202]

Somehow Doris was also managing to fit in some cabaret performances. Her performance at the Roadhouse Cabaret Club, Leicester Square, in January 1931 elicited this review in *The Era*: 'Miss Doris Hare, one of the most brilliant of present-day comediennes, did wonderfully well all last week. There is joie de vivre, vivacity, intelligence, charm and talent here, and she has some very clever material too.'[203]

After the end of the tour of *The Show's the Thing*, she returned to variety and cabaret, again with Winnie playing the piano for her. But things were about to change. In the summer of 1932 Noël Coward would cast her in his new revue, *Words and Music*, catapulting her to a new level in the theatrical hierarchy.

ACT TWO

STAR OF STAGE,
RADIO AND TELEVISON

CHAPTER 6

INTO THE WEST END

There is surely no more versatile revue artist than
Miss Doris Hare and why she is not a celebrity I do not know.
Perhaps she will be soon.[204]

A fortuitous meeting in Singapore played a key role in Doris's big break. The story begins a couple of years earlier, and again her sister Betty is at the heart of it. In 1929 Betty was touring overseas with R. B. Salisbury's Far Eastern Tours. Also in the company was John Mills, a young actor who would go on to stardom and a knighthood. But in 1929 he was at the very start of his career. He describes the enterprise he joined in his autobiography:

> Mr Salisbury had been taking a company out to the Far East for years. It was in reality a concert party consisting of about twelve people, which, for some reason best known to himself, Mr Salisbury called 'The Quaints'. They had become very well-known and successful, and R. B., when he decided to move with the times and provide musical comedies and straight plays, including Shakespeare, for the enjoyment and edification of British sahibs and mem-sahibs, flatly refused to change the name.[205]

In fact the name 'The Quaints' is typical of concert party names during and after the First World War. Betty had appeared in 'The Cubists', 'The Qualities', and 'The Topics'. Fashions, however, had changed since then.

I have been unable to track Betty's career in the years between 1923 and when she joined Salisbury's company in any detail, but I know she had a passion for travel and would regularly sign up for overseas tours. One faded theatre programme from February 1925 lists her as a member of *The League of Notions*, an 'intimate revuette', that week playing the Kursaal Theatre in Alexandria. When she took off on one of her tours, Kate, resigned to her daughter's wanderlust, would remark, 'She's got that itchy bum again.'

Salisbury demanded considerable versatility from his players. They needed to 'acquit themselves creditably in modern straight plays, musical comedies (which called for quite expert tap dancing), and Shakespeare's tragedies [they played *Hamlet* and *Julius Caesar*] all in the same week'.[206] It was in Singapore that, purely by chance, they were seen by someone who would change Mills', Betty's, and ultimately Doris's theatrical fortunes: Noël Coward. He happened to be travelling in the region on one of his periodic recuperative trips that often followed a spell of intense work, when his companion developed a serious case of amoebic dysentery and was confined for a month in a Singaporean hospital. As Mills tells the story, Coward was looking around for something to do while waiting for his friend to recover, 'when he saw to his amazement a bill' which read: 'TONIGHT AT 7:30 / THE QUAINTS / in / HAMLET. This was too good to miss. What exactly did it mean?'[207]

The giant of the English stage decided to find out. That night the Quaints were not actually playing *Hamlet* but *Mr Cinders*, a musical comedy version of *Cinderella* that reverses the genders; the House Manager had forgotten to change the bill. Mills played the put-upon son forced to work as a menial by his evil stepmother and her two sons, Betty the forceful young daughter of an American millionaire who becomes his Prince Charming. Learning that Coward was going to be in front, 'The Quaints were in a state of unsuppressed excitement. ... incredible though it seemed this man of magic [Coward] was actually coming to see the show tonight. The tension built up during the day.'[208] In the event, as Mills writes:

> There are, happily, some rare occasions in the theatre when every-thing seems to go right and nothing goes wrong. That performance of *Mr Cinders* at the Victoria Theatre, Singapore, was one of them.

Betty Hare and I stopped the show with 'Just A One Man Girl'. Betty was wonderful that evening; her timing was immaculate and we found laughs that had been undiscovered for weeks.[209]

The 'man of magic' was impressed and whisked the whole company off to Singapore's famous Raffles restaurant. For the next few weeks, as he waited for his friend to leave hospital, Coward and the Quaints were inseparable. They became so close that when one of the company's actors became ill, Coward volunteered to take over his leading role in *Journey's End*, a famous play set in the trenches of World War I. A year later, in 1931, Coward would cast both Mills and Betty in his play *Cavalcade*, an extravagant pageant of British history, which covered the first thirty years of the twentieth century through a single family, the Marryots. Betty's part, however, was considerably smaller than Mills's.

Betty was a talented actress with a wide range, and very pretty, but although she made a reasonable living in the theatre, she never achieved anything close to Doris's success. I have often wondered why. One reason may have been that she lacked Doris's drive. Like Doris, she had little in the way of formal education; she never talked about attending school, and my sister and I never thought to ask. She read widely, however, and was intellectually curious. She also loved the visual arts. I remember her taking me to many museums and galleries when I was a child. Of all Kate's children, she was the one I have always felt who if, given a choice, would not have chosen the stage as a career.

Coward remained fond of Betty throughout his life. He would find parts for her in his shows, even if these were small, trying to give her at least one line so she would get a credit in the programme. In his last play, *Waiting in the Wings* (1960), set in an actors' retirement home, he gave her a poignant little cameo as the maid of an old actress (played by Sybil Thorndyke) fallen on hard times.

Betty was an untiring champion of her little sister. This paid off in April 1932 when Coward was preparing a new revue, to be produced by his usual producer C. B. Cochran. On Betty's recommendation – 'You should meet my kid sister, she'd make a cat laugh and she's on at Holborn Empire next week' – Coward arranged for someone from Cochran's office to check out Doris's act. The funny little sister was then summoned to audition for Coward. He promptly engaged her as one of the principals of the new revue, *Words and Music*.

'brains in a desert of mediocrity'

Coward was riding high. His four most recent shows, all with Cochran as producer, had been hits: *This Year of Grace*, *Bitter Sweet*, *Private Lives*, and *Cavalcade*. He was in a position to call the shots and this time he decided his new revue would not follow the standard Cochran model. Sheridan Morley, author of one of the most perceptive Coward biographies, explains:

> Coward was determined that this next production would be all his own work: not the usual amalgam of writers, composers and lyricists all brought together under Cochran's ample banner, but instead a one-man revue of which he would be the sole author, composer, lyricist and director. The numbers would not include the traditional ballet or slapstick set-pieces, nor the usual lavish panoramas of old Spain or New Mexico; instead they would be intimate, unspectacular and witty with rather more concentration on the words than the sets. But even that did not guarantee enough autonomy for what Coward had in mind; he decided that the cast would include no stars of the [Gertrude] Lawrence/[Beatrice] Lillie calibre, whose special talents demanded special material which they then moulded into their own peculiar style, but instead less celebrated actors and actresses who could be shaped by Noël into what he wanted for each number.[210]

Doris and Mills would be two of those less celebrated principals. Betty, too, would be in the show, although not as a principal.

Coward wanted *Words and Music* to have a coherence revues normally lacked. In pursuit of this, everything was worked out in advance,

> Arriving for the first rehearsal, the company had been amazed to find that, contrary to all revue practice, the running order of *Words and Music* was already planned and typed as were the scripts for all

the sketches. From then on, it was rehearsed to all intents and purposes like a play, with none of the usual last-minute alterations in the placing and timing of numbers.[211]

Words and Music opened in London at the Adelphi Theatre on 16 September 1932 to almost uniformly ecstatic reviews. *The Bystander* gushed, 'As for the pattern, the homogeneity, the wit, the décor, the tunefulness, the immaculate style, the abundance of the revue, I have never seen, nor hope to see, a more compact, coherent, better balanced, better dressed, better anything show.'[212] Coward, it was agreed, had come up with something new. For the *Theatre World*

> this revue strikes a definitely new note in conception and execu-
> tion; where others rely on big "names" who struggle valiantly to
> overcome the handicap of uninspired material, this one takes a few
> clever people little known to the general public and makes them
> into stars through the brilliance of the sketches and songs
> entrusted to them. In short, *Words and Music* is an overwhelming
> success of brains in a desert of mediocrity.[213]

In many reviews, as here, Doris is referred to as a newcomer. The *Brighton and Hove Illustrated Weekly News* mentioned confidently, 'Doris Hare, a young English comedienne never seen before in the West End'.[214] In reality, her cabaret career with Henry de Bray and ten years of variety, had frequently featured performances at London theatres such as the Coliseum and the Holborn Empire. That she was seen as a newcomer, 'little known to the general public', is evidence of the gulf that separated the prestigious world of sophisticated West End revue from the despised nether regions occupied by the 'low' genre of variety. Tony Warren often stressed to me how extraordinary it was for a performer to make the leap from variety to the West End. 'It just didn't happen', he would say. That it happened for Doris was due to the fortuitous coming together of Coward's enforced stay in Singapore, his meeting with The Quaints, and his interest in finding 'less celebrated' actors.

The 'braininess' of *Words and Music* should not be overstated. Coward always wrote for an essentially middle-brow audience. 'I've

Fig. 20 – 'Mad about the Boy' as staged in *Words and Music*, 1932.
The sketch begins outside a cinema from which an audience is exiting, having just seen 'the boy' (Guy Fortesque) in his latest film, *Her Soul's Avenger*. The audience includes the society lady (Joyce Barbour), the schoolgirl (Nora Howard), the street walker (Steffi Dunn), and the cockney servant (Doris), who will each sing a verse about her obsession with 'the boy'.

never', he wrote in 1960, 'written for the intelligentsia. Sixteen curtain calls and closed on Saturday.'[215] As John Lahr observes in *Coward: The Playwright*, 'Coward was not a thinker ... His genius was for style. ... Only when Coward is frivolous does he become in any sense profound.'[216] A perfect illustration of this is the song 'Mad about the Boy', first sung in *Words and Music*.

In *Words and Music* 'Mad about the Boy' was sung by four women, a society lady, a schoolgirl, a streetwalker, and a cockney scullery maid. Doris was the scullery maid. The song was singled out by many reviewers. For *The People's* reviewer it was 'the real song hit of the show'.[217] Seventy years later, it was listed on the Noël Coward Society website as 'the pre-eminent royalties earner in the Coward repertoire'.[218] It was given a huge boost by its use in a 1992 ad for

Levi's Jeans in which a version sung by Dinah Washington is the soundtrack to images of a muscular, bare-chested, youth, clad only in a pair of jeans, repeatedly diving into swimming pools against backgrounds of entranced – and distinctly less beautiful – onlookers. It was an early subject of *Soul Music*, a 2004 BBC Radio 4 series that explores 'pieces of music with a powerful emotional impact'.

Nowadays 'Mad about the Boy' tends to be sung, as Barry Day notes in his exhaustive compilation of Coward's lyrics, 'as a torch song with the implication that it is the yearning of a mature woman for a younger man', but 'the context in the show was quite different.'[219] The setting was first the facade of a cinema showing *Her Soul's Avenger*, starring Guy Fortesque, a matinee idol. Among the exiting crowd are the society lady (Joyce Barbour), the street-

Fig. 21 – Doris as the 'skivvy' obsessed with 'the boy', *Words and Music,* **1932.** Doris devised a bit of business in which on the lines 'I'm fired with cupid's arrow/every Wednesday from four to six', she flung out her arm and a pot went flying. At first Coward disapproved, but she persisted and eventually he admitted, 'darling, you were right.'

walker (Steffi Dunn), the schoolgirl (Nora Howard), and the scullery maid (Doris). Each of them is then shown in her home environment where she sings about her obsession with the film star. Now singers usually only sing the society lady's verses and chorus. Occasionally they may include some of the streetwalker's verses, but never the schoolgirl or the scullery maid.

There has been much speculation about the identity of the 'boy': who is the real film star Coward had in mind? For me, the song is not about a particular individual. Written at a time when the whole cult of film star celebrity was still relatively new, it is about the nature of that celebrity and the intense, but ultimately illusory, relationship fans have with their idols, the unreality of which those fans often themselves recognise. Coward nearly always wrote songs in a major key, this one, however, is in a minor one, which helps give it its complex yearning quality. The three adult women, so different from one another, all acknowledge the unreality of the relationship. The society lady has actually met the 'boy':

> I met him at a party just a couple of years ago
> He was rather over-hearty and ridiculous
> But as I'd seen him on the Screen
> He cast a certain spell
> ...
> If he was real or not I couldn't tell
> But like a silly fool I fell

The streetwalker sings ruefully:

> My particular kind of Fate
> Has taught me such contempt for
> Every phase of love,
> And now I've been and spent my last half-crown
> To weep about a painted clown.

Doris as the scullery maid also recognises the absurdity of her passion:

> I know I'm potty but I'm mad about the boy.

Only the schoolgirl lacks this self-awareness, but she is given lines that reveal the deluded nature of her obsession, as well as being an example of how Coward would insert little 'queer' titbits into his songs that would likely pass unnoticed by most of the audience but be picked up by the more sophisticated:

I know that quite sincerely
Housman really
Wrote *The Shropshire Lad* about the boy.[220]

When the song finishes Guy Fortesque makes a brief appearance. He sits, looking bored, soaking his feet and receiving a manicure, as his secretary shows him his fan mail. To each letter he gives the same formulaic response: 'Send her a photo.' This is a song about the fantasy relation at the heart of celebrity.

Guy Fortesque was played by Edward Underdown, a handsome young actor from an aristocratic background. In another number with Doris, 'Three White Feathers', he is a guardsman. This time the relationship portrayed is real. He and Doris are sitting in a carriage on London's Mall while they wait in line for her to be presented at Court. Presentation at Court was a ritual, part of a debutante's 'coming out', in which upper-class young women, wearing a head-dress of three white feathers, were presented to the Monarch. This young woman, however, is not a debutant but an actress from humble origins being presented at Court because she is marrying into the peerage. Underdown plays her future husband, whose role in the sketch is simply to listen as his future bride sings of her unlikely ascent:

I can't help feeling
Fate's made a fool of me rather.
It placed me where I shouldn't be
And really couldn't be by rights.
...
We lived at Ealing.
Me and me mother and father.
...

119

We had a pawnshop on the corner of the street,
And father did a roaring trade.
I used to think those rings and necklaces were sweet,
Now I wouldn't give them to my maid.

In the case of 'Three White Feathers' Coward needed to do little shaping to fit Doris to the song. It reflects her humour and down-to-earth personality in real life; like her, the soon-to-be ennobled actress approaches life through the prism of the stage:

Though my beginnings were humble
I've studied each small movement of my self-improvement
From the start;
I've toured for ages,

Fig. 22 – An actress sings 'Three White Feathers' to her future husband as she waits to be presented at Court, *Words and Music*, 1932. The fashion reporter from *The Tatler* (28 September 1932) was in raptures over 'the lovely Court dress' Doris wears: 'it appears to be of miroir velvet of a delicate mauve nuance, its sculptured folds increasing its dignity; certainly débutantes will envy the manner in which the plumes and veil are kept in place.'

I'll never falter or stumble;
I'll give an air of breeding
And a first-rate reading of the part;

She is also conscious of a certain absurdity:
You must forgive me if I kid myself a bit
In me tiara and me gown,
And though my accent may not always fit,
Don't be afraid I'll let you down.

Her feet remain firmly on the ground, she won't forget the pawnshop and its sign of three balls, her journey summed up in the last lines of the refrain:

Today it may be three white feathers
But yesterday it was three brass balls.[221]

The song is not perhaps one of Coward's greatest, included on the Noël Coward Society list of those nowadays 'sporadically performed'. A number of the reviewers of the original show mention it, however, *The Era* writing: 'This trifle is brilliantly done by Doris Hare, who is consistently good throughout the revue.'[222] *The Tatler* notes how

For once thrown out of poise, [the actress] waves to the crowd from her car, then snaps into correctitude for the Guardsman-husband she must not let down. Memories from childhood in a pawn-broker's shop ... A lovely, excellently-written incident, with splendid performance in cameo by Doris Hare.[223]

Nevertheless, that up-market publication's reviewer, familiar with Court rules and regulations, felt compelled to add 'an absurdly pedantic fact – Guards Officers must retire from the terrific Brigade if they marry stage performers.' A nice indication of the still somewhat questionable position of all actors, regardless of whether they performed in low or high genres.

While the critics may have been enthusiastic about Coward's revue – 'a great entertainment', as *The Era* put it, ' for intelligent grown-ups'[224] – the paying public was less so. Perhaps it was a little too brainy? At first business was good but after a few weeks it began to drop, and the show closed in early February 1933 after a run of six months. It then went on a short provincial tour with most of the London cast, including Doris and Betty, but even so it failed to recoup its costs, the first Cochran-Coward production not to show a profit.

From Cochran and Coward to Charlot

For several years after *Words and Music* Doris would continue to straddle the worlds of revue and variety. She also appeared in a number of now forgotten British films, but usually in small, cameo parts. The most notable one I managed to track down is *Discoveries* (1939) in which she played the wise-cracking secretary of the film's star, Carroll Levis. The film was a spin-off of Levis's popular radio programme, also called *Discoveries*, in which he introduced unknown performers discovered by him through his touring stage show. In the film Levis played himself. The plot involves him continually being accosted by individuals (played by variety stars of the day, such as Afrique, Ronald Shiner and Kathleen Harrison) all desperate to be 'discovered'. Despite a weak script, Doris gives a strong performance; but unfortunately, good as Levis may have been as spotting talent, he was not a very good actor, and the film seems to have come and gone without attracting much attention. It did, however, introduce the song 'There'll Always be an England', sung in a patriotic finale by the boy soprano Glyn Davies. It would go on to be recorded by Vera Lynn and become a wartime anthem.

Immediately after the Coward revue, Doris, billed as 'C. B. Cochran's great Comedy find from the London Production *Words and Music*',[225] was the chief attraction of a touring variety show, *The Merry-Go-Round*. One sign of her ascent was that she was now accompanied by Ivor Weir, a considerably more accomplished pianist than her sister Winnie. She was soon back in a London revue, however, not a Cochran production this time but one by the other major revue producer of the interwar years, André Charlot. The show was called *How D'You Do?*. Many years later Charlot's biographer interviewed Doris and she recalled that she was so charmed by the impresario, she quite forgot to ask about money, only discovering later that her weekly salary would be £15, a huge drop from the £25 a week Cochran had paid her: 'He paid terribly. But his shows were so pretty.'[226] While performing in *How D'You Do?* Doris also found time for cabaret, appearing, 'by kind permission of André Charlot', at the Café Anglais, where she is billed immediately below Drina Beach, 'the wonder dancer from the Josephine Baker Revue'.[227] Later she would feature as one of the regulars in Charlot's radio programme, *The Charlot Hour* (See Chapter 8). The impresario also cast her in his next revue, *Hi Diddle Diddle*. And this time, probably thanks to Doris, her brother Bertie was also a member of the cast, playing small parts in a number of sketches.

Hi Diddle Diddle opened in London in October 1934 after a brief pre-London tour. Like *How D'You Do?*, it was a modest success, provoking *The Illustrated Sporting and Dramatic News* to wonder why Doris was not a celebrity, while *The Sphere* pronounced her 'one of the cleverest all-round performers that ever adorned a revue cast; there seems to be nothing on the stage she cannot do well.'[228] According to *The Sketch* in her number 'Mamie of the Chorus' she scored 'a hit as a funny bundle of humanity vainly striving to become a chorus girl'. Also included in the show was one of her urchin characters, Little Willie Trampleasure,

Overall *The Sketch* found the show to be

> a typical Charlot revue. A long menu – thirty courses all told; pretty girls; pretty costumes; pretty little fantastic scenes ... and a bucketful of nonsense which, when handled by Mr Douglas Byng or Mr John Tilley ... turns hotch-potch into spicy dish.[229]

Douglas Byng (also one of the stars of *How D'You Do?*) was a veteran performer. Born in 1893, he was most famous for his drag personas. Drawing on the pantomime dame tradition – he played dames in pantomimes throughout his career – he developed a style of drag performance that featured songs, all composed by himself, which were, in the words of Sheridan Morley, 'a curious mixture of sophistication, schoolboy humour and double entendre'.[230] In *Hi*

Diddle Diddle his drag personas included Nell Gwyn, La Belle Chi Chi (a seventy-five-year-old French cabaret performer who still insists on dancing the can-can), and Lizzie, the Pre-War Flivver (a female incarnation of a veteran motor car), all of which can sound rather dated to modern ears but which in 1934 were known and loved Byng personas to his many fans. But he also sang Cole Porter's 'Miss Otis Regrets' (the first public performance of the song), not in drag but as the stereotypical upper-class butler. The song tells a familiar story of a woman taking her revenge on a man who 'done her wrong'. The twist is that in this case the woman is a high-class society lady. Written as a private joke, it started life as a party piece performed by Porter and Monty Wolley at their friends' parties. But over time it has become much more than this. The many different singers who have recorded it are evidence of the song's strange haunting power. As with 'Mad about the Boy', 'Miss Otis Regrets' is a song whose meaning transcends its creator's intention. Porter may have written it as burlesque of country music, but his musical genius succeeded in infusing the song with a genuine pathos, while the burlesque element saves it from descending into sentimentality.

After *Hi Diddle Diddle* closed in March 1935, Doris's next London appearance was again in a Charlot production, *Dancing City*. This was not a revue but a 'musical play'. Set in the court of Empress Maria Theresa in eighteenth-century Vienna, it told a story of the scandalous new dance, the waltz. Doris played the Empress's maid. The music was composed by Hans May, a native of Vienna who fled Austria after the rise of the Nazis. Later he would become well known for his film scores, including for *Brighton Rock*, one of the best film adaptations of a Graham Greene novel. *Dancing City*, however, was not a success. The reviews were generally poor. For the *Birmingham Gazette*, '*Dancing City* is as dull and stupid a musical comedy as the scenery is wonderful.'[231] Doris, however, got some good notices, such as this one from the *Yorkshire Post*: 'the cheerful gutter-sniping of Miss Doris Hare' adds to the appeal of Hans May's 'delightful songs'.[232] The show lasted no more than a few weeks in the West End and Doris returned to variety shows presented as revues. In September she was one of the stars of *Voila*

Les Dames, a 'non-stop revue' at London's Prince of Wales Theatre. *The Era* wrote of her in this: 'Doris Hare's work ... is as artistic as possible – her sense of the burlesque is admirable.'[233]

Competing with the Cinema

Non-stop variety and revue were a response to the increasing challenge films posed to live entertainment. In an attempt to compete more effectively some variety theatres began to copy their rival's format; four shows at day (often a mixture of variety and revue) running continuously from 2pm to midnight, which patrons, as with cinemas of the day, could enter and leave whenever they wanted. This allowed the theatres to lower their seat prices. *Voila Les Dames* was a show of this type. The pioneer of the format was the Windmill Theatre in London, which after switching to showing films for a time, decided to experiment with this new idea at the beginning of 1931. The experiment was an immediate success and other theatres soon followed the Windmill's lead. These included the London Pavilion, which tried to reassure nervous performers at a time of economic depression that

> variety artists should understand that there will be no cutting of artists' terms, as far as the London Pavilion is concerned.
>
> Performers will have to work harder for the same money, but that is not an unprivileged position in these days when most people have to work harder for less money.[234]

Doris continued the gruelling schedule of four performances a day, six days a week, until February 1936.

In general entertainment journalists seem to have approved. *The Bystander* noted that 'Non-stop revue , with its "popular" prices and its come-as-you please atmosphere, is about as good an answer to the talkies as the theatre has yet produced'.[235] Writing in *The Era*, W. J. Bishop agreed:

> It was the talk of the town – those crowds besieging the London Pavilion and unable to get in! ... Even the lay Press – usually so strangely reticent about variety matters - devoted columns, head-

lines, and special articles to the new boom in entertainment circles - non-stop variety. ... [John Southern, the general manager of the London Pavilion] told me, "It didn't pay as a cinema so we started running variety bills there. We put on good bills, and found immediately that there was a real big demand for vaudeville of the right type today."[236]

A few months later Bishop celebrated – with some exaggeration perhaps - the effect on employment, writing an article with the headline: 'Non-Stop Variety Creates an Employment Boom: Less Profit for Hollywood but More Wages for England'. Producers he spoke to told him of their problems in finding artists. He quotes one 'very prominent man' as saying, "'It is almost impossible to get girls nowadays for troupes – non-stop variety has solved the problem of unemployment in the variety profession, as far as the chorus and small-part people are concerned, at all events.'" At the Pavilion he was told, for non-stop variety, including artists, front of house and stage staff, they employed 215 people, when they were showing films, it was about forty. The article ends with a patriotic reminder of the benefits to the British economy:

> When one considers the indirect employment created by the non-stop boom – the hundreds of frocks, and the quantities of scenery, for they are changed so often – one begins to realise the immensity of labour required ... And that the British public realise that to give our own flesh and blood artists a chance of earning a living, entailing as it does the employment of so many more people, is once again evidence of our unfailing patriotism. What used to fill the coffers of American film magnates is now being circulated among our own people. ... And that, surely, is to everyone's advantage.[237]

In part non-stop revue was following the pattern of French cabaret music halls such as the Folies-Bergère and the Casino de Paris: alongside comedy there was always a chorus of scantily clad women. *Voila Les Dames* followed this formula. It had 'obviously been conceived', *The Bystander* concluded, 'to appeal primarily to the not-too-tired businessman who enjoys broad humour and has an appreciative eye for the female form'.[238] *The Tatler*, with its keen eye for class, took issue with the 'tired businessman' as the audience:

> This lively show has been publicised as 'for the tired businessman'. On the night I was there, the stalls were occupied mainly by young, active and hearty folk from Melton Mowbray, the Cavalry Club and other wide open spaces, I expect they came to study Gillie Potter [one of the starring comedians].[239]

Whether or not it was catering to home counties hearties, or businessmen, tired or otherwise, its imagined audience was male rather than female, and not working-class, even if the comedy was low rather than sophisticated.

After leaving *Voila Les Dames*, Doris went back touring in variety for a few months, doing impersonations, and singing with Ivor Weir again as her pianist. She was also busy broadcasting. She was one of three performers announced for a new weekly programme *Music Hall*, 'the flagship Variety programme of the mid-1930s'.[240] In the summer of 1936 she was part of the BBC's star-laden radio version of *Cavalcade*. This was the Coward show in which both Betty and John Mills had appeared after he had 'discovered' them in Singapore.

The broadcast roused *The Era* critic Edward Betts to apoplectic fury. Nowadays the BBC under John Reith is often thought of as a pillar of the Establishment. Betts's review reminds us that in the mid-1930s a number of those in the media saw it quite differently, more akin to an apologist for Bolshevism. The headline of the review was 'Defeatist "Cavalcade": Bolshie, Bolshie, All the Way'. Its first line reads: 'So the "Bolshies" managed to get their peace programme after all – but they called it "Cavalcade"!'. Val Gielgud (the brother of John Gielgud and the senior drama producer at the BBC) and Felix Felton were castigated for their supposed anti-war message:

> Emphasis was quite unnecessarily and inartistically laid on the horrors of war; the causes of these particular wars [the South African War, at that time commonly referred to as the Boer War, and World

War I] were minimised, so that what emerged was practically an accusation of jingoism against those who took part in them.

Betts concluded that the broadcast, 'which so many people had anticipated with keen expectation', was a 'sad anticlimax'. Those disappointed people 'had overlooked the fact that in most BBC quarters, if patriotism is mentioned it is a sure sign to them that "the world is going mad".' The furious critic did have some kind words at the very end: 'Musically, the production was more satisfactory ... Doris Hare [the only performer mentioned by name] deserves special mention for her acting and singing in the "20th Century Blues" episode.'[241]

'Twentieth Century Blues' – a song Coward acknowledged as 'exceedingly difficult to sing'[242] – is the play's final song. Sung in a nightclub in 1930, it has a world-weary tone, and lyrics that still seem applicable in our twenty-first-century world:

> Why is it that civilized humanity
> Can make the world so wrong?
> In this hurly-burly of insanity
> Our dreams cannot last long.
> ...
> In this strange illusion,
> Chaos and confusion,
> People seem to lose their way.
> What is there to strive for,
> Love or keep alive for,
> Say, 'Hey, hey!'
> Call it a day?[243]

'*You* can't *be English, you're* alive'

In the late summer of 1936, Doris's career would take yet another turn. For the first time since her days as Little Doris Hare acting in melodramas, she would return to the straight theatre. The play was *Night Must Fall* by Emlyn Williams. A big success in London, it was now headed for New York. Doris joined the cast for the New York production, the only new addition to the cast. Understudying

Williams would be her brother Bertie. This was the same Emlyn Williams who as a child had sat entranced watching the 'Bing Babes', a connection, as I far as I know, of which neither Williams nor Doris was aware. And their lives had indirectly come into contact on yet another occasion: the night of the public dress rehearsal for *Words and Music* at the Adelphi Theatre. The triumph of *Night Must Fall* was still years away, Williams and his friend Bill, unknown struggling actors. Bill claimed to know the front-of-house manager and hoped to get them in to see the show. Williams watched through the Adelphi's glass doors

> while [Bill] went in and up to a forbidding Cochran minion who looked like a warder in a dinner jacket.
>
> The man shook his head and Bill came out red in the face, 'Sorry old boy, no go, he didn't recognise me.'
>
> Dressmakers and understudies hurried in. I felt we were refugees who had been refused a landing permit. In the middle of the foyer, a luminous figure in slacks and blazer, blue shirt open at the neck, scarf impeccably tied at the throat, a brilliant smile. A host receiving at the party of the year. Noël Coward, through glass.[244]

In the years since this painful demonstration of his exclusion from the world of Coward and Cochran, as Williams established himself as an actor and a playwright, he had become friendly with Doris and the entire Hare family. Winnie, who remembered him listening avidly to Kate's stories of her travelling theatre days, would tour with three of his later plays: *The Corn is Green* (1940); *The Light of Heart*, with Williams himself (1941); and *The Druid's Rest* (1944).

Night Must Fall is a psychological study of a psychopathic murderer, Dan, who having impregnated the maid of a tyrannical old lady, worms his way into the affections of her employer Mrs Bramson. He also half seduces the old lady's young niece and paid companion, despite her recognition of his evil nature. Ultimately he murders his benefactor for her cashbox, stowing her head in a hatbox. Williams played Dan, with the veteran Dame May Whitty as Mrs Bransom. The audience knows of murderer's guilt from the start – the play opens with a prologue in which his appeal against his death sentence is turned down. Its power lies in the psychological exploration of a murderer and his complicated relationships with different women. To leaven the darkness there was some comic relief, provided by Mrs Bransom's cook, Mrs Terence, and the maid Dora. Doris played Mrs Terence.

Prior to *Night Must Fall* opening in America, there was a brief tour in Britain. The provincial papers were enthusiastic about both the play and the performances. The *Birmingham Gazette* pronounced the play 'a masterpiece ... You must see Emlyn Williams as he unfolds little by little the mind and purpose of the murderer, unfolds it with uncanny skill to a great crescendo of fascinating devilry.' And the comic relief was not only praised for comedy: 'You must see and hear the priceless comic relief, and yet sincere interpretations of Doris Hare and Betty Jardine [who played Dora].'[245] The *Evening Dispatch* agreed, the two women 'gave performances which were more than cameos: they were triumphs, in more than a small way, of the dramatic art'.[246] The reception was rather different, however, when they got to New York. According to his biographer, Emlyn feared the worst when he discovered on landing in New York that his play was being promoted as 'The Spine-Chilling British Melodrama'.[247] His fears were justified. The play opened in September to distinctly lukewarm reviews. John Anderson's in the *New York Evening Journal* was typical in its faint praise for the play and Emlyn's acting: 'Mr Williams is mighty frightening at first in "Night Must Fall," but it is all so long drawn out, so labored in its elaborately sinister effect that the fright wears off. ... Nor, I may add, is Mr Williams' acting quite as fresh and inventive as it ought to be for such solo playing.' The rest of the cast was more to Anderson's taste, 'notably Doris Hare, who is immensely amusing as a quarrelsome cook with none of this "Yes M'am" nonsense about her'.[248] Not surprisingly, given the weak notices, the play only survived eight weeks. Bertie returned to Britain almost immediately, but Doris decided to stay on and try her luck in the States, either in film or radio.

During her time in America she had an active social life. Tilly Marks, the Marks and Spencer heiress,[249] was a good friend of the Hare siblings, and she provided letters of introduction to her social set in New York. Those Doris met responded to her warm, outgoing, personality. She seemed to defy so many of their stereotypes about the English that people would say to her, as she told a *Daily Express* interviewer on her return to London, 'You *can't* be English, you're *alive.*'[250] Her stay in New York was made all the more enjoyable because not only did she have her brother with her, but in October her favourite sister, Betty, arrived as part of the cast of Coward's *Tonight at 8:30*. After Coward and Gertrude Lawrence's great success in *Private Lives* audiences were keen to see them together again. To capitalize on this, Coward wrote nine short plays, all starring the two of them but varying in genre and mood; some were comedies, some serious, some had music. On any given night, a selection of three of the plays would be performed. Coward cast his old friend Betty in a small part in *Still Life*, a poignant story of an impossible love affair, later expanded and filmed by David Lean as *Brief Encounter*. Betty played Mildred, the chatty friend who interrupts the final meeting of the two lovers before they part for ever. She also understudied Lawrence in *Red Peppers*, a comic piece described by Coward as 'a vaudeville sketch sandwiched in between two parodies of music hall songs',[251] that featured a second-rate husband and wife variety act, the kind of act that both Lawrence and Betty were familiar with from their early careers. After a successful run in London, *Tonight at 8:30* opened on Broadway in November.

Betty and Doris stayed at the Wentworth Hotel on West 46th Street, close to Broadway and popular with theatre people. The building is still there today, and still a hotel, although it is now The Hotel at Times Square. The two sisters attended parties together, seeing the sights and generally having a good time. Their time together was cut short, however. *Tonight at 8:30* was a success, but in March Coward collapsed under the strain of a performance schedule that had the two stars performing three different plays every night, six on matinee days, and the show closed a month earlier than scheduled. A few weeks later, in early April, Betty sailed for home. Doris felt the departure of her sister keenly. While she was in New York she kept a diary, as far as I know the only time she did so, at any rate this is the only one that survives. In the diary she rarely says much about her feelings. It is mostly a record of where she went and what she did, but the day she saw Betty off she writes: 'Betty left in floods of tears. I felt awful. I miss her very much.'

The Beatrice Lillie Problem

Doris's performance as Mrs Terence in *Night Must Fall* had aroused some interest and she was hopeful that other offers might follow. In the diary she records that Gummo Marx, the 'unknown Marx brother', who, like his brother Zeppo, had become an agent, 'liked me in the show and is going to see what he can do'. She had at least one screen test, for MGM, but nothing came of it. By this time she was thirty-one – although she seems to have knocked a few years off her age, claiming to be twenty-six in a number of interviews – and at that time the opportunities in Hollywood for a British woman known for comedy rather than romantic roles were limited. She had more luck with radio where she already had years of experience broadcasting for the BBC. Her first broadcast in New York was on the Rudee Vallee Hour on NBC. Also appearing was Spencer Tracy. She remembered his kindness. As she recalled in her later *Daily Express* interview, while she was sitting nervously waiting for her turn at the microphone, he came up to her and asked:

> "What's the matter, frightened?"
> Frightened? Boy, I was terrified, and told him so.
> "Listen, girlie," said Tracy, "I may be a big star, but if it's any consolation to you I'm terrified too."

Her performance went down well enough to secure her some more broadcasts. She was signed up by NBC for a short series of fifteen-minute programmes featuring 'intimate character sketches and songs',[252] and by WOR for another series of fifteen-minute programmes for Rolls Razor. The months of trying to establish herself in the States seem to have been something of a roller coaster ride. Everything would seem to be going well, and she would get her hopes up only to be disappointed. 'I'm a bit fed up of all the lies they tell you here' she writes in her diary on 4 February 1937, and on 7 February, 'I've made up my mind to go home.' She was still

Fig. 23 – Doris broadcasting for NBC, 1937. In America it was difficult for Doris to escape being compared, often unfavourably, with Beatrice Lillie.

despondent a couple of days later when she saw someone at Twentieth Century Fox: 'More stuff about tests etc. and more lies ... I'm just sick of them.' But then on 15 February there was the audition for Rolls Razor, and the next day she writes 'Rolls Razor O.K. am thrilled'. In the end, however, she was unable to secure a long-term sponsor and in late April, after a little more than seven months in America, she returned to London.

While Doris's American broadcasts were praised by the critics, looming over her was the inescapable presence of another comedy import from Britain, Beatrice Lillie, with whose estranged husband, Sir Robert Peel, Doris had earlier toured in Britain. Lillie had conquered New York ten years earlier in *Charlot's London Revue*. The *New York Times* enthused, 'There is no one in New York comparable to Beatrice Lillie.'[253] Although born in Canada, Lillie had made her career in Britain and seemed to Americans quintessentially English. When Doris began broadcasting, she was hailed as 'the funniest comedienne to come from England since Beatrice Lillie arrived'.[254] But the comparison was not always to Doris's advantage:

> Miss Hare is sure to be compared with Beatrice Lillie – and likely not too favourably. ... [she] has something very definite to offer Yankee dialers, but must veer from the Lillie line if she wants to impress the rank and file, and incidentally a sponsor. While her ozone type is typically that of the English music hall comedienne, on this side of the water, Miss Lillie landed first and hence all followers are sure to be classed as copy-cats.[255]

Another critic noted approvingly that on her WOR programme, 'she sounded less like a Beatrice Lillie impersonator than she has on NBC'.[256]

In reality Doris was not the same kind of comedienne as Lillie. It was generally agreed that Lillie was, as Brooks Atkinson (one of the major American theatre critics of the mid-twentieth century) wrote, 'a comic genius'.[257] Coward agreed but, as his companion and biographer Graham Payne remembers, with a caveat: Coward 'always insisted that [Lillie] had "star quality, moments of genius and little ... acting talent".'[258] Doris, while not that kind of comic 'genius', had great acting talent. In everything she did, Lillie was always herself. Early in 1939, a few months before the war began in Europe, she starred in a version of *Words and Music*, now called *Set to Music*. The biggest hit of the show was a new song Coward wrote specially for her, 'I Went to a Marvellous Party', which Lillie sang dressed in 'slacks, a fisherman's shirt, several ropes of pearls, a large sunhat and dark glasses'.[259] The song capitalised on her particular strengths, outrageousness and an endearing eccentricity. The song, still one of Coward's most popular, lists a wonderful array of bizarre characters – many with a distinctly queer slant to them. This comes from the second refrain:

I went to a marvellous party

...

Dear Cecil arrived wearing armour.
Some shells and a black feather boa.
Poor Millicent wore a surrealist comb
Made of bits of mosaic from St Peter's in Rome,
But the weight was so great that she had to go home.
I couldn't have liked it more.[260]

Lillie dominated *Set to Music*. According to Sheridan Morley, 'for most critics Bea was the show and it became an evening with Beatrice Lillie rather than another Coward revue.'[261] This is a long way from what Noël had originally intended, a revue with unknowns he would mould to fit his ideas. Indeed, when planning *Words and Music*, as Morley noted (see above p. 114), Coward explicitly excluded casting 'stars of the [Gertrude] Lawrence/[Beatrice] Lillie calibre'. Doris's comedy, unlike that of Lillie, was rooted in the portrayal of realistic and relatable characters: the movie-mad skivvy in 'Mad about the Boy', the slightly self-mocking actress of 'Three White Feathers' marrying into the peerage. These were both songs that Lillie sang in *Set to Music*, but I have difficulty imagining her singing them, just as 'I went to a Marvellous Party' does not seem right for Doris.

Back to Britain
Once she was back in Britain, Doris was soon busy broadcasting for the BBC. In the next few years she would make many radio broadcasts, mainly but not exclusively for variety programmes. In July 1937, for instance, she could be heard in *Nikki Makes News*, a musical radio play by Spike Hughes. In a blurb for the programme the *Dundee Evening News* noted with some exaggeration perhaps that 'a welcome feature is the return of Doris Hare, fresh from her radio triumphs in the States'.[262] Chapter 8 considers her history with the BBC in in more detail.

She also returned to the live stage. In November she was back in the West End in *It's in the Bag*. This was billed as 'musical-play-revue', but it seems to have been essentially a standard revue consisting of songs and sketches strung together around a wafer-thin plot involving a Russian theatre company looking for backers. Two of Doris's siblings, Betty and Bertie, were also in the show. Betty appeared in a number of the sketches playing small parts, Bertie stage-managed the show, and he played Doris's lover in one sketch. Another principal in the show was the singer Elisabeth Welch. One review writes of her and Doris:

> Elizabeth Welch, singing with her customary charm and persuasiveness in the kind of Southern-American numbers she understands so well; and Doris Hare, a pretty and nimble English comedienne, as clever with her feet as she is melodious in voice and amusing in stage drolleries.[263]

A few years earlier Welch, a singer with a rich smoky voice, had introduced London audiences to the song 'Stormy Weather' in the revue *Dark Doings* in 1933. More than forty years later she would sing it at the end of Derek Jarman's 1979 film of *The Tempest*, a wonderful version in which, dressed as a goddess in a golden gown, she sings in a room full of cavorting sailors.

Overall the reviews for *It's in the Bag* were mixed and the show closed after a couple of months. Doris returned briefly to cabaret, appearing with Vic Oliver at the Paradise Club. Born in Austria and trained as a violinist, Oliver had built an act around self-deprecation and pretending to play the violin badly. For the *Era* reviewer she and Oliver were a breath of fresh air:

> Did a round of the niteries. With one exception the same gang and the same stick-em-up dreariness. Soho isn't Soho any more ... The exception was the Paradise – staging a tiny but excellent revue with Doris Hare and Vic Oliver. Full marks for chorus presentation. The Hare girl singing songs witty enough to make one believe they were written to be sung by Beatrice Lillie on Broadway ... But for the rest. Oh, boredom![264]

Notably, while Doris's songs remind the reviewer of Beatrice Lillie, as a performer she is not compared, favourably or unfavourably, with Lillie. In Britain they were simply two different comediennes.

Later in the year there was another short-lived review at the Saville Theatre, *Pélissier's Follies of 1938*, which for the first time since *Words and Music* would reunite her with John Mills. After a very promising start in British films in the years after *Words and Music*, Mills's career was in something of a slump, as was the whole of British cinema. A good friend of his was Anthony Pélissier, the son of Harry Pélissier, whose Pierrot troupe, the Follies, had enjoyed huge success in London before World War I. The younger Pélissier was also going through a difficult time in his career. He and Mills decided to console themselves with a trip to Switzerland, and there they hatched the idea for a new revue. Mills tells the story in his autobiography: 'After the second bottle of heavy Swiss red wine had been consumed we decided that London was ready and waiting with bated breath for a revival of his father's famous Follies.' Once back in London a show was put together: 'An excellent cast was assembled including my old friend Doris Hare, Gene Gerrard and an enchanting young musical comedy actress, Roma Beaumont.'[265] The notices were mixed, but generally good if not raves; Mills and Doris got some of the best notices. 'Miss Doris Hare', Herbert Farjeon noted, 'I would almost term indispensable to any revue.'[266] Nonetheless the show did not run, closing at the beginning of July. In Mills's view the show was doomed by a negative but perceptive review by the influential critic James Agate, 'the one critic who at the time was powerful enough to make or break the show'.[267] For Agate (who misspelled the name of the famous concert party, the Co-optimists) with the death of Harry Pélissier in 1912,

> all genius in his kind was not eclipsed but extinguished as far as we can see forever. The co-optivists who followed in 1921 were a pale echo of the follies and the Pélissier Follies of 1938 are a still paler echo of the co-optivists.[268]

The failure of this attempt to hitch what most of the critics agreed was a perfectly good, unpretentious revue, to the past glories of the Follies is another demonstration of popular entertainment's inherent restlessness, the need continually to come up with something new, and the rapid consignment of today's successes to an outdated past.

Doris's next venture took her into some genuinely new territory. She would play Toinette, the pert maid in *The Robust Invalid*, an English version of Molière's *Le Malade Imaginaire*. We tend to think of the pre-war commercial theatre as a desert devoid of the classical repertory, particularly foreign classics, but occasionally there was more adventurous fare. The end of 1937, for instance, saw the beginning of John Gielgud's series of four classic plays, *King Richard II*, *The School for Scandal*, *Three Sisters*, and *The Merchant of Venice* at the Queen's Theatre. A year later the Frenchman Maurice Sachs proposed a short series of French plays at the Apollo Theatre, the main play to be an English translation with a curtain raiser in French. In the event it seems that only the first double bill, *The Robust Invalid* with a curtain raiser by Sacha Guitry, *Les Deux Couverts*, was actually produced. The translation Sachs used, an anonymous nineteenth-century one, seems to have been as unfortunate as the English title; most of the reviews mentioned its poor quality; and a number of them were none too sure about the quality of Molière himself. The pre-war London theatre was a very parochial place.

Sachs strove for a supposedly authentic seventeenth-century style by having the actors use what one reviewer termed the 'familiar French method of classical production ... The characters stand or sit in line and address us. Occasionally they chase each other round the room and then line up again.'[269] While the critics may not have liked the translation and have had their doubts about the play itself, they generally praised the performances (which included the theatrical debut of the seventeen-year-old Joan Greenwood). 'Miss Doris Hare, a godsend to any revue', the *Sphere* reviewer wrote, 'here brilliantly struck out in what I fancy must be an entirely new line and made good as the perky soubrette of classic comedy.'[270] The *Illustrated London News* went even further: 'Miss Doris Hare caught the spirit of the pert lady's maid to the life. Her performance was the only one that might have stepped out of the seventeenth century.'[271] Was Doris perhaps channelling something of her early experience of melodrama, and its performance style? In Donald Sinden's Foreword to Richard Fawkes' Boucicault biography he remembers the 1970 *London Assurance* production's adoption of an older acting style: 'it was not until 1904 that Gerald du Maurier had become the first actor to face another actor when he spoke to him. Before that, an actor listened in profile while the other actor faced the audience and spoke his lines. We actually tried this with *London Assurance* and it worked superbly.'[272]

It would be more than twenty years before Doris would again be given the opportunity to act in the classics. After *The Robust Invalid* she returned to more standard pre-war theatrical fare: musical comedy. A popular star at the time was Bobby Howes, the original Mr Cinders in the eponymous musical that so impressed Noël Coward when performed by the Quaints in Singapore. Howes had just had a big success in the West End with *Bobby Get Your Gun* and, following its run in London, he was taking it on a short provincial tour. Doris replaced the American singer and comedienne Gertrude Niesen (the first person to record 'Smoke Gets in Your Eyes') as a Cuban 'gun-moll' who attempts (unsuccessfully) to vamp Howes when he visits Havana to retrieve his birth certificate, which will prove his claim to an earldom. In the view of the *Liverpool Evening Express*, 'Doris Hare, another London "star", is a comedienne whose dancing is an outstanding feature of the show.'[273] The *Yorkshire Post* was also impressed by her dancing: 'praise should be given to Doris Hare, who, as Lupe, a Cuban dancer, made a great success of the tango and the conga.'[274]

Meanwhile as the 1930s drew to a close, political tensions were mounting; it became ever clearer that it was only a matter of time before war broke out. During the war Doris's career was to take yet another turn, but before telling this story, there is another one that deserves to be told: her brother Bertie's brief career as manager of a repertory theatre, an adventure which began in the months leading up to the war.

CHAPTER 7

HARE PRODUCTIONS

We were also joined by a young gentleman called Peter Ustinov.
He was lovely but he did insist on playing everything in a different
accent every night. ... Bertie, who was our leading man and
manager, remonstrated with him and Ustinov replied ... "If I can't
experiment in weekly rep, where can I experiment?"

Hilary Mason[275]

After the *Uxbridge and West Drayton Gazette*'s appreciative notice of his rendition of 'Father bob your whiskers ere the robins nest again' in the 1925 Actors' Orphanage's pantomime, the first reference I could find to Doris's brother Bertie as an actor is in a 1927 touring production of Edgar Wallace's *The Ringer*.[276] In one review he is credited as both actor and stage manager (a classic entry position in the theatre).[277] In 1930 he joined the Bristol Repertory Players for a ten-week season in Bath,[278] and over the next ten years he managed to scrape a living in the theatre. When Doris was in a show, she always tried to get him some small part, as she did in *Hi Diddle Diddle*.

When he was young Bertie was very handsome, but unfortunately, as his sisters admitted privately, he was no more than adequate as an actor. At some point, however, he learnt to play golf and became quite a skilful player. This would benefit him in later life when his professional life would revolve around pantomime in the winter and summer variety seasons. The star comedians in these shows were often keen golfers, and were happy to have a proficient player in the company. Over the years he also acquired a competency in theatre administration, and in addition to playing small

Fig. 24 – Bertie Hare in pantomime. This undated photo from an unknown pantomime comes from some time in the 1950s or 1960s. During these decades the pantomime format, and the roles Bertie played, changed little.

parts, was often employed as company manager, or something similar. His second wife, Dorothy Dampier (daughter of Claude Dampier, a famous music-hall comic), was also a seasoned pantomime performer, specialising in roles such as the fairy godmother in *Cinderella*, and assorted witches. In the post-war years, the two of them made a comfortable, if modest, living, rotating between summer seasons and pantomime.

The years leading up to the war were more difficult. In January 1937, after Bertie returned from New York, he joined another rep company, Collin's Repertory Players. This was a short-lived experiment in staging plays at Collin's, a long-established music hall in Islington. The experiment seems to have lasted less than a year. A couple of years later Bertie and his soon-to-be first wife, Lisa

Desterre, decided to launch their own repertory theatre. For his debut as an actor manager Bertie chose the small market town of Aylesbury, some thirty-six miles from London, taking an initial three-month lease on the Market Theatre, formerly a cinema.

The Repertory Movement

Theatres with resident companies performing a different play each night, commonly referred to as stock companies, have a long history. The old portable theatres were a down-market version of these, playing small towns without permanent theatres. The repertory theatre emerged in the early years of the twentieth century as a new form of theatre with resident companies. The repertory movement was born out of a dissatisfaction with the 'drama' presented by the theatrical establishment based in London. Its pioneers envisaged companies that would present, as George Rowell puts it, 'a wide-ranging programme of plays each season chosen on merit rather than commercial profit-making potential and representing the best of the old drama and the new',[279] and present it at affordable prices. This theatrical vision, however, required some form of financial subsidy. As one theatre historian has written, 'without adequate subsidy repertory theatre is a fragile project.'[280] In the early years such support usually came from ideal-istic wealthy patrons such as Annie Horniman (the granddaughter of the man who invented packaged tea), who founded her pioneering Manchester repertory theatre in 1907. In the interwar years the number of repertory companies grew, but the number of wealthy patrons interesting in adventurous, challenging plays did not. Eventually various forms of state subsidy would take the place of private patrons but not in the 1930s. Rather it was commercial companies who identified a new opportunity. The coming of the 'talkies', according to Rowell, both challenged theatres and offered a new niche:

> there was a growing demand for "live" drama ... Theatrical managers stepped in to supply this demand with twice-nightly repertory companies playing "popular" programmes at "popular" prices. The product offered was cheap in every sense ... But it met a need.[281]

One of the most prolific and successful commercial repertory managers was Alfred Denville, a key figure in the founding of the Travelling Theatre Managers' Association of which Doris's parents had been founder members. The 'popular' programmes presented by Denville and the other commercial repertory managers relied heavily 'on the well-tried popular West End hits irrespective of the worth or variety that they contributed to the season'.[282] It was this repertory tradition, focussed on giving audiences what it was assumed they wanted, rather than introducing them to new, challenging drama, to which Bertie's theatre adhered, although they performed once not twice nightly. The story of the short-lived Market Theatre, Aylesbury is worth telling both because it shows yet again how Doris and her siblings saw themselves as part of a single, family enterprise, and because it reveals something of the reality of the less storied, and less written-about companies at the bottom of the repertory hierarchy.

Bertie and Lisa's company was certainly 'cheap in every sense'. As in rep generally, salaries were far from lavish. Peter Ustinov, who joined Bertie's company as an eighteen-year-old, recalls in his memoir being paid £2.10 a week: 'There was just enough for my digs and a single chocolate-covered peppermint cream bar per week.'[283] There was no shortage of recruits aspiring to a theatrical career, however: rep was one way of getting a foothold in the professional theatre, and access to the all-important Equity card. From 1929 only those who were members of the actors' trade union, Equity, were allowed to perform professionally, but in order to become a member, an actor had to demonstrate that they had already worked in the theatre. Provincial Repertory companies were allowed to hand out two new Equity cards each year, and this was how most young actors got their card. As a result, reps were able to charge newcomers a premium for the chance to work professionally. In the case of the more prestigious reps these could be hefty. Richard Pasco, later a distinguished classical actor, recalls his father paying a hundred guineas to the 'Q' Theatre in the early 1940s for his sixteen-year-old son 'to do a nine-month season as an apprentice'.[284]

Training Ground or Trap?

Many older actors tend to view the old reps with nostalgia, and to mourn their demise. In 2019 Ian McKellen went so far as to warn that Britain 'will never again produce actors of the calibre of himself, Michael Gambon or Judi Dench because of the disappearance of the regional repertory system'.[285] Kate Dunn's history of rep, *Exit Through the Fireplace*, collects a wide variety of actors' memories of their days in rep. Interestingly, we can hear echoes of the old debates as to whether acting in portables ruined an actor or provided valuable training difficult to acquire in any other way. Derek Jacobi, like McKellen a theatrical knight and rep advocate, spent three years at Birmingham (one of the most prestigious reps):

I didn't in all honesty miss drama school. They could have taught me a lot of things, but what they couldn't have taught me, and what they can't teach anyone, is how to be an actor. You either are or you aren't. And I thought I was, something inside me told me I was, and all I needed was to learn through experience. In rep I had three years of something that I thought was of infinitely more use to me than a drama school.[286]

In the 1950s and sixties a stint in a weekly rep was seen by many as a necessary part of an actor's training. Peter Bowles recalls how

Albert Finney famously turned down *Lawrence of Arabia* in order to go to Birmingham Rep. He said, "If I do *Lawrence of Arabia*, I will become a star and it will be too soon. I want to go into rep." We were all advised and recommended after drama school to go to rep. It was like a university after your drama school.[287]

According to Peter Hall, it gave actors technical expertise:

Of all the great actors I've worked with, and I've worked with nearly all of them, the most consummate technician was Paul Eddington [chiefly remembered now for the classic television series *Yes Minister*] and that was because he'd worked for twenty-five years in rep.[288]

The theatre critic and Pinter biographer, Michael Billington, argues it was not only actors who benefited from working in rep: 'it's no accident that the two best dramatists to have emerged in the late 1950s – Pinter and [John] Osborne - were both products of the educative treadmill of weekly rep.'[289] Its advocates argued that rep allowed actors to take risks. As Richard McCabe puts it,

> The great thing about rep was that you could go and fail. You weren't aware of that at the time, you gave the best that you could give, but you could experiment more. I'm sure if I'd given the kind of performances I gave then at somewhere like the RSC [Royal Shakespeare Company] with the nation's press there, the pressure would have affected me, it would have hemmed me in.[290]

Some of those in Dunn's book, however, are more sceptical. Paul Daneman, who was having difficulty finding work and had been invited back to Birmingham Rep, asked John Gielgud if he should accept. Gielgud was adamant: 'No, no, no, don't do any more, stay with what you've done, it gives you a kind of spurious authority.'[291] And Joss Ackland recounts a cautionary tale:

> There was an actor in the company when I was at Wolverhampton. He was absolutely wonderful. He was brilliant, he would turn in the most fantastic performances. Eventually, after about seventeen years in rep, he went to the West End to do a play and they rehearsed and after the first week everyone thought, my God this is extraordinary, then the rehearsals went on and there was nothing there. He had got into this habit over the years and it was sad because there was no development.[292]

Bertie the Actor Manager

In 1939, struggling to find work in London, Bertie must have found the idea of running his own company with his partner Lisa appealing. He leased a cinema and set about renovating it to accommodate live theatre: the stage was altered, extra lighting was installed, and the cinema's 648 seats modified. He named his production company Hare Productions. It was very much a family enterprise with Doris providing some financial backing. Having achieved greater success than any other member of the family, this was a way Doris could help not only Bertie but also her sisters; in the course of its short life all the Hare siblings would appear at Bertie's Market Theatre. It is unclear, however, how substantial Doris's investment was. Certainly in later years her chief memory was the steady stream of cheques she wrote to keep the enterprise afloat.

Bertie, however, was confident. As he explained to the *Bucks Herald*, if the Hare Productions' Repertory Theatre 'can give them the right plays (and I mean to) Aylesbury will prove a good centre for acting', promising that his sister, 'Miss Doris Hare, who is a well-known radio artiste' and other stars from the West End would make guest appearances.[293] Despite Bertie's brave words, Hare Productions was always a modest enterprise at the lower, commercial end of the rep hierarchy – no theatrical knights began their careers at the Market Theatre. The £25 premium it charged aspiring actors reflected its modest status. Twenty-two-year-old Hilary Mason – later to have a solid career as a character actor that included playing the blind psychic in Nicolas Roeg's film *Don't Look Now* – got her start with the Market Theatre. She tells the story of her arrival, £25 in hand, in Dunn's book. Initially the company had a business manager, Federic Baugh, but within a month or two, and prior to Mason's arrival, he was gone, and Lisa took over his responsibilities.

> I handed my twenty-five pounds over to the leading lady, who was sitting in the ticket office clad in brassière and a pair of khaki shorts. It was a very hot day. It was 6 June 1939 – not a good year to start a career. They seized my twenty-five pounds with alacrity because they were all very poor and I played ten wonderful parts. I played Queen Victoria from eighteen to eighty and stage-managed the play as well. At the end of my ten weeks they did take me on and they paid me three pounds a week.[294]

As with the Alexandra Portable Theatre, the overriding need was to attract paying customers. The Market Theatre's audience may have been more middle-class, but its patrons' preference was for plays that ran along familiar and predictable narrative grooves, a little titillation perhaps but nothing too adventurous or challenging. The 'right' plays that Hare Productions gave the people of Aylesbury were mainly West End successes, generally lightweight, with the odd sprinkling of more substantial fare, such as Ibsen's *Ghosts* (Hilary Mason was Mrs Aveling). A playbill announcing the forthcoming weekly attractions for November 1939 (saved by Hilary Mason) gives a sense of the range: 'J. B. Priestley's comedy drama *Laburnum Grove*; *White Cargo*; George Bernard Shaw's *Pygmalion*'; and the 'funniest play for years, *George and Margaret*'.[295]

White Cargo, revived by 'public demand', is another example of the omnipresence of 'Empire' in interwar culture, often, as here, supplying both exoticism and titillation. The play, first produced in 1923, is a steamy, and racist, tale of lust and rivalry among white rubber planters in West Africa. The cause of all the trouble is the seductive, but manipulative 'native' woman, Tondelayo. It would later be filmed with Hedy Lamar as Tondelayo. In Aylesbury, Tondelayo was played by Lisa Desterre, suitably browned up: 'Miss Desterre', the *Bucks Herald* informed its readers, 'will have to colour every night. Two gallons of brown stain have been ordered for the week.'[296] Admission to this daring play was restricted: 'Adults Only' was included in prominent type on the large ad placed in that week's *Herald*. Also in the cast was the eighteen-year-old Peter Ustinov. It was in this play, in which the very young Ustinov played the doctor who tends to the warring rubber planters, that he adopted a different accent each night, fending off Bertie's remonstrations with the question: "If I can't experiment in weekly rep, where can I experiment?". In his autobiography Ustinov refers to playing 'the depressing doctor in that superb piece of far-flung Empire kitsch, *White Cargo*,' a play that even then seemed to him hopelessly 'out of date'.[297]

Bertie's experiment running a repertory theatre lasted just over a year, from February 1939 to March 1940. All of his sisters appeared as guest performers. Winnie starred in Frank Vosper's *Love from a Stanger*, an adaptation of an Agatha Christie short story in which Bertie played a homicidal maniac. Betty was the star of the West End success, *The Wind and the Rain*, a comedy by Merton Hodge. Both sisters appeared in another West End success, George Savory's *George and Margaret*. Not surprisingly, given the family's association with Noël Coward, the company's repertory included several of his plays, *Hay Fever*, *Private Lives*, and a performance of three of the short plays of *Tonight at 8:30*: *Hands Across the Sea*, *Still Life*, and *Fumed Oak*. This compilation starred Doris, billed as 'The Radio, Stage and Screen Star'.[298] It also included Betty, but Doris was the main attraction. Written as a vehicle for Gertrude Lawrence, *Hands Across the Sea* featured the scatterbrained Lady Maureen, married to Commander Peter Gilpin. The couple are thinly veiled caricatures of Coward's friends Lord and Lady Mountbatten, who were not amused: 'It was a bare-faced parody of our lives ... Absolutely outrageous.'[299] For the local paper's reviewer: 'Doris Hare enjoys herself and delights the audience as Lady Maureen (Piggie),' while in *Still Life* 'Lisa Desterre and Ian Cunningham give an accomplished performance as the lovers who meet weekly on Milford Junction Station, but Doris Hare, complete with red wig, sneaks [*sic*] the show again as Myrtle Bagot the "refained" buffet manageress who is adored by Albert Godby, the ticket collector.'[300] It seems that Doris was at home both in the high comedy of *Hands Across the Sea* and the low comedy of Myrtle Bagot.

Even Molly, the family outsider, was summoned to Aylesbury at one point. She was familiar with the demands of a rep, her entire career was spent moving between rep and touring companies. In early 1940 she was with one of the companies run by Frank Fortescue, like Denville a major commercial producer of repertory companies. In February the Market Theatre had scheduled a production of *Gaslight*, the famous thriller from which the term 'gaslighting' derives, in which a husband tries to drive his wife mad. Lisa was to play the besieged wife, but shortly before the opening night she succumbed to flu, and Bertie appealed to his sister. According to the *Bucks Herald*, 'Molly Hare undertook the very difficult task of filling the part at short notice, and gave an excellent performance as the nerve-wracked wife, which gained her well-deserved applause.'[301]

The Theatre and the Community

Repertory theatre, like the old portables, needed the support of the local community, and Bertie and Lisa used similar tactics to gain that support: contributions to local charities, competitions in which audience members won prizes, and participation in local events. To raise funds for the local hospital, the town had a Carnival Week in July. 'Outstanding among the items on the programme', the *Bucks Herald* informed its readers, would be 'the Empire Masque and Mart to be held in the Market Square ... Stalls representing both eastern and western parts of the Empire will intermingle and lend colour and a touch of the bizarre to Aylesbury's historic centre.'[302] Bertie and his company would play a prominent role in the Carnival, contributing 'a Masque of Empire ... including episodes from the history of the Empire and scenes from plays by Shakespeare, Houseman [*sic*] and Noel Coward'. For the Carnival's grand finale, the theatre organised a variety concert. All the Hare siblings (with the exception of Molly) took part, and there were also guest stars, such as Billy Russell, a popular comedian of the day (we will meet him again in Chapter 9). The local paper printed an account of the Chairman of the Hospital's Extension Committee's lengthy speech of thanks after the concert. It included fulsome praise of the company:

> Mr and Mrs Hare are the prime movers in the concert to whom special thanks is due. (Applause). Also Hare Productions Ltd. Mrs Hare, better-known as Miss Lisa Desterre and beloved by us all, and Mr Ian Cunningham [a leading member of the company] have been absolutely indefatigable during the past week. Each evening they have attended one of the dances which have been held in the villages in the Hospital area. ...
>
> I ask you all, if you appreciate their efforts, and I think you do, to give them the best of your support at the Market Repertory Theatre during the coming weeks.[303]

The *Bucks Herald*'s report of the concert in aid of the hospital also noted that 'Billy Badrick, who won the local talent competition at the Market Theatre, was included in the bill, and sang some yodelling songs with great success'. Another of Bertie's experiments was 'lucky seats'. People sitting in those seats would receive a present: 'On Monday night one lady got a leg of lamb, another a clothes horse and a third a frying pan.'[304]

Despite all their efforts the Market Theatre always struggled financially. It was the war, however, that finally put an end to it. The Market Theatre's last mention in the *Bucks Herald* is in March 1940. Bertie would go into the army, serving with the Eighth Army in the Italian Campaign, and the theatre itself would be requisitioned by the Ministry of Food for use as a warehouse.

Fig. 25 – Bertie Hare as a soldier, c.1945. Bertie is wearing a genuine military cap, but not an official army uniform. The photo was probably taken as a publicity shot after he returned from service in Italy and was re-establishing his career.

CHAPTER 8

RADIO HOSTESS OF THE RED ENSIGN

In broadcasting your audience is conjectural, but it is an audience of one.
Millions may be listening, but each is listening alone, or as a member
of a small group, and each has (or ought to have) the feeling that you
are speaking to him individually.
George Orwell, 'Poetry and the Microphone'[305]

As war loomed in the late summer of 1939, it was assumed that on the outbreak of hostilities Germany would immediately launch a massive bombing campaign. Anticipating this, on the declaration of war on 3 September 1939, all theatres, cinemas, sports grounds and other public places were immediately closed to minimise casualties. However, the expected bombing of British cities did not begin until the following September, and within a few weeks the order was rescinded. In these months of anxious waiting, often termed the phoney war, theatres and cinemas began to reopen, although public gathering places had to close by 10pm. C. B. Cochran took the opportunity to put on a revue, *Lights Up!*, with sketches that referenced wartime topics, and a little less lavish than his pre-war efforts. The show starred Evelyn Laye, a popular musical comedy star. Doris was one of the principals and Betty a supporting player. *The Sunday Times'* James Agate judged Doris 'the show's best comedian'.[306] According to *The Stage*, 'Two outstanding achievements must be placed to the credit of Doris Hare. In "The Understudy" her gift of low comedy characterization is only excelled later by a further exhibition as a gamin-evacuee singing "I Didn't Really Never Oughter 'Ave Went".'[307] One of the responses to fears about imminent, catastrophic bombing raids was an initial

"I DIDN'T REALLY NEVER OUGHTER 'AVE WENT"

Fig. 26 – Doris as a reluctant evacuee in *Lights Up!*, 1940. Doris's urchins seem to have been more convincing males than were her Aunt Winifred's principal boys (see Fig. 4).

mass evacuation of children from urban areas. 'I Didn't Really Never Oughter 'Ave Went' has Doris, dressed as an urchin from the slums of London, singing about his culture shock on encountering rural life, where milk comes from none-too-clean cows rather than glass bottles. It would be one of the few *Lights Up!* numbers to be recorded. But even though the show received positive reviews, wartime conditions, the mandatory blackout, petrol rationing and the general anxiety, limited audiences, and it closed in London after a few months. A short provincial tour ended in June. During its run, Evelyn Laye, like many stars in wartime, was determined to do her bit by organising concerts for service men. She was particularly attached to the navy. As a teenager during World War I she had performed for the troops in Portsmouth and fallen in love with a young sailor who died in the war. During World War II the British Navy's main base was the remote Orkney port of Scapa Flow. As she recounts in her autobiography, Laye had heard about the isolation and miserable life of sailors stationed there from a sailor – perhaps her dead love? – in the previous war. She was determined to travel there and perform for the men. Mobilising various contacts in high society, and in the face of considerable official opposition, by February 1940 she had succeeded in organising a concert with herself, Doris, two of the men from *Lights Up!*, Clifford Mollison and Martyn Green, and her pianist, Gordon Whellan. She and Doris, Laye explains in her memoir, were 'to provide the glamour'. It was a memorable occasion for all of them: 'We got there despite the admiral's warning that it was no place for women, that we couldn't come because of a gale which made flying dangerous, and that he obviously thought we were all mad.'[308] Buffeted by a storm in a tiny plane on the last leg of the flight to the island, all the performers were airsick. As they staggered off the plane into a freezing Orkney winter they were greeted with the news that their luggage with their costumes and props had been left behind. Also left behind was Laye's make-up case. Doris remembered her saying in horror, 'But I can't sing to the sailors in the face I've just been sick in.' Doris had carried her own, far more modest make-up kit with her, and Laye ended up making do with what Doris described as 'my Woolworth's make-up'. Laye never forgot the rapturous welcome the men gave them:

> We were the first outsiders they had seen for months; the first concert party that had ever been to Scapa. We had no costumes, no make-up, no props; but we sang, gagged, played the piano to them for two hours, to the greatest audience any of us had ever known.[309]

A little less than a year after the Scapa Flow concert, Doris would again be entertaining sailors, this time merchant seamen rather than the Royal Navy, and on a more regular basis as host of the BBC programme *Shipmates Ashore*, a now forgotten programme but enormously popular at the time. The programme, and its reception within the BBC and by its audience, reveals a lot about this relatively new medium, radio, and the shifts brought about by the war.

The Pre-War BBC

The BBC was founded in 1922 as the British Broadcasting Company with the puritanical Presbyterian, John Reith, as its general manager. Five years later it became the British Broadcasting Corporation with Reith as its Director General, who would remain in command until his resignation in 1938. Reith was committed to providing a public service available to everyone who wished to listen; the idea that you should give the masses what they wanted, however, was anathema to him. The BBC, he insisted, had a mission to elevate and educate. Nonetheless, popular music and variety were a part of the programming from the beginning. Such fare was tolerated by Reith, although since he was a lifelong Sabbatarian, not on Sundays. His attitude to popular entertainment on the radio is reflected in a talk he gave to the Manchester Luncheon Club in 1927 in which he got an appreciative laugh from his audience with this line:

> Don't judge our programmes by children's hours or variety enter-
> tainments. I know they're dreadful. I haven't much opportunity of
> listening in my own room, but there are occasions when I cannot
> get across the room quickly enough to turn my set off.[310]

The first reference I have found to a broadcast by Doris comes from July 1931, when she was on a variety bill at London's Metropolitan Music Hall. The broadcast was one of a series of BBC's 'Vaudeville' programmes. There seems to have been no attempt to craft a programme for the radio; acts were simply broadcast as they were performed on the stage. These acts included among others, 'Doris Hare (light songs and character impressions); the Hulbert Brothers; Irene de Noiret (folk songs and chansons); Billy Thorburn (pianoforte syncopations)'. Playing music throughout the programme was 'Len Fillis's Novelty Hawaiian Orchestra'.[311]

After her success in André Charlot's *How D'You Do?*, Doris became one of Charlot's regular stable of performers. As early as 1928 the impresario had produced *The Charlot Hour* for the BBC, a series of programmes he devised, directed and compered, which gave listeners 'a revue of the air'. This had proved extremely popular, generating a flood of letters. The fledgeling BBC was distinctly unimpressed. Charlot recalled one of their officials telling him, 'We pay no attention to correspondence of that sort.'[312] Despite his success, Charlot was wary of the new medium. As a theatre producer he recognised the threat it posed to live theatre. Some years later in an article he wrote for the *News Chronicle* he explained, perhaps a little disingenuously, why he nonetheless began broadcasting:

> In 1923 when listeners numbered only a few thousand, I made a report to the Society of West End Managers, predicting that radio would do irreparable damage ... The damage that I predicted has been done. Then why did I allow myself to be swallowed for a time ... by the radio octopus? Because ... I realised how much pleasure broadcasting could bring to invalids and to people who lived 50 miles or more from a theatre or a cinema. I shook hands with the enemy.[313]

Charlot's innovation was to create a *radio* programme rather than simply recording bits of a show performed in front of a live audience. In 1933 Charlot agreed to reprise *The Charlot Hour*. Doris, Beatrice Lillie, and Frances Day (a popular nightclub singer) were members of his radio company. An indication of the formality expected by the Corporation, was that the performers wore evening dress for the recording. In contemporary radio listings in the newspapers, the programme would often be highlighted. It was, according to the *Middlesbrough Daily Gazette*, 'one of the most popular wireless features of recent years'.[314]

As radios became cheaper and more convenient, listened to through a speaker rather than headphones, they were soon to be found in almost every home. Rather than the male hobbyist listening in isolation on his headphones, the listening experience became communal, and the radio a central part of family life. At the same time inherent in the new medium was an intimacy different to that of live theatre and cinema.

Doris also began appearing on television as soon as BBC began experimenting with this new medium in 1934, two years before they began regular transmissions from Alexandra Palace. At this point just a few thousand people, all in the London area, possessed television sets. In the BBC archives there is a contract with Doris for *Linoleum*, a floor show transmitted from Alexandra Palace and presented by Reginald Smith, dated 16 June 1937. This would have been very soon after her return from New York. For this television appearance she was paid £18.18.0., a not inconsiderable sum for a radio performer at this time. The experiment with television came to an abrupt end with the declaration of war. With no prior notification to the 20,000 homes with a television set, the service was shut down for the duration.[315]

After her return from America, Doris could be heard regularly on the radio. In May and June her NBC shows, recorded in New York, were included in the shortwave listings, immediately following 'Negro Revue with Louis Armstrong's Orchestra'.[316] In addition to variety and radio revues, there were plays and comedy shows, including one by Arthur Marshall, famous for his spoofs of the popular novels of Angela Brazil, tales set in girls' boarding schools avidly devoured by adolescent girls. Entitled *The Giddiest Girl in the Coll*, it is described by the *Sunderland Daily Echo* as 'a girls' school burlesque' with Arthur Marshall as the Headmistress, and 'Doris Hare, Hermione Gingold, Shelia Kaye, and Adeline Hook as his assistants of mirth'.[317] Much to my regret, there is no surviving recording of this. Collie Knox, the *Daily Mail*'s radio critic, had no doubts about Doris's potential, writing in 1936, 'In Miss Hare we have an artist of unusual versatility who could, if the BBC felt like taking the trouble to do such things, be developed into a first-class radio personality on her own.'[318] Knox was prescient, although it would be several years before she would become a major radio star, and it would take the changed context of the war to bring this about.

The BBC at War

The war years transformed the character of the BBC. By 1939 close to 80 percent of British households had access to a radio. And with wartime paper restrictions limiting the size of newspapers, radio would play a major role in the dissemination of information. The Corporation was very conscious of its responsibility. For the radio historians James Curran and Jean Seaton,

It is clear that the BBC, almost certainly the most important instrument of domestic propaganda during the war, conducted a campaign intended to convince the public of its own endurance and solidarity. The BBC emerged from the war as both a symbol and an agent of the victory. More than at any other time, the BBC was part of, and seen to be part of, the history of the nation.[319]

On the outbreak of war, responsibility for the BBC had been shifted from the Postmaster General to the new Ministry of Information. Exactly how much control the Ministry should have over the BBC was never clearly defined. In general the BBC saw itself as part of the war effort, at the same time it was determined to retain its independence. For its part the Government was concerned that the BBC be seen as a trustworthy purveyor of truth, not a propaganda arm of officialdom. The result was a complicated dance as the Government sought to get its message out and the BBC sought to retain control of its programmes. A memoir written in 1977 by Howard Thomas, the BBC producer who would play such an important part in Doris's radio career, takes us into the world of the BBC at war, and the transformation of what he terms the 'Gentleman's Club' BBC of the pre-war years.[320]

In the uneasy lull of the phoney war, there was, Thomas explains,

> growing anxiety about the German propaganda broadcasts from Hamburg, and the increasing audience (particularly among the troops) for the insidious broadcasts of Lord Haw-Haw, as the Daily Express had dubbed the traitor broadcaster, William Joyce.
>
> The BBC controllers were relieved to be able to respond to these pressures, and a second channel, the Forces Programme, was officially launched in February 1940. At Broadcasting House the programme planners welcomed the challenge and the Forces programmes were designed to compete for audiences against the dreary Home Service.
>
> Predictably it was an instant success, not only with the audience for whom it was specifically designed, but with the civilian public, equally disenchanted with the colourless and unadventurous radio programmes they had suffered since the outbreak of war.[321]

Asa Briggs, the official historian of the BBC, makes the point that 'the theory behind the contrast between the Home Service and the Forces Programme was not so much that civilians' and soldiers' tastes differed as that their listening conditions did'.[322] These were programmes that could be listened to with half an ear, in a busy canteen or while also doing something other than listening to the radio.

Radio did not have the theatre's immediate, direct relationship of performer and audience. Cinema might also lack this live contact, but films were watched in the company of others; individuals and families more often listened to the radio in their own private spaces. In his first autobiography, Emlyn Williams captures the new sense of intimacy of the early headphone-listening days, as well as demonstrating, as Charlot put it, the 'pleasure radio could bring to invalids and those living far from other sources of entertainment' (see above p. 155). In 1926 Williams had retreated back to his family home in Wales after suffering a nervous breakdown at Oxford. Radio, he writes, 'coaxed him back to health'. His father had bought one of the early crystal radio receivers, listened to with headphones.

[A]fter the Whispering Baritone, the tinkle of a piano turned the parlour into a cool spacious country-house, then Gwen Ffrangcon-Davies spoke poetry – listening, I would look unbelievingly out at weed and brick – then a great orchestra before which the parlour faded into air and left not a rack behind. ...

I enjoyed best the night sessions, when I would sit in the dark, one tiny light glowing and ear-phones tight, like a spiritualistic operator in weird touch with Debroy Somers and the Savoy Orpheans.[323]

As radio ownership became increasingly widespread it also created its own form of collectivity. Eric Hobsbawm notes:

For the first time in history people unknown to each other who met knew what each other had in all probability heard ... the night before: the big game the favourite comedy show, Winston Churchill's speech, the contents of the news bulletin.[324]

Of course, newspapers, too, created a similar kind of collectivity, but now for the first time the content was transmitted through the intimacy of a human voice, something that had previously demanded spatial proximity. But which voices were appropriate? The powers-that-be at the pre-war BBC were clear. Like the rest of the country, the Corporation of the 1930s was, in the words of the broadcaster Edward Stourton, author of a history of the BBC during the war, 'rotten with class privilege and snobbery'.[325] It was generally agreed that the appropriate voice for broadcasts with any claim to seriousness or authority was educated, male, and spoke the Received Pronunciation of southern England.

During the war things began to open up a little, at least as regards male voices. In 1941, for instance, the Yorkshire novelist and playwright J. B. Priestley delivered a series of *Postscripts* reflecting on Britain and the British. They were broadcast after the Nine o'clock News at the same time as Lord Haw Haw's infamous, but apparently very popular, German propaganda broadcasts. Priestley's warm northern tones, and his down-to-earth folksiness, proved to be enormously popular. The programmes would make him one of the first genuine radio celebrities. Also in 1941 the BBC briefly recruited another Yorkshire man, Wilfred Pickles, as a news-reader. But while the range of male voices may have been expanded during the war, there was a general consensus that women's voices, whether or not they spoke RP, did not lend themselves to radio, except as singers and entertainers, and even then not always.

Siân Nicholas in her book on the wartime BBC gives a nice example of the belief that only messages conveyed by 'a serious male voice' would carry conviction. The two comedians Elsie and Doris Waters broadcast a series of short sketches called *Feed the Brute*. As Gert and Daisy, two working-class housewives, they propagated, but always with humour, Ministry of Food guidelines, 'recommending nourishing alternatives to meat, suggesting how to adapt favourite recipes to new foods or leftovers, underlining the importance of green vegetables, and advising on how to save fuel'.[326] The sketches, given prestigious slots after the One o'clock and the Six o'clock News, were extremely popular, and unlike other BBC programmes on coping with shortages and wartime rationing, their audience contained a large proportion of working-class housewives. None-theless, as Nicholas notes (quoting from a Mass Observation report) 'official approval was qualified: "the *full impact* of Gert and Daisy's talks *has not been achieved*. There has not been that extra something which has crystallised interested listening into universal action. If there had been a brief summary in a serious male voice at the end, this effect might have been more fully achieved."'[327]

A voice that the BBC establishment particularly detested was that of the crooner, who, thanks to the microphone, sang in a new intimate style. Crooning, whether practised by women or men, was condemned as sentimental, that great bugbear of the cultural elite: this was not the stuff to inspire fighting men. In the summer of 1942 with the war going badly, the BBC decided it was necessary to act to stem this menace. A new Dance Music Policy Committee was formed, and on 22 July an edict went out to BBC staff, publishers, bandleaders and the press. It included the exclusion of 'any form of anaemic or debilitated vocal performance by male singers', and 'an insincere and over-sentimental style of performance by women singers'.[328] Fortunately for Doris, her voice was not heard as tainted by 'crooning'. She sang in a style shaped by her years in variety and revue, performing to live audiences in large theatres with no microphone to help her. As early as 1934, the suitability of Doris's voice for radio had been noted. In an otherwise critical review of the BBC's Charlot Hour, she is exempted: 'Full marks go to Doris Hare for her song; her voice is ideal for the microphone and she has studio style.'[329]

Marriage

To prevent enemy bombers using the BBC's radio transmitters to help them locate targets, the various regional services were consoli-dated into a single Home Service, the ancestor of today's Radio 4. In 1940 a new Forces Service was added, aimed, as the name suggests, at those fighting. With the threat of the bombing looming, most of the corporation's departments were moved out of London. The Drama Department was relocated to a stately home in the Cotswolds, Variety to Bristol. The move to Bristol would be significant for Doris's personal life. It was there sometime in late 1940 or early 1941 that she met a research scientist, John Fraser Roberts, at the time stationed in

Bristol as a consultant in Medical Statistics to the Royal Navy. They would marry in March 1941. Up to this point she had been romantically involved with several men but had rejected marriage. As she recounted in later life, she might have sung her heart out in some torch song while madly in love with some man, but her career had always come first. She explained this to Jim Mollison, the pioneer aviator, then married to fellow aviator Amy Johnson.

In 1936 Mollison was a passenger on the ship taking the *Night Must Fall* cast to New York. Doris later described how she was waiting to board the ship when, 'suddenly down the gangplank who should come but Jim Mollison. Yes, high as a kite ... I'd met him at odd parties with Tilly Marks and then around places.' He was travelling to New York before making a solo flight back across the Atlantic. As the ship made its way to New York, she and Mollison had something of a flirtation. She remembered one evening when the sea was particularly rough, the two of them sitting together and looking out over the sea as mountainous waves crashed up and down. 'I loved it' – Doris was always a good sailor – 'he looked at the sea and said to me, "Yes, it's great, Doris, and you know, in five days' time I've got to fly over this bloody ocean." ' He then invited her to his cabin, '"Oh, come down to my cabin," and I thought, oh yes, hello, hello, hello and I said, "What are you going to do? Show me the etchings?" He said, "No, no, of course not. I'd just like to show you the plans of my aeroplane," After what Doris described as a 'gentle grope'- effortlessly deflected by her – he told her of his longing for a son; his wife's inability to have children, he claimed, was why the marriage was in trouble. The fact that Mollison was a raging alcoholic might also have had something to do with this. Doris was quick to disabuse Mollison of any thought that she might be interested in giving him children, saying, 'And don't look at me, dear. I have no intention of supplying your needs. I've got a lot of things to do and a career in front of me. '

Her attitude would change when she met John Fraser Roberts. My sister, Susan was born in October 1942, followed five years later by me. In many ways they were complete opposites. He was an academic with what he sometimes described as 'a vulgar profusion of degrees', who would later become a Fellow of the Royal Society.

And while he was an introspective man with a quiet wit, essentially a homebody, she was an actress with almost no formal education, outgoing, always up for a party and determined to enjoy life to the full. She remembered Dame May Whitty, who played the old lady victim in *Night Must Fall*, saying to her on the voyage to New York, perhaps a little wonderingly, 'I've never seen anybody enjoy themselves as much as you do, Doris.' These two people with diametrically opposed personalities, however, also complemented each other. Each had immense respect for the other's professional accomplishments, and since they inhabited quite separate professional worlds, there was no competition. Something that I very much appreciated in my father was his belief in the talents of women. He always maintained that the greatest pool of untapped talent was among women, and in his own professional life he supported and advanced the careers of many women. There was never any question of Doris relinquishing her career. Her commitment, even in the first flush of passion, is indicated by a memo from the Variety Department concerning her appearance in a programme in March 1941, in which it is noted that while she was planning to get married on March 8th, if the show cannot be put off, she will have to put off her wedding. And indeed she did. The marriage took place a week later on March 15th. Doris and John remained married for over thirty years, mostly happily, although towards the end they began to grow apart; and in 1975, when Doris was seventy and John seventy-five, they divorced.

Shipmates Ashore

A few months after her marriage Doris would begin hosting a new programme, *Shipmates Ashore*, one of the high points of her career. *Shipmates Ashore* would turn Doris into the 'first-class radio personality' Collie Knox had predicted she could become. But there was at least one false start. Early in 1941 Doris starred in a new comedy show, *Dial Doris!*, which seems to have been devised to capitalise on Doris's comedy skills. It was written by Ted Kavanagh, scriptwriter of one of the most iconic of wartime radio shows, *ITMA*. The 24 January 1941 *Radio Times* carried an article promoting the programme:

Do you want your children met at the station and conducted safely across London? Are you looking for a chauffeur? Does your debutante daughter need ushering into society? Are you a lonely bachelor who wants to meet a nice girl who cooks well and looks glamorous into the bargain? ...

You do? Then dial Doris!

Doris will arrange anything you wish for a small fee, and she will take everything under her personal supervision. ...

She has an office boy, and perhaps an assistant, but she does all the important work of the bureau herself. She is willing, quite incredibly willing and industrious, but shockingly inept, one of those loveable muddlers who, with the best intentions, frequently wreck everything with which they come into contact. It is her principle never to turn anything down, even the most impossible of requests. She always does her best and is indefatigable in her endeavours to help her clients. It isn't her fault if her efforts often end in disaster, and the difficulties she gets involved in are worse than a kitten's most intricate entanglements with a skein of knitting wool. But by the end of the day she comes out on the right side – somehow. ...

There will be music in the programme, for Doris has on her books a collection of musicians, a most elastic band, which is capable of being stretched to almost any capacity and can provide appropriate music for any type of function. There will be singers too to give you the kind of songs your mother sang, or, if you are of a younger generation of the kind you sing yourself, or wish you could sing.[330]

This kind of comedy would seem a good fit with Doris's personality and, as evidenced by *ITMA*, Kavanagh was a brilliant scriptwriter, but for whatever reason *Dial Doris!* did not take off. There were just six episodes. A year later, however, came *Shipmates Ashore*.

The creator of the programme, Howard Thomas, was one of the first imports to the BBC from the world of commercial radio – an opening up spurred by the new wartime demands on the BBC. Like Doris, he was born in the South Welsh Valleys. Four years younger, he, too, left the Valleys at an early age, never to return. Brought up in Manchester, he began his professional life there, turning to advertising when he failed to secure a job on a newspaper:

> My lucky star guided me to a job writing copy for a small but tough Manchester advertising agency. F. John Roe, the one-man boss of this little outfit, had me doing everything from putting my foot in shop doors soliciting new clients and standing alongside Mr Cohen of Henry's Store to check whether the superlatives in my advertisements for women's underwear actually brought in customers, to organising publicity stunts for our clients.[331]

After a few years Thomas moved on to London and more prestigious agencies, although he never forgot Roe's lessons: 'Thus I gave up my happy situation with F. John Roe, the showman advertising-salesman who taught me more in three concentrated years than I was to learn in the ten subsequent years in London.'[332] At the London Press Exchange he was given the task of starting up their Commercial Radio Department, writing and producing most of their programmes himself. Once war broke out, however, advertising work dried up and Thomas's department was closed down. He had already been producing some programmes for the BBC, and a few months after the new Forces Programme was launched, he was hired full-time as a producer.

Thomas challenged the Corporation's staid complacency. Eventually, after numerous battles with executives who, like Reith, wanted to 'educate and elevate' listeners rather than giving them what they wanted, he would resign from the BBC. Later he would have another successful career in the pioneering years of British commercial television. As a producer he had a genius for devising programmes that caught the public mood, creating two celebrated wartime programmes that attracted huge audiences: *The Brains Trust*, which brought together three contrasting speakers – mainly those we would describe today as public intellectuals – to discuss questions sent in by listeners; and *Sincerely Yours*, the programme that made a star out of Vera Lynn. Almost every book, television or radio programme about Britain during the war includes a mention of these two programmes.

Lynn may have been hugely popular with listeners, but the BBC establishment was less enamoured. A minute in the record of a meeting of the BBC governors after the fourth programme reads: '*Sincerely Yours*; deplored, popularity noted'.[333] Thomas remembers Sir Cecil Graves, Deputy Director-General of the BBC, fulminating in a meeting at Broadcasting House:

> Why should we hear so much of Vera Lynn? ... How could men fit themselves for battle with these debilitating tunes in their ears? The BBC cannot avoid some responsibility for making this lady popular and so depreciating the morale of fighting men. Besides the theme of most of these songs is sentimental sex and this mood at the best of times should not be encouraged.[334]

When the second series of *Sincerely Yours* ended in 1943, 'High up in the Corporation no tears were evident', Thomas writes, 'No mutinies had broken out but at the War Office and elsewhere the feeling remained that there had been some undermining of morale. "Let's have some virile stuff," the BBC was told. "Haven't you got chaps who can sing some decent marching songs?"'[335] Thomas did his best: 'Now I had to produce vigorous, healthy, noisy music so I asked Debroy Somers to assemble a combined orchestra and military band, with a male voice choir.'[336] Somers found a young man, Charles Dorning,

> an ordinary young man ... who could sing at professional standard but who had never broadcast ... One Sunday in July we had him on the air in a belligerent and full-bloodied programme, I am John Citizen [punctuation *sic*], billed in the *Radio Times* as the "The Voice of the People – the man with something to say, something to sing". He was the man-in-the-street set to music, and we played him on with Elgar's "Song of Freedom" section of "Pomp and Circumstance". In between military marches and rousing songs from the more masculine musicals we gave him some rousing descriptive ballads.[337]

The programme was not a success and only lasted a few weeks, one of this brilliant producer's rare failures.

Thomas's programme *Shipmates Ashore* is rarely mentioned in the histories of wartime broadcasting. In his own words, '*Shipmates Ashore* had no claims to be a distinguished BBC programme, in fact at times it could have been criticised as artless and commonplace.'[338] Nonetheless, he writes, 'It was the programme that I was most sorry to give up when I resigned from the BBC.'[339] Just what kind of a programme was this 'artless', 'commonplace' programme? Thomas's account in his memoir may not be totally objective, but it provides a plausible account of how the programme came about, the aims that lay behind it, and its development over time. It also tallies with the records of the programme's history in the BBC's written archives.

Shipmates Ashore was the result of a request to the BBC by the Ministry of War Transport for a programme for the Merchant Navy, which, despite providing an essential service, did not receive much recognition. Not formally part of the armed services, merchant seamen suffered horrendous casualty rates during the war, higher than any of the armed forces. The historian of the Merchant Seamen's war, Tony Lane, writes, 'By 1943 it would have been hard to find a merchant ship which did not have among its crew men who had survived a sinking or an aerial or a surface attack.'[340] The initial, not very successful, response to the Ministry's request was a programme was called *Blue Peter*. Thomas was given the task of revamping it. He began with a visit to the East End docks to see for himself 'the places where merchant seamen are "welcomed" back to London after the perilous voyages in convoy from Murmansk and across the Atlantic'. He found that 'the only comforts and entertainments ranged between austere Seamen's Mission Halls and sleazy brothels'.[341] This gave him the idea to create a Merchant Navy Club in the West End from which the programme would be broadcast. The name of the programme would be changed from *Blue Peter* to *Shipmates Ashore*. Its 'prime aim' would be

> to draw together the merchant seamen as a group, keep them informed of developments in their own interest and welfare, and make them feel wanted and welcomed when they came back to British ports. A secondary objective was to stimulate interest in and respect for the Merchant Navy among the general public and the

rest of the Forces. *Tales of bravery and hardship were strictly out. We had no heroes.* Beside the entertainment there was a good proportion of information; an ex-ship's carpenter, George Ralston, collected seamen's news and there was a ship's newspaper read by Freddy Allen, one of the matiest of the BBC newsreaders. The hub of it all was 'In the Clubroom", a trenchant discussion platform where officers and men were able to have candid exchanges with officialdom, from civil servants to cabinet ministers, on the vital subjects of pay, pensions, food and working conditions.[342]

As Thomas makes clear, in addition to providing practical support for seamen in the form of relevant, reliable information, *Shipmates Ashore* was intended to increase recognition of their vital role in the war effort. Reading his summary of the programme's aim with twenty-first-century eyes, the explicit rejection of 'tales of bravery and hardship', and the insistence that 'we had no heroes', is striking. The ethos of *Shipmates Ashore* was deliberately unheroic. Its narrative was closer to the one Angus Calder sees as underpinning 'The Myth of the Blitz': 'the assumed invincibility of an island race distinguished by good humour, understatement and the ability to pluck victory from the jaws of defeat by team work, improvisation and muddling through'.[343]

The entertainment element of *Shipmates Ashore* was to consist of dance music, songs, and comedy acts. The resident orchestra would be Bill Debroy Somers and his band – in an earlier incarnation the Savoy Orpheans (who had brought comfort to Emlyn Williams after his breakdown [see p.158]) – with whom Doris had often appeared on variety bills. A crucial component for Thomas was a hostess who would hold the combination of variety and information together, and create a genuine club atmosphere:

I chose earthy Doris Hare as hostess, in preference to lovely film actresses who would have jumped at such a job, because Doris was much more than an actress reading her lines. This was a warm-hearted woman who greeted the men with real warmth and affection. In distant oceans they responded to her husky voice and made a mental note to have a 'date with Doris' when they got to London.[344]

The skills required of the *Shipmates Ashore* hostess were a perfect fit with Doris's expertise as a performer: her 'earthiness', and warmth, spontaneous wit, and well-honed skills in responding to live audiences – she was 'well able to deal with any over-exuberance from the sailors'.[345] She embodied a sincerity particularly well suited to radio, and her 'low' comedian's persona suited this programme designed to create a link between ordinary seamen and home.

The committee set up to oversee the revamped *Blue Peter* included representatives from the Ministry of War Transport, the Ministry of Labour, the National Union of Seamen (representing ordinary seamen), the various Merchant Navy officer unions, and the Ship Owners Federation. Thomas explained the format of the show to the BBC:

> We'll hire a dance hall. Put on a band and get stars from the theatres. This will be the Merchant Navy's first port of call when they get to London and we'll give them a big show, female company and free beer [to be provided by local breweries, not the BBC]. There'll be some serious stuff as well.[346]

Initially, the decision to locate the club in the London's West End was questioned: 'Speculation was that the men would be happier and more at home in the East End; and there was also the implication that some of them might not always behave themselves.'[347] Thomas remained firm, however, and ultimately prevailed. Combatting the stereotype of the irresponsible, drunken sailor remained central to the programme.

Shipmates Ashore began broadcasting in early January 1942. It took Thomas a little while to get the format right:

> One mistake I certainly made was to hire the Hammersmith Palais de Danse for our first recording on a Friday morning. The big ballroom was cold and draughty, and the girls who came along to sit at the tables were also chilly and aloof. They were chorus girls from a London theatre and I soon found out that the last people to welcome lonely sailors were tired and un-made-up show girls at the dawn of their day. This miscalculation was adjusted at once and

I imported groups of girls from the Forces and Civil Defence services. Most popular of all were the London Transport clippies, who became regular visitors.[348]

Once they switched to the more intimate Astoria Ballroom in Charing Cross Road things began to improve. Tickets were allocated through the unions, and soon sixty or seventy merchant seamen were finding their way to the club each week. But it was still a virtual not a real club. Thomas and Charles Jarman, General Secretary of the National Union of Seamen, and its representative on the *Shipmates Ashore* committee, pressed the relevant government ministries to turn it into a real club. It so happened that the International Ladies' Garment Workers Union of America had (prior to Pearl Harbour) donated $75,000 to be used in this time of war to benefit merchant seamen. Thomas and Jarman suggested to the Minister of Labour, Ernest Bevin, that this would be an appropriate use of the funds. The American Ambassador agreed. Thomas found an empty restaurant on Rupert Street, just off Shaftesbury Avenue, and an actual, open-every-day club was established on its five floors. With two bars and rooms where the men could stay, it was envisaged as somewhere seamen could come and relax while on leave and entertain their wives or girlfriends. Once a week *Shipmates Ashore* would be broadcast from the club. Broadcast from 5:30 to 6pm on Saturdays, a peak time, the programme was not only popular with merchant seamen but also the audience at home. By the end of its first year it had an audience of six million.[349]

Not everyone, however, was happy with the programme. From the beginning the spectre of class loomed. Lane quotes a revealing letter from the general secretary of the Navigators and Engineer Officers Union when the programme was still *Blue Peter*. In its earlier incarnation the programme had included broadcast messages to seamen from their wives, a feature dropped by Thomas. The letter voiced concern about these messages:

We noted that there were no messages from Masters' or Navigating Officers' wives and only one from an Engineer Officer's wife. In our view, this is not surprising as we imagine there will be some

Fig. 27 – Doris at the Merchant Navy Club, 1943. Doris with merchant seamen and a London Transport clippie on the occasion of the presentation of a cheque for one hundred guineas (collected by the London Transport Sports Association) to the Chairman of King George's Fund for Sailors.

reluctance on the part of Masters' and Officers' wives to have their messages indiscriminatingly "mixed up" with those from the wives of the Seamen.

We see no reason why the person chosen to disseminate messages to either Officers or Seamen should be characterized by the type of voice and accent used in this section of the broadcast. We feel that the impression which this feature must leave with the general public is that the standard of culture and education in the Merchant Navy is of an unusually low order. We consider that if it is decided to continue broadcasting messages ... a little ingenuity should make possible some separation of those messages from those of the men's wives without causing offence to the 'lower deck'.

Recognising that the 'lower deck' might not be happy about these comments, the author was careful to include the request that 'this letter not be the subject of discussion at any conference at which the representatives of the National Union of Seamen are present as it ...

is unlikely that our point of view would be appreciated and we naturally do not want to offend the susceptibilities of ... the Seamen's Union on what may be described as a social issue'.[350]

Similar concerns were raised about what some saw as the programme's 'low' character', and Doris's suitability as hostess. Listening with twenty-first-century ears to the few, brief clips of the programme that survive, Doris does not sound at all lower class – accents have shifted considerably over the years – but apparently she did in the 1940s. A *Sunday Pictorial* reporter who interviewed her was surprised to find that 'Hearty, hail-fellow-well-met Doris Hare is not half so rough and tough as she sounds in *Shipmates Ashore*'. He was aware that 'A few Merchant Navy officers wives and BBC governors wrinkle noses at the Hare huskiness, but for sailors Doris is the sound of home'.[351] A cartoon by Norman Mansbridge, who had himself served in the Merchant Navy, captures the disdain of certain officers when they heard Doris's signature welcome, 'Hello Shipmates!'.

The Florence Nightingale of the Merchant Navy

'The radio hostess of the red ensign (the merchant navy flag)', as Doris was sometimes introduced, with her signature sign-off, 'love from Doris and smooth sailing', was certainly a favourite of the 'lower deck'. When the Seamen's Union (NUS) sent out a circular to their branches to gauge their feelings, Jarman, always a strong supporter of Doris, wrote to Thomas that the feedback was that 'with the exception of two Branches, our officials all endorse my contention that she just fills the bill'.[352] To settle the matter Thomas suggested that the BBC's Listener Research Director send out a short questionnaire to get the response of the officers. Writing in a memo dated August 4 1943, he explained:

> One of the main reasons for my suggesting a questionnaire was that there is a certain amount of controversy about the suitability of Doris Hare. The ratings are all for her and she is, in fact, an enormous favourite with them. On the other hand, some of the officers (and particularly these officers' wives) think that Doris is inclined to sound too much like a barmaid.

"Hullo, shipmates!"

Fig. 28 – Norman Mansbridge cartoon showing the response of some officers to Doris's signature opening to _Shipmates Ashore_, c.1943. Mansbridge served in the Merchant Navy during the war as a radio operator and roving war artist. This cartoon seems to have been drawn for use as a private card.

My answer has always been that it would be easier [*sic*] to get someone who sounds more refined than Doris, but in the process we would lose the warmth and sincerity which has done much to make this programme popular.[353]

According to Jo Stanley, who has studied the Union's archives, 'In the 85 years of its twentieth-century existence, the NUS journal had more pictures of Doris than any other woman, by far.'[354] An article by H. E. Hancock published in _Sea Breezes_ (a magazine devoted to the worldwide shipping industry) in 1946 when the programme had been running for four years, reflects both the affection in which Doris was held, and the programme's down-market appeal. It begins by noting the popularity of _Shipmates Ashore_:

Originating as a feature for the officers and men of the Merchant Navy, it has become one of the most popular broadcast items, not only with the men at sea but the listening public. ... [T]he Listener Research Department of the BBC has found that "Shipmates Ashore" often has the largest listener audience in the light programmes [after the war the Forces Programme was replaced by the Light Programme] broadcast on Saturdays.

For Hancock, Doris was the perfect hostess: 'It is through her that the intense enjoyment and happiness which pervades the whole performance goes with such spontaneity over the air.' He himself, he writes, 'find[s] this half-hour vastly entertaining. It may be that my tastes are "rather plebeian".'[355] The programme also had its non-plebeian fans. One day Howard's office received a call from Buckingham Palace 'to say that the King and Queen listened to *Shipmates Ashore* regularly' and would like to visit the Merchant Navy club to watch a recording. A visit was duly arranged. It seems to have been a great success, particularly the band's rendition of 'God Save the King'. Since the day of the recording was shifted to accommodate the royal schedule, Joe Loss and his band were standing in for Debroy Somers:

When the royal visitors entered the club 'studio' the band rose to its feet and played the National Anthem with their usual fortissimo and swingy style. ... Queen Elizabeth was delighted. "What a relief," she said, "to hear that played in such an original and lively way".[356]

The programme's 'spontaneity' lauded by *Sea Breezes*, it should be noted, was a 'performed spontaneity'. It was a scripted programme; all wartime scripts had to be approved by the government's censors. Doris's skill was to make the words written by Thomas sound spontaneous and sincere. In addition to introducing the various artists, the information items, and generally providing continuity, Doris also sang one or two songs. Tolchard Evans, probably most famous as the composer of 'Lady of Spain', wrote two theme songs for the programme for her to sing, first, 'Sailor, Sail Me Round', then 'Sailor Who Are You Dreaming of Tonight'. Soon she was christened 'the sweetheart of the Merchant Navy'. Seamen would besiege her for her autograph, something that then, and throughout her life, she was always happy to provide, sometimes a little too enthusiastically; she was sent an official memo asking her to refrain from signing seamen's identity cards 'love from Doris'.

The good feeling towards merchant seamen generated by the programme is evidenced by the flood of donations for the men at sea that listeners sent to Doris. In addition to money, scarves, sweaters, and socks poured in. There was even a donation of raffia toy animals for the children of merchant seamen who had lost their lives at sea from the villagers of Ikotekpene in Nigeria, then a part of the British Empire. This was despite the BBC's strict rules against any on-air solicitation. The money went to a fund Doris set up in support of the seamen's Surrey convalescent home, Limpsfield. After the war she would be awarded an MBE for her fund-raising efforts, which included numerous charity concerts and other events. Some of the money raised went to fund the first of three cottages built at Limpsfield to house elderly seamen. This opened just after the war and was named Susan Jane, after my sister. Doris had taken time off from hosting the show in the later stages of her pregnancy. She was determined that neither marriage nor pregnancy would derail her career, insisting, as Thomas recalls in his memoir, 'on working at the club until the very last minute. Patricia Burke was very popular as a substitute on the few occasions when Doris was absent, and I think Doris was determined to hold her to her favourite job of Merchant Navy hostess, babies or not.'[357] In keeping with the conventions of the time, her pregnancy was never mentioned on the air. It was simply explained that Doris would be taking a 'rest', during which time the programme would be hosted by Stanley Holloway, later to achieve international fame as Eliza Doolittle's father in *My Fair Lady*. On her return a few months later, no mention was made of Doris's new baby. Once the link with pregnancy was safely behind her, there were occasional mentions of Doris's little daughter.

Evidence of the rapport she established with the 'lower deck' is provided by the National Union of Seamen making her an honorary member – the first woman member in the union's

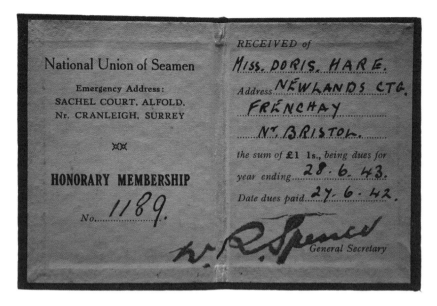

Fig. 29 – Doris's NUS membership card issued in 1942. Doris was the first female member of the National Union of Seamen.

history - when her pregnancy forced her to temporarily relinquish her hosting role. Many of the seamen who listened to her during the war did not forget her. More than forty years later, a stage version of *On the Buses* with Doris, Mike Robbins and Anna Karen was put on Canada. Karen had vivid memories of Doris being mobbed by elderly service men who had served in the Merchant Navy, and for whom she was still 'the sweetheart of the Merchant Navy'. For Karen this made the opening night in Canada 'a living nightmare. [Doris] went on and the audience went... and I thought oh my God, we're going to be working ourselves to death and she's going to get all the laughs because it was chock-a-block with the Navy. Every person who'd ever fought in the war in Canada was there.'[358]

After her death my sister and I found among her papers a letter to her written in pencil at the Merchant Navy Club on one of the 'letter-folders' provided to seamen by the Seamen's Welfare Board. It captures the bond she seems to have created with many seamen and is worth quoting in full.

Dear Miss Hare,

Please forgive the Pencil, but I could not find a Pen in the Merchant Navy Club. Would you kindly accept these [I assume some form of donation was included] as a token of my very best respects for all the wonderful things you have done for my mates in the Merchant Navy and Merchant Seamen of the last war who were forgotten by their country. As you know there are 1,000 ex-Merchant Seamen in mental hospitals all over the world who never received a visit from any seamen's missionary or other seamen's organization. These men have never received a penny, pension, or gratuity from the country or the ship owners. No wonder we call you the Florence Nightingale of the M. N. after the way you have spent time and money on our behalf. On behalf of all M. N. men and myself I wish you health eternal.

Jimmie Stewart

The Radio Voice

After *Shipmates Ashore* had been running for a year, Thomas wrote a reflection on the programme's first year. He included a tribute to Doris:

Over and above all was the sweet and genial Doris Hare, the Merchant Navy's sweetheart, if ever there was one. There are a good many radio programmes with comperes and com-meres, but there is something entirely different about Doris Hare's handling of *Shipmates Ashore*. The great thing about her is that she is not just a Radio artist acting a part, but she is a woman, meeting you and greeting you with all her heart. One of the great pleasures I get out of making *Shipmates Ashore* every week is to watch the grins and smiles on your faces as you sit in the Club listening to Doris Hare.[359]

As hostess of *Shipmates Ashore*, Doris was exempt from the requirement that she sound authoritative. Her task was to provide 'warmth and sincerity', to remind men, living with the ever-present threat of torpedo attacks, of home and family, and reassure them they were not forgotten. Hers was a quintessentially female role. If women on the radio attempted to step beyond accepted 'womanly' roles, they immediately lost their credibility. So ingrained was this conviction that even to Thomas, who was certainly not part of the traditional BBC boys' club, women's voices on the radio somehow sounded inauthentic, or insincere. The only exception was 'entertainment', and even then he thought 'sincere' women broadcasters were rare. He defines the problem in a piece in the popular paper *Reynolds Illustrated News*, written in February 1944, a few weeks after he had parted ways with the BBC.

In the article, entitled 'The BBC Must Come to YOU for Talent', the now ex-BBC producer reflects on how the BBC might better cater for the Forces. Above all, he argues, radio needs 'new personalities'. 'Under present conditions', he laments, 'broadcasters of the C. H. Middleton [pioneer of gardening programmes in the 1930s] calibre emerge very rarely.' Mentioning several of the contributors to his own programme, *The Brains Trust*, he goes on to note the qualities successful broadcasters have in common: 'An entire absence of speech affectation, the easy use of everyday expressions, the colour of a local "twang"'. For Howard, women – all women it seems – lack these qualities:

It is extraordinary that in the whole history of British broadcasting there has not emerged one woman talker with the "human interest" quality of the men I have mentioned.

When a woman gives a radio talk the microphone seems to do something to her. Somehow she seems to become "socially" conscious; she puts on her "best voice" and often the voice undergoes a physical change, pitching higher than normally. The essential quality of femininity seems to disappear.

Analysing the merits of the men broadcasters named in this article you will notice the one thing they share in common – sincerity, and that is the quality which seems to be most lacking in the broadcasting style of many BBC women talkers.

Occasionally it comes through on the entertainment side, with Vera Lynn and Doris Hare and Gracie Fields as examples, and then the success is tremendous.[360]

The Sweetheart of the Merchant Navy Remembered

Shipmates Ashore gave Doris her first mass audience. Its six million listeners in Britain, an unknown number of men at sea, and its many overseas listeners, constituted an audience many times greater than any she had reached as a live performer. After the war the programme continued for a time, but in 1947 the format was changed to a more straightforward information programme for merchant seamen, and Doris was let go. It would be some twenty-three years before she would have another audience on that scale, this time on television in the sit-com *On the Buses*.

When commercial television was introduced in Britain in 1955, Thomas was appointed to lead ABC TV, one of the new, regional commercial stations. He proved to be equally skilled at television production as in radio. Together with Sydney Newman, who would later create *Dr Who* for the BBC, he was responsible for the very British, cult series *The Avengers* in which Patrick Macnee's crime-fighting dandy was aided and abetted by a series of feisty, independent women, first Honor Blackman and then Diana Rigg. In the first series, however, the star of the series had been a doctor played by Ian Hendry with Macnee as his sidekick. The show took time to build an audience, and this first series is largely forgotten.

As was customary at the time, the tapes of most of the episodes were wiped and reused. Just three survive, and in one of them, 'The Frighteners', Doris has a cameo role. 'The Frighteners' was broadcast in 1961, when many viewers might be expected to remember her from *Shipmates Ashore*. She plays an elderly actress employed by Hendry to help unmask a villainous, but smooth conman about to elope with a rich young heiress. Pretending to be the conman's disowned, cockney mother, she confronts him in the presence of the heiress with a pitiful tale of his dying father, desperate to see him one last time. When the bewildered 'son' is revealed to have, just as his 'mother' claims, a horseshoe-shaped scar on his back (actually seen by Hendry earlier when attending to the conman), the scales fall from the eyes of the young woman, and she tearfully returns to her father. Defeated, the conman slinks off into the night. Left alone with the two heroes, the old 'mother' then reveals her real identity. She is Doris Courtney, as Hendry informs

Macnee, 'the best old trouper in the business'. The 'old trouper' explains that she's known Hendry for years, 'I knew him when I was the forces sweetheart', a little nod to Doris's wartime fame.

I am happy this episode survives since the last few minutes when the false cockney mother drops her act and becomes Doris Courtney, provide a rare recording of Doris playing herself. Particularly when she eyes the bottles of booze on a table, saying to Steed, 'We're not going to leave all this lovely gin are we?', and pours a brandy for him as the episode ends.

CHAPTER 9

A WORKING-CLASS MATRIARCH

If we want to capture something of the essence of working-class life ...
it is the 'dense and concrete life', a life whose main stress is on the
intimate, the sensory, the detailed, and the personal.

Richard Hoggart, *Uses of Literacy*[361]

When Doris died in the summer of 2000, the obituaries in all the major broadsheets (*Guardian, Telegraph, Times* and *Independent*) began with her role, thirty years earlier, as Mrs Butler, mother of Reg Varney's bus driver Stan Butler in *On the Buses.* One of ITV's longest running sitcoms (there were seven series), it ran from 1969 to 1973. It featured the trials and tribulations of Stan and his bus conductor best mate, Jack Harper, ever chasing nubile young women, ever seeking to outwit the authoritarian Inspector Blake. Stan, unmarried, lives at home with his widowed mother (Doris), and his sister Olive and brother-in-law, Arthur Rudge, locked together in unhappy wedlock. There were three spin-off films.

The programme was hugely popular: in 1970 it was the top television comedy show with more than seven million viewers; and in 1971 the first film, called simply *On the Buses*, was the highest grossing film at the British box office. The critics, however, almost to a man (or woman), loathed both the series and the films, seeing them as the nadir of British comedy. Reading David Parkinson's *Radio Times* capsule review of the final film, *Holiday on the Buses*, you can almost hear him gathering his skirts in disgust: 'one of the worst films you'll see this or any other year. ... the film's only achievement is the sheer amount of smutty sniggering it manages to cram into 85 minutes. ... Absolutely abysmal.'[362] I am not sure when this diatribe was

Fig. 30 – The *On the Buses* Core Cast, 1969. The Butler family, Stan Butler's mate Jack Harper, and Stan and Jack's nemesis, Inspector Blake.

published, but it could have been any time after the film's debut in 1971. Nonetheless, in the ensuing half century all three films have frequently been reshown on television during holiday seasons. When I was writing this book, the television episodes were continuing to be rerun and there was still a flourishing fan club. Professional reviewers have tended to be mystified by this popularity. Even the television critic of the *Daily Mirror* – a tabloid with a readership that undoubtedly included many *Buses* fans – was grudging in his praise, writing in 1970 when the show was already a success,

> Behind the jokes – and they ranged over such topics as inhalers stuffed up girls' noses, birthmarks on bottoms, baldness, glandular deficiency and woollen vests under see-through nighties – there has been a touch of genuine social observation.
>
> The reality behind the jokes has got to ring true otherwise the jokes, however awful, don't work.

Perhaps it is this kind of accuracy in reproducing the world of hair-curlers, false teeth, and the unlovely sound of the lavatory in full flush, that has won the series its popularity.

It surely can't be the jokes.[363]

The Sancho Panza Side of Life

Buses was written by Ronald Chesney and Ronald Wolfe. Much of the humour was slapstick comedy that drew on a long tradition of music hall and variety clowning. This wordless, physical comedy was crucial in papering over the scripts' weaknesses. All the regulars were good at physical comedy, particularly Varney, a late product of that variety tradition. Although *Buses* rarely gave Doris much opportunity for this kind of clowning, there is one nice routine in the episode 'Mum's Last Fling', in which she short-sightedly attempts to apply mascara. First she tries without her glasses, but cannot see what she is doing. She then puts on her glasses, but now her eyes are out of reach.

Buses is a quintessentially British show. Viewed through twenty-first-century eyes it is undeniably misogynist, homophobic, and sometimes racist. Its scripts lack the comic genius of such writers as Dick Clement and Ian La Frenais (*Porridge, The Likely Lads*), Ray Galton and Alan Simpson (*Hancock's Half Hour, Steptoe and Son*), John Cleese and Connie Booth (*Fawlty Towers*), or Johnny Speight's *Till Death Us Do Part*. And unlike those acknowledged highpoints of a golden age of comedy, *Buses* never dealt with the crucial issues facing a rapidly changing Britain, such as race or shifting gender and family relations. It remained locked in a comfortingly familiar white, working-class world very little changed from that conjured up by Richard Hoggart in *Uses of Literacy* – a book rooted in the author's childhood memories growing up in the 1930s in Leeds. Both book and television series evoke a lifeworld, frozen in a time that is already past, and yet strangely timeless. As Hoggart explained in a 1991 interview in which he reflects on *Uses of Literacy*,[364] he started writing the book before commercial television became so dominant in popular culture, and it does not feature in his account of working-class culture. Nonetheless, because the portrayal of working-class life is so similar, the working-class attitudes documented in *Uses of Literacy* provide an illuminating commentary on *Buses* and its working-class characters.

The working-class world of *Buses*, like that described by Hoggart, is an almost exclusively *white* world. This despite the fact that when *Buses* was first shown there were many people of colour working in public transport, both Afro-Caribbean and South Asian. *Buses* does nod to this reality. In one episode the wife of a South Asian employee takes over as the cook in the Bus Depot canteen. Predictably, when she begins offering South Asian food the results are disastrous; the series was made before South Asian food, and other 'ethnic' cuisines, had established themselves as an accepted part of the British diet. All the core characters in *Buses*, however, are white. The scriptwriters' main acknowledgement of diversity takes the form of including people of colour as extras in the Bus Depot scenes; there are often a number of Sikhs milling about wordlessly in the background, easily identified by their turbans. There is one Afro-Caribbean at the Depot, who is given the occasional line, and the clichéd (and racist) nickname Chalky. Nonetheless, *Buses* takes place in an overwhelmingly white, working-class world that rarely admits the new realities of an increasingly multi-cultural Britain. One of the reasons perhaps for its continued appeal.

The Comedy in *Buses* is heir to a long tradition of bawdy British humour stretching back to nineteenth-century music hall and beyond. One of the most insightful commentators on this tradition is George Orwell, a writer whose attitude to the British working-class culture was similar - although not identical – to Hoggart's. Interestingly, Hoggart talks in his 1991 interview about his uncomfortableness with what the academic commentators were writing about popular culture:

> I was much more impressed by the short essays of George Orwell such as the one on boys' weeklies or even more the one on the art of Donald McGill, where it takes what might look like repetitive trash and traces it back to the impulses behind it or being called up in people.[365]

Orwell's writings on popular culture speak to the nature of the humour in *Buses* and its staying power, particularly his celebrated 1941 essay, 'The Art of Donald McGill', which explores the appeal of

Fig. 31 – Donald McGill postcard, 'Astonishing the Natives', 1933. McGill's caricatures are essentially good-natured. The woman here may be being ridiculed, but she looks comfortable with herself and her size.

one strand of this comic tradition, the British seaside postcard. For much of his long life Donald McGill (1875-1962) was one of the most prolific producers of the quintessentially British seaside postcard, traditionally sold in holiday resorts. He continued creating new postcards with their simple artwork and a double-entendre caption right up until his death. They were still being sold in the 1970s when *Buses* was first shown. As with *Buses*, there is a timeless-ness about McGill. In 1941 Orwell could write, 'they are exactly what comic postcards have been any time these last forty years.'[366] This seems to me true also of *Buses*. The series may have debuted at the end of the 1960s, and continued into the early 1970s, but the underlying assumptions about the relations between men and women, workers and authority figures - the assumptions on which the jokes depend – hark back to the world before the Swinging Sixties changed mores for ever. The young women ogled by Stan and Jack may wear miniskirts, but the show's jokes are close kin, as Orwell noted about McGill's, to those of 'the revue and music-hall stage'.[367]

Orwell makes no aesthetic claim for McGill's postcards:

Anyone who examines his postcards in bulk will notice that many of them are not despicable even as drawings, but it would be mere dilettantism to pretend that they have any aesthetic value. A comic postcard is simply an illustration to a joke, invariably a "low" joke, and it stands or falls by its ability to raise a laugh.[368]

Nonetheless he had a definite affection for the 'low' comedy tradition:

In the past the mood of the comic postcard could enter into the central stream of literature, and jokes barely different from McGill's could casually be uttered between the murders in Shakespeare's tragedies. That is no longer possible, and a whole category of humour, integral to our literature till 1800 or there-abouts, has dwindled down to these ill-drawn postcards, leading a barely legal existence in cheap stationers' windows. The corner of the human heart that they speak for might easily manifest itself in worst forms, and I for one should be sorry to see them vanish.[369]

The low comedy of McGill and *On the Buses* acknowledges that we all inhabit bodies - bodies that have their own needs and desires not under the control of our 'higher' natures. In low comedy, the body is, to quote one commentator, 'notoriously treacherous ... it fails, breaks wind, looks unintentionally ridiculous when it should look its best.'[370] But is it possible in the twenty-first century, with its very different sensibilities, to recuperate this very British comedy tradition, with its recognition of inescapable bodily demands and the absurdity of human existence without robbing it of its earthy vigour? The 2011 National Theatre production *One Man, Two*

Guvnors suggests that it can be done. Rapturously received by the critics and garlanded with awards, the show was a popular success in Britain and America. Based on Carlo Goldoni's *The Servant of Two Masters* (written in 1746), *One Man, Two Guvnors* updates the play's action to 1963 Brighton. For *Guardian* critic Michael Billington, Richard Bean's translation turns Goldoni's original into 'a riotous farce combining the original's structure with a particularly Anglo-Saxon verbal and physical humour' to produce 'one of the funniest productions in the National's history'.[371] Watching the show, I could not help thinking how much Doris would have loved this production that took the British comedy tradition, preserving its Sancho Panza truth, while stripping it of its misogyny, racism and homophobia. While the translation is very free, Bean keeps the play's basic structure and its archetypal low comedy hero, here called Francis Henshall, and played with comedic genius by James Corden. Henshall, a classic Sancho Panza character, is driven by his basic needs for food and sex; he never aspires to any higher aims than that of satisfying his bodily demands. Love is brought down to earth as the response to urgent bodily needs. When asked by his love-interest if he prefers eating or making love, he ponders the question before uttering an aside to the audience, 'Tough one that, innit'.[372]

Women and Comedy

A year before he wrote 'The Art of Donald McGill', Orwell was briefly employed as the theatre and film critic for the feminist journal *Time and Time*. During his stint he wrote a review of a show at the Holborn Empire, *Applesauce*, a revue starring the raunchy comedian Max Miller. In his review he argues that low comedians like Miller, like McGill's postcards, 'express something which is valuable in our civilization':

> Anyone wanting to see something really vulgar should visit the Holborn Empire, where you can get quite a good matinée seat for three shillings. Max Miller, of course, is the main attraction. ...
> Max Miller, who looks more like a Middlesex Street hawker than ever when he is wearing a tail coat and a shiny top hat, is one of a

long line of English comedians who have specialized in the Sancho Panza side of life, in real *lowness* [Orwell's emphasis]. To do this probably needs more talent than to express nobility.

.... Quite apart from the laughs they give one, it is important that such comedians should exist. They express something which is valuable in our civilization and which might drop out of it in certain circumstances. To begin with, their genius is entirely masculine. A woman cannot be low without being disgusting, whereas a good male comedian can give the impression of something irredeemable and yet innocent, like a sparrow. Again they are intensely national. They remind one how closely knit the civilization of England is, and how much it resembles a family, in spite of its out-of-date class distinctions. The startling obscenities which occur in *Applesauce* are only possible because they are expressed in double entendres which imply a common background in the audience. ... So long as comedians like Max Miller are on the stage and the comic coloured postcards which express approximately the same view of life are in stationers' windows, one knows that the popular culture of English is surviving. Meanwhile, *Applesauce* is a first-rate variety show, with only the minimum of "glamorous" songs between the comic acts.[373]

Orwell's revulsion at the very idea of a low female comic reflects perhaps his middle-class sensibility. Working-class audiences, according to Richard Hoggart - and Hoggart grew up in a working-class milieu – very much appreciated low women comics: 'The working-classes have always loved a "comic", as their biggest music-hall names indicate. They love the men who are "fair Irish", full of a cock-eyed fun, and the women who are uninhibitedly and irrepressibly vulgar, like the late Nellie Wallace.'[374]

One of those performing the 'glamorous' songs that Orwell seems to have found tedious was Vera Lynn, not mentioned by name in his review, and still some months away from *Sincerely Yours* and radio super-stardom. This staunch defender of low comedy does, however, single out one of the other principals: Doris. Ten years earlier she had appeared with Max Miller in the revue *Fools in Paradise*. *Applesauce*, in the words of the *Sunday Pictorial*, 're-unites two scintillating wags, Max Miller and Doris Hare'.[375] A number of the critics pointed out that *Applesauce* 'is not really a revue at all, although that is what it claims to be. Actually, it is an elaborately-presented music-hall entertainment.'[376] Something that was also true of *Fools in Paradise*. *Applesauce* was most definitely a show in the low comedy tradition with Max Miller as the main attraction. Doris was part of what Orwell termed its 'good supporting programme with some brilliant sketches'. *Theatre World* agreed:

> Doris Hare gets a big chance in this show and seizes it with both hands. For a long time one of our cleverest comediennes, Doris has too often been neglected or cast in some spectacular show in which her comedy work could not receive the proper scope. Here she has a chance to show the public what a very clever comedienne she can be, and the audience was quick to show its appreciation.[377]

Orwell, too, appreciated her. One of the two 'brilliant sketches' he mentions by name in his review features Doris: 'Doris Hare does a skit on a strip-tease act.' Tantalisingly, he does not elaborate on its content. I do not know what kind of 'skit' this was, but it was unlikely to have been sophisticated high comedy. Throughout her career Doris's comedy was repeatedly described as low or broad. In the previous chapter I quoted the review of Cochran's *Lights Up!* extolling 'her gift of low comedy characterization'.[378] But even though performed by a woman, it seems that Orwell did not find Doris's low comedy in *Applesauce* 'disgusting'.

A Working-Class Sitcom

Almost thirty years later when Reg Varney, Wolfe and Chesney were deciding who should play Reg Varney's mother in *Buses*, this same 'gift of low comedy characterization' stood her in good stead. A couple of years earlier Doris had played a small part in an episode of *Beggar My Neighbour*, another sitcom starring Varney. She only had one line but her comic timing so impressed Varney that he at once thought of Doris and her delivery of that one line: 'your timing of it was superb ... magic', as he wrote in his tribute for her celebratory Ninetieth Birthday Book. She was also Wolfe and

Chesney's first choice, as they explain in their Foreword to *On the Buses: The Complete Story*,

> We did not have to look too far for an ideal actress to fill the role of Stan's Mum – the first and immediate choice was Doris Hare. Alas, she was out of the country with her husband a Professor of Medicine, who was attending a seminar. ... So Cicely Courtneidge was booked for the first series on the understanding that, if the show was successful and continued, she would be replaced by Doris. And that is how it turned out.[379]

Wolfe (born 1922) and Chesney (born 1920) both had long careers in entertainment. In the early 1950s Wolfe began writing scripts for the radio programme *Educating Archie* that featured the ventriloquist Peter Brough and his dummy Archie. I still find the idea of a radio programme based around a ventriloquist bizarre, but it was extremely popular, running from 1950 to 1960. It was on this programme that Wolfe and Chesney met. Chesney had first come to fame as a harmonica player; beginning in the 1930s he toured extensively in variety and was soon regularly broadcasting on the BBC, becoming one of Britain's most celebrated performers at a time when this instrument was at the height of its popularity. During the war he broadcast a programme on the Forces Network called *Let's Play the Mouth-Organ* that provided on-air lessons for seamen and others. Doris and he first met when he was a guest on *Shipmates Ashore* talking about his programme. He was also one of the celebrity guests included in a 1944 concert, 'Doris Hare's Convoy of Stars', that she organised to raise funds for the Limpsfield Convalescent Home for Merchant Seamen. At that time many radio comedy shows would have musical interludes; Chesney's original role in *Educating Archie* was to perform harmonica solos. However, he soon began collaborating with Wolfe on the scripts; and a writing partnership was born. Once they had achieved writing success, Chesney abandoned his musical career.

By the time they wrote *Buses*, Wolfe and Chesney already had five successful sitcoms to their name, the most successful being *The Rag Trade*. Set in a small garment factory, this was the show that made Reg Varney a household name. Much of the comedy revolved around the never-ending battle between Varney's foreman, the factory manager (played by Peter Jones), and the seamstresses' feisty shop steward (Miriam Karlin). *Buses*, like *The Rag Trade*, was focussed on workplace tensions but this time Varney is a worker, the bus driver Stan Butler, not a supervisor. The on-going workplace struggle is now between Stan Butler, his conductor Jack Harper (Bob Grant), and the authoritarian Inspector Blake (Stephen Lewis). In addition there are the Butler household's family tensions. All the struggles play out in a solidly working-class world.

A central comedy dynamic in so many British sitcoms, such as *Steptoe and Son*, *The Likely Lads*, and going back to *Hancock's Half Hour*, is the social aspiration, continually thwarted, of a working-class or lower-middle-class character. *In Beggar My Neighbour* Varney played a prosperous blue-collar worker, comfortable in his working-class identity, living next door to his wife's sister and her husband, an aspiring, but impoverished junior executive. But this kind of class tension was never part of the *Buses'* narrative structure. All its main characters are working-class and have few if any social aspirations. The very choice of the bus and bus workers as the heart of the sitcom signals a working-class location, although one that reflects the earlier stable working-class world of Orwell and Hoggart, rather than that of the 1960s. Apocryphal or not, Margaret Thatcher's famous declaration that 'a man who, beyond the age of twenty-six, finds himself on a bus can count himself as a failure', reflects the assumption that travelling by bus is not for the prosperous.

It is now more than forty-five years since the last episode of *Buses* first aired, and despite the almost universal disdain of the professional critics, both the television programmes and the films remain stubbornly popular, continuing in these very different times to attract new viewers. What explains this enduring popularity?

Part of the answer, it seems to me, are the basic, underlying tensions on which the jokes are based. As Peter Brook – an avantgarde director whose work could hardly be more distant from *Buses* – notes, 'The strongest comedy is rooted in archetypes.'[380] The world of the bus depot has essentially shrunk to Stan and Jack, two single working-class men whose lives revolve around their perpetual search for erotic pleasure, and the foiling of their supervisor, Inspector Blake's attempts to discipline them. Blake, or Blakey, is not a manager but a promoted bus driver. In a sense he represents the worker who has betrayed his class. Focussed on his Sisyphean struggle with Stan and Jack, Blakely exhibits few signs of social aspiration. Young nubile women conductors in mini-skirts – it is the end of the 1960s, beginning of the 1970s – appear but only to be ogled, chased, occasionally caught, before disappearing to be replaced by other, virtually identical young women in the next episode. Significantly, managers, those who wear suits, not a uniform, rarely appear. The never-ending, epic struggle between Stan, Jack and Blakey, is the same eternal struggle as that between the cartoon characters Tom and Jerry, Wile E. Coyote and Road Runner. And like Tom and Wile E. Coyote, Blakey is subjected to all kinds of physical assault; he is soaked with dirty water, tripped, hit on the head, but, as in the cartoons, there is no blood, and he always emerges unscathed. Even if he is seen at the end of an episode bruised and bandaged, in the next episode he will appear with no sign of injury, ready once more to do battle. This is an image of the unceasing struggle of the everyman (or woman) worker in a world stacked against them, not to achieve social mobility, just to survive and wrest a little fun from life. This is a working-class attitude to life that Hoggart, writing in the 1950s, but drawing on his memories of his pre-war childhood, characterised as one that puts a particular value on pleasure: 'Pleasures are a central part of life, not something perhaps to be allowed after a great number of other commitments have been met.'[381]

The tensions in the Butler household are similarly old, familiar tensions, those that stem from living in close proximity to family members not out of choice, but because of financial need. As with the Bus Depot, the comic geometry of Stan's home life is structured around a small core of characters. Crammed together in a small terrace house are Stan; Stan's Mum, Mabel Butler, the owner of the house (Doris); his sister Olive (Anna Karen); and Olive's husband, Arthur Rudge (Michael Robbins). Money is always short, the gas or electricity always in danger of being cut off because of unpaid bills. Occasionally there will be visitors but almost always such visitors represent a disruptive force that must be expelled, as when the snobbish Sally, to whom Stan is briefly engaged, and who happens to be Inspector Blake's niece, comes to tea with her uncle. Sally continually corrects Stan's pronunciation and grammar - particularly important signifiers of class in Britain - and insults Mum's cooking. When her proposed daughter-in-law makes it clear she could not countenance living in the Butler home, and starts correcting Mum's grammar, the family matriarch's polite facade crumbles and Sally and the Inspector are soon routed. The engagement broken off, the episode ends with Stan and Mum laughing about Sally's social pretensions.[382]

Matriarch of the Butler Family

Conflict for the writers of *Buses* is the bedrock of comedy. 'The first trick in writing comedy', Wolfe explains in his manual on writing comedy scripts, 'is conflict. Without conflict a scene is flat. With conflict, however small, it comes to life.'[383] At the heart of the comedy dynamic of Stan's home life are the warring relationships between Olive and Arthur, and Arthur and Stan. Arthur continually verbally abuses Olive, while Olive continually, but unsuccessfully, seeks his sexual attention. The warring relation is in contrast to the relationship between Stan and his mother. As Wolfe explains, 'We needed someone in the house for Reg to clash with, as he was basically a nice cockney guy, he couldn't be in conflict too much with his mum.'[384] This is why the role of Stan's brother-in-law is so crucial.

Mum is the matriarch of the Butler family. She is a strong, working-class woman whose life is devoted to her family. In this she very much resembles the strong women at the heart of working-class families described by Hoggart in *Uses of Literacy*.[385] Her late husband is never mentioned, he seems to have died some time before the start of the series. She owns the house in which she lives with Stan, Olive and Arthur, and even though Stan is the main breadwinner, this gives her a certain authority. Rarely if ever is she the butt of misogynist jokes. She is also a firm upholder of family loyalty, one of the few ways in which Doris's own character overlapped with that of Mum. In one episode her sister Betty plays

Mum's sister, Aunt Maud, and there are several episodes where the oldest Hare sibling, Winnie, is seen behind the counter of the Depot's canteen. Like Doris, Mabel Butler expects family members always to be ready to help each other out. She causes Stan problems at work by getting him to run errands during his work day and insists that he pick up her sister Maud from the station in his bus. She is also an upholder of conventional morality, holding the line against 1960s permissiveness. One of her roles is to foil Stan's attempted seductions. She will, for instance, suddenly appear, bearing cocoa and kippers, just as things are about to reach their climax with his latest conquest. She is also perfectly comfortable in her working-class identity. Like all the core characters in *Buses*, she has no social aspirations.

Mum is not, however, portrayed as a harridan mother-in-law. Her son-in-law's venom seems only to be vented on the hapless Olive. Mum's role is usually that of peacemaker between Olive and Arthur, always concerned to maintain family solidarity. With its young, sexy women, somewhat unaccountably attracted to two rather homely middle-aged men, *Buses* may nod to 1960s permissiveness, but all the jokes against Olive, and the confining home that frustrates desire, are underpinned by an old-fashioned morality. As Orwell remarks of the 'nagging wives and tyrannous mothers-in-law' of McGill's postcards, 'They do at least imply a stable society in which marriage is indissoluble and family loyalty taken for granted.'[386] Arthur might continually abuse Olive but there is no suggestion that he would ever leave her, or at least not until Michael Robbins, tired of playing Arthur, left at the end of the sixth series. At the beginning of the seventh series we discover that Arthur has indeed left Olive; the first episode is about her getting a divorce. This, however, does not alter the reality that the misogynist jokes aimed at her by Arthur in the first six series, and in the spin-off films, are underpinned by the assumption that marriage is indissoluble.

Notably, not only is Mabel Butler not the stereotypical harridan, she is even occasionally allowed a sex life. In the episode 'Mum's Last Fling' she takes up with one of the conductors at the Bus Depot. This threatens to disrupt the Butler household, as she begins to spend her pension money on herself rather than household expenses, and neglects her domestic tasks, forcing the incompetent Olive to take over the cooking, and Stan and Arthur to perform other tasks designated as female. One way the inappropriateness of this is signalled is by showing Arthur doing the ironing in a frilly, feminine apron. But while Mum's new sartorial ambitions, a 'fun' wig, thigh-length leather boots, a fashionable maxi-coat, are ridiculed by the men of the household, and played for laughs, she is not subjected to the savage misogynistic jokes that Olive is. She may be dressing somewhat inappropriately for an older woman but, unlike Olive, she does not embody the gross and leaky female body with its disgusting neediness. Mum's determination to enjoy her 'fling' to the full may be played for laughs and her new wardrobe ridiculed, but she remains a self-confident woman in charge of her own life. Inevitably, the affair ends badly; the new beau, Wilfred, is revealed to be married and something of a con man. We do not see, however, the moment when this is revealed to Mum, or the confrontation with the false beau; we jump to a chastened Mum sitting with Stan at the kitchen table. The family bond restored, he comforts her. She reflects ruefully on the experience but remains resilient. As in the working-class world evoked in *Uses of Literacy*, the Butler home is the solid, reliable centre of an ultimately stable, reliable world.

In the final *Buses* film *Holiday on the Buses* (1973) Mum once again gets to enjoy a little sexual adventure. According to Craig Walker, uber-*Buses* fan and author of *On the Buses: The Complete Story*, *Holiday on the Buses* 'is widely regarded among the fans as their favourite film of the three'.[387] The film was made in 1973 after the television series had ended. All three films take place in something of an alternate reality to that of the television episodes. Despite their apparently dire sex life, Olive and Arthur have managed to produce a son, and there is no talk of divorce. The film's premise is that Stan, Jack and the Inspector have all been sacked from the Bus Depot; Stan and Jack are now in charge of a holiday camp bus in North Wales where Blakey has been hired as Head of Security. The entire Butler family, complete with Olive and Arthur's son, and Mum, arrive for a holiday. Mum hooks up with a holidaying pensioner, Bert Thompson (Wilfred Bramble, best known as Steptoe Senior in *Steptoe and Son*). This time, far from her being taken advantage of, she seems to be the one in

Fig. 32 – Doris and Wilfred Bramble in *Holiday on the Buses*, 1973.
'Mum' as a sexually confident older woman.

control, getting Bert to buy repeated rounds of drinks for the whole Butler clan, for instance. It is clear that Mum has no illusions that this is anything lasting, she is just out for a bit of fun. Seeing an older woman being allowed to be sexually active, without being ridiculed for this, or ultimately punished, is refreshing.

'the most abject female figure in British comedy'

Mabel's hapless daughter Olive is anything but a self-confident working-class woman. Her defining characteristic is her unattractiveness. She is overweight, wears glasses with thick pebble lenses (without which she cannot see anything), has lank hair, and wears hideous clothes. Her pathetic attempts to make herself more desirable, an inappropriately sexy new nightie, false eyelashes, just make her more ridiculous. The oversized eyelashes, Arthur tells her, 'are too big – every time you blink, you'll knock your glasses off'.[388] She is the polar opposite of the sexy young women Stan and Jack are perpetually chasing, the unappealing wife of the McGill postcards, the unlovely creature nubile young women turn into. It is a convention of these postcards, as Orwell puts it, that 'Sex-appeal vanishes at about the age of twenty-five. Well-preserved and good-looking people beyond their first youth are never represented.'[389] *Buses* is rooted in this dichotomy between young and attractive, and past their prime and unattractive – a dichotomy that only applies to women, however. There is no suggestion that the lecherous male pursuers of young women are, or need to be, young and physically attractive. Varney was fifty-three (just eleven years younger than Doris), and Bob Grant thirty-seven, when *Buses* began, although Stan was supposed to be much younger. Neither of them was in any conventional sense good-looking.

It is interesting to contrast Mabel Butler's strong family matriarch – the quintessential, female pillar of strength within the working-class family, found in both Hoggart and Orwell – with the hapless Olive, a much-abused doormat, incapable of standing up for herself. Olive belongs to a quite different tradition to that of the often-romanticised working-class mother, the tradition of the monstrous wife ridiculed by generations of variety comedians.

Olive's place is firmly within the four walls of the Butler home. The only times she works outside the home are when there is a financial crisis in the household. And when she gets a job as a clippie at the Bus Depot, or helping out with its newly opened nursery, it ends in disaster. At home, too, she is the cause of continual disasters. She is lazy and greedy, and incompetent at all the normal female tasks; she cannot cook – her terrible cooking is the source of many jokes – she does not make the bed properly: 'I don't think she's ever made our bed', Arthur complains, 'She just pulls the bed clothes up.'[390] She is dim, fails to understand much of Arthur's abuse, and frequently dissolves into tears. Compared to McGill's jolly, self-confident large, women (see Fig. 31), Olive presents a pathetic, ground down figure. She is always the butt of jokes, never the instigator. In short, she is, as Leon Hunt writes in *British Low Culture*, 'the most abject female figure in British comedy'.[391]

The jokes against Olive belong to a long music-hall and variety tradition of misogyny. There were scores of male comedians who would deliver monologues about their monstrous wives and mothers-in-law. Billy Russell is a good example. We met Russell in

Chapter 7, when he was a guest artist in the concert the Aylesbury Repertory Company organised to benefit the local hospital almost thirty years before *Buses*. When Russell appeared in Aylesbury he was a star comedian who performed in the character of Old Bill, the old soldier of the Bruce Bairnsfather World War I cartoons, a character given theatrical life in *A Better 'Ole* – the show that Doris joined after her return from Ireland in 1921. By the 1930s Old Bill, dressed in tattered clothing and with a walrus moustache and a clay pipe, was no longer a veteran but a working man, billed as 'Billy Russell, On Behalf of the Working Classes'. Russell told jokes about married life and 'the wife' that are the direct ancestors of the jokes later aimed at Olive. In a routine he performed during World War II he would talk about his wife like this,

> what a size! What a figure! She's like a venetian blind with the cord broke, It's remarkable how far the human skin with stretch without bursting ... To see her with the nose-bag on, it's an education – her stomach's got no memory! She sat down today, she had a beefsteak, if it had been any bigger she could have milked it! Worrying about her figure – four hours yesterday up at the beauty specialists. I don't think she got served. ... she's been worrying about these air-raid precautions. She wasn't satisfied – she went up to the Town Hall, the bloke give her a gas mask, she put it on, it's an improvement.[392]

Russell, however, was not performing in a sitcom. Old Bill's wife was an unseen presence. The comedians doing their variety acts were up on stage alone. They talked *about* 'the wife', not *to* her. How the absent wife might respond is left unsaid and unknown. The jokes against Olive are said to her face. Her passivity in the face of them is at least in part because they belong to this tradition of male comics addressing unseen women.

Shortly before he died in 1971 - at the time when *Buses* was first being shown – the seventy-nine-year-old Russell was interviewed by Stephen Dixon for his website 'Voices of Variety'.[393] Like many older comedians he fulminated against young comedians whose stock in trade is blue jokes that use explicit sexual language. He recalled being on a late-night television show: 'A young comic went on and

he started up with bloody awful dirty gags. Not one clean gag.'
Asked if humour had changed much since his day, he responded:

> Don't mention it in the same breath! ... What we just heard wasn't
> humour. It belongs in the tap room or the barrack room, not in a
> place of public entertainment. You just wouldn't be allowed to say
> that sort of thing in the old days.

In the days before blue jokes conquered the comedy world, the
saucy double entendre was a bedrock of British humour. The
naughty word that was never actually uttered, the salacious meaning
that was denied, allowed audiences to enjoy a delicious frisson of
transgression while not actually transgressing the sexual taboos. As
Russell puts it, 'Suggestion, yes. Innuendo, yes. Obscenity, No.'[394]
Max Miller was a master of this art, insisting that it was the audience
that gave the joke its obscene meaning: 'I know exactly what you're
saying to yourselves ... you're wrong! I know what you're saying! Ooh,
you *wicked* lot! You're the kind of people who get me a bad name!'[395]

There may have been strict taboos in Russell's day surrounding
sexually explicit language, but there was no such squeamishness
about misogyny. As he explained to Dixon, in contrast to the jokes
of young blue comics,

> My stories were always inoffensive. I told stories about 'the wife'. I
> used to say she was too big to get in the bath. Well, she *could* get in,
> but there was no room for the water. We have to take her out into
> the backyard of a Friday and swill her down with the hosepipe.
> When it's a bit cold, we can't manage that so I go over her a few
> times with the Hoover. That sort of humour. Inoffensive.[396]

The jokes directed at Olive echo Russell's 'inoffensive' humour:
Stan asks what's in the bath, Mum tells him she is soaking some
sheets. He then asks what's in the bathroom sink: 'My smalls,' Olive
replies. 'I thought those were the sheets,' responds Stan.[397] To me, a
woman shaped by the feminism of the 1960s and 1970s, these kinds
of jokes *are* offensive. The 'Me Too' movement has drawn attention
to the real-life consequences of the unspoken assumption that

underpins Stan and Jack's relentless pursuit of all 'attractive' (unlike Olive) women: men are predators, women are prey – prey that ultimately wants to be caught. The novelist Anne Enright gives a telling example, pertinent to *Buses*:

> Last year, I spoke to a young female doctor who has on occasion been sexually assaulted or insulted by men under her care. What were they thinking? One answer is that they think she is a nurse and that they are, by long-standing comic tradition, entitled to molest nurses.[398]

All societies have their taboo subjects that must not be joked about, and words that must not be said, but these shift over time. Nowadays, for instance, the N-word is taboo for anyone except people of colour, and even for them there are many spaces, such as mainstream television, where it is frowned on. In Russell's day, he told Dixon, a comedian could be barred for saying 'damn' or 'hell', whereas the N-word in pre-war Britain, and for many years thereafter, was considered uncontroversial, and used casually and unselfconsciously by journalists and elite authors, as well as popular entertainers. Orwell, for instance, reflecting in 'The Art of Donald McGill' on the hidden-in-plain-site quality of comic postcards, writes: 'many people seem to be unaware to the existence of these things, or else to have a vague notion that they are something to be found only at the seaside, like nigger minstrels or peppermint rock.'[399]

The critics' disparagement of *Buses* never worried Doris; she was just delighted to be in such a popular show. She may have been stage struck and her theme song may have been 'There's No Business Like Show Business', but she had lived with the theatre's unpredictability, a world of harsh competition and fickle audiences. A story Anna Karen told my sister and me is revealing. Karen was having a bad day during a *Buses* rehearsal. As she began to moan, Doris turned to her and said, 'You know what you need, dear,' pausing for a response. 'No, what?' said Karen, expecting Doris to say something like 'a nice cup of tea'. The response she got came from a professional life that had seen plenty of hard times. What she needed, Doris told her, was 'a nice, long spell out of work'.[400] Success was never to be taken for granted.

'*Watching* On the Buses *makes me feel I've got my Nan back.*'
For many, a defining characteristic of *Buses* is – to quote David
Parkinson's memorable putdown - its 'smutty suggestiveness'. And yet
when its fans talk about the programme, the word that comes up time
and time again is its 'innocence'. My accountant, a big fan, explained
to me that he loves the programme, and watches the repeats when
they are shown on television, because 'it was so innocent'. This is close
to Billy Russell's insistence that his jokes about 'the wife' were inoffensive. It seems that what makes Russell's jokes 'inoffensive', and *Buses*
'innocent', to quote Wright's introduction to his *Buses* book, is that
'*On the Buses* never resorted to any swearing or sex scenes to gain
laughs'.[401] Leering at mini-skirted clippies as they reach up to adjust a
bus's destination, speculating on their availability, and all the sugges-
tive remarks, are fine as long as the fulfilment of desire is not shown,
and, above all, there is no swearing. The use of sexual swear words may
no longer be taboo in the way, for instance, the N-word and ethnic
slurs now are, but it appears they still have the power to make many
people uncomfortable enough that their reliable absence in a show
like *Buses* is notable and appealing.

A letter written to the *Daily Mirror* in 1972 captures the sense that
Buses represents a holdout against a threatening deluge of permissiveness. The paper had asked its readers to respond to the question: Is
Mary Whitehouse really necessary? At the time Whitehouse, founder
of the National Viewers' and Listeners' Association, was leading a
campaign against what she saw as the collapse of moral standards
across the media. The overwhelming majority of the readers
responded 'No!' to the *Mirror*'s question: 'Many readers point out
that all sets have an "off" switch should anyone be offended by a
programme.'[402] But there were some who agreed with her. One reader
wrote, 'We need Mrs Whitehouse to put over the public's point of
view. We applaud and want such healthy shows as "On the Buses"
and "Love thy Neighbour".' *Love thy Neighbour*, a show about an Afro-
Caribbean couple who move in next door to a racist white working-
class man and his wife, ran from 1972 to 1976. From 1973 to 1975 it
was the most successful British sitcom, although the 1994 *Guinness
Book of Sitcoms* describes it as 'controversial', and nowadays its treat-
ment of race would be considered far from 'healthy'.

To try and get a better understanding of *Buses* fans' deep attachment to the television programmes and film spin-offs, in 2017 my sister and I attended a weekend event celebrating the final film, *Holiday on the Buses*. Organised by Walker and Richard Coghill (another Buses uber-fan), it was held at the Pontins Holiday Camp (now Prestatyn Sands Holiday Park) where the location shots were filmed. The weekend included a bus tour of all the local place where scenes were shot; there was a lot of earnest discussion among the attendees as to exactly where the camera had been placed to film the sequence where Arthur's motorbike, with Olive in the sidecar, comes off the road, tipping them and their luggage into the river. *Holiday on the Buses* was shown in a nearby cinema, followed by a Q&A with a few of the surviving cast members. In 2017 Anna Karen (she died in 2022) was the only one of the core cast still alive but Walker and Coghill had managed to round up a few of the women who had played small parts, once nubile young women chased by Stan and Jack, now elderly matrons. Sue and I represented Doris. The following day there was a session where fans could take photos with Anna Karen and the others, and get signed publicity photographs. Sue had put together a slide show of some of the highlights of Doris's long career, which ran on a loop. She had also dug out of her children's dressing-up box the gold lamé trouser suit Doris had worn on one of her dates with the pensioner Bert in 'Mum's Last Fling', and we posed for selfies with *Buses* enthusiasts holding the sacred relic.

Over the course of the weekend we tried to talk to as many of the fans as we could. The attendees, of course, represented a small sample of self-selected fans. In total there were about a hundred of these, almost all white, ranging in age from a few elderly people, who watched *Buses* when it was first shown, to teenagers, usually accompanied by one or both parents, who had discovered it relatively recently. *Buses* was first shown in the days before VCRs; if you wanted to watch a programme, you had to watch it when it was broadcast. Television viewing was often still a family event, not unlike the wartime experience of listening to the radio in the days of *Shipmates Ashore*. A number of people had warm memories of this kind of family viewing.

I was most struck by how many people told us that the Butler family conjured up the family they remembered from their childhood. And here it seems Mum resonated particularly strongly. Typical was this comment: 'Doris could have been my mother, she had a lovely smile, she could have been everybody's mother.' For middle-class *Guardian* journalists, like Andrew Roberts, *Buses* may seem 'as bleak as any offering from Ken Loach, with its London of rusting Hillman Minxes, bare light bulbs and kitchens reeking of congealed fat',[403] but to many, it would seem, it embodied the warm embrace of a world governed by family, A. E. Housman's 'land of lost content'.

One incident in particular stays with me. Sue and I were sitting in the minibus that was to take us back to Pontins after the showing of the film. The only other person on the bus was a young woman, in her late twenties or early thirties. Rather shyly she came up to us and said: 'I just want to tell you how much your mother meant to me. My mother died when I was young and I was brought up by my Gran. Watching *On the Buses* makes me feel I've got my Nan back.'

Much of the programme's enduring appeal can perhaps be explained by the combination of accomplished comedy performers, and plots based on time-honoured, structural tensions within the family and at work, played out in a safe space, saturated with nostalgia. To borrow Hoggart's formulation (quoted on p. 183), this sitcom that seems such a throwback to older comedy traditions takes 'repetitive trash and traces it back to the impulses behind it or being called up in people'.

Another 'Mum'

After *Buses* Doris would play another Mum in a new, and very British, film genre that emerged in the 1970s: the sex comedy. In 1970 the British Board of Film Classification (responsible for certifying all films publicly distributed in Britain) made major changes to its ratings system that made possible a new sexual explicitness. As Simon Sheridan, a cultural commentator and self-confessed fan, writes:

with the arrival of *Confessions of a Window Cleaner* in 1974, there was no turning back. The era of the stupefying, phenomenal, magnificent British sex comedy was upon us. The *Confessions* films and the legions like them combined all the successful elements of TV situation comedies (knockabout plots, gross sexual stereotypes, *double entrendres*, familiar suburban settings, crusty old character actors and pretty girls) with a gigantic dollop of nudity [but never full-frontal *male* nudity] and simulated sex. The mix was irresistible to the general public, whose seemingly insatiable appetite for titters and tits knew no bounds.[404]

There were four *Confessions* films: *Confessions of a Window Cleaner* (1974); *Confessions of a Pop Performer* (1975); *Confessions of a Driving Instructor* (1976); and *Confessions from a Holiday Camp* (1977). Like *Buses*, the films were set in solidly working-class milieu; the plot structure was always the same: the sexual escapades of the young working-class Timmy Lea, who, like the *Buses*' Stan, lives at home with his family, but unlike Stan is allowed to have sex with the succession of attractive and eager women he is continually encountering. Timmy is also less of a predator than Stan or Jack, more of an innocent in the tradition of Voltaire's Candide, who simply goes along with whatever is offered to him. It helps that the *Confessions* star was the attractive twenty-three-year-old Robin Askwith rather than the considerably less attractive fifty-three-year-old Varney or thirty-seven-year-old Grant.

As Hunt notes, that this came across as 'good clean fun' was greatly aided by the hero's family having 'a sitcom familiarity about them'.[405] The sitcom family here harks back, albeit rather faintly, to stereotypical portrayals like Orwell's rhapsody about the manual labourer's home written forty years earlier: 'Father, in shirt-sleeves, sits in the rocking chair at one side of the fire reading the racing finals, and mother sits on the other with her sewing, and the children are happy with a pennyworth of mint humbugs.'[406] Timmy's parents were played by Bill Maynard, and in the first film, Dandy Nicholls; his sister by Sheila White; and her ne'er-do-well cheating husband, instigator of many of Timmy's misadventures, by Anthony Booth. Nicholls and Booth were both regulars in *Till*

Death Us Do Part (the British sitcom remade in America as *All in the Family*). When Nicholls was unavailable for the second film, Doris was an obvious choice; she would play Timmy's Mum in the rest of the series. Sheridan judges the *Confessions* films, 'undoubtedly the best sex comedy series of the 1970s',[407] and for him the best comedy in the films was provided by the family scenes: 'Aside from Askwith's continuing sexcapades' in *Confessions of a Driving Instructor*, 'Bill Maynard's performance as Timmy's uncultured, oafish, flat-capped father was rapidly becoming the funniest turn in the series, and his interplay with clucking wife (Doris Hare) and whining sour-faced daughter (Sheila White) is as marvellous as ever.'[408] In *Confessions from a Holiday Camp*, 'as usual, the most chucklesome scenes are reserved for the Lea family, immortalised by Doris Hare, Bill Maynard and Sheila White.'[409]

When she made *Confessions of a Pop Performer* Doris had not seen the previous film. She knew what her role was, another lovable cockney Mum, but had not read the rest of the script with any care. She was all too familiar with being out of work, and her philosophy was always to accept whatever work she was offered. Since she was only in the family scenes, she was not present when they were filming the more explicit stuff. It was only when she went to the film's premier, dressed, as she felt an actress should be, in her full finery, that sinking further and further into her mink coat in embarrassment, she was heard to exclaim: 'Gawd, I'm in a porn film.' Her realisation did not, however, prevent her signing on to do two more *Confessions* films, even securing bit parts for her three siblings, Winnie, Betty and Bertie, as mourners at a funeral in the final film, *Confessions from a Holiday Camp*.

The critics did not share Sheridan's enthusiasm for the films, they were just as scathing as they were about *Buses*. The *Daily Mirror's* review of *Confessions of a Pop Performer* captures the general feeling:

> Only those happy to settle for the most basic tittering will be amused by *Confessions of a Pop Performer*. ... It's a grovel and grope film, about as sexually stimulating as the spectacle of Russian fishwives working through a Leningrad winter. ... Forget the X rating. It deserves a double S – Shuddersome Stinker.[410]

There were plenty of film goers, however, happy to settle for the 'most basic tittering'. The first of the series, *Confession of a Window Cleaner*, was the highest-grossing British movie of 1974,[411] and all three of the subsequent films did well at the box office – a popularity for which some critics blamed the British public. David Robinson in *The Times* sniffed that 'the sexual infantilism of a sufficient proportion of the public' promised to give *Confessions of a Pop Performer* 'the same box-office success as its predecessor'.[412]

Having looked at some high points of Doris's trajectory as a low comedian, in the next chapter we return to the period between the final years of *Shipmates Ashore*, and the beginning of *Buses*. The post-war years, and particularly the 1950s, were not always easy for her. But then came the moment in the late 1950s and 1960s when the British theatre was transformed by new playwrights and actors challenging the old models of comfortable, bourgeois theatre – the theatre in which Doris was so at home. Somewhat surprisingly perhaps she was to find a new home in those bastions of high culture, the Royal Court, the Royal Shakespeare Company and the National Theatre. I tell that story in the final chapter.

ACT THREE

A "LOW" COMEDIAN GOES LEGIT

CHAPTER 10

THE YEARS OF TRANSITION

Perhaps the worst that can be said of the theatre of the early post-war years was that it was a fallow period.

David Pattie,
Modern British Playwriting in the 1950s[413]

At the end of Chapter 8 we left Doris about to step down as hostess of *Shipmates Ashore* early in 1947. This chapter tells the story of her career after *Shipmates* as she confronted the changing theatrical landscape of the 1950s.

The Allies may have declared victory in 1945 but the Britain that emerged from the war years was not the world imperial power it had been before the war. In reality its pre-eminence had long been in decline but the harsh realities of post-war austerity as the country struggled to recover from the legacy of debt left by the war, brought this home in a new way. Britons asked themselves what kind of country would, or should, post-war Britain be. There were those, like W. Somerset Maugham, who were horrified at what they saw as a retreat from all that had made Britain 'great', and 'the impregnable bastions of the class system' surrendering to 'a cadre of social inferiors'.[414] But there were many who looked forward with optimism to the creation of a new, more equitable Britain that would offer the opportunity for a decent life to all. The landslide victory of the Labour Party in 1945 with its rejection of Churchill and the Tory Party, reflected this vision of a fairer, more modern Britain which embraced the challenge of building the future.

Despite the doom-saying of the likes of Maugham, the 'bastions of the class system', might be shaken, but they were still standing. As regards the theatre and the other arts, the immediate post-war years and the decade of the fifties can be seen as a time when there were indications, green shoots we might say, of new, radical forms, the hints of which tended to produce hysterical apoplexy in the right-wing press. It would not be until the next decade, however, that the fundamental shifts in the tectonic plates underpinning the landscape of British culture would become apparent. The theatre of the immediate post-war period and the 1950s continued, for instance, to be run almost exclusively by those seeking maximum profits.[415] It was only in the 1960s that the idea of state-subsidized theatres began to be accepted. In 1961 the critic Kenneth Tynan, champion of John Osborne's *Look Back in Anger* – the staging of which at the Royal Court in 1956 had supposedly changed British Theatre for ever – concluded despairingly, 'A decade ago, roughly two out of three London theatres were inhabited by detective stories, Pineroesque melodramas, debutante comedies, overweight musicals, and unreviewable revues; the same is true today.'[416] This was the theatre world which Doris confronted after leaving *Shipmates Ashore*.

Back to Live Performance

Even while hosting *Shipmates*, Doris never abandoned live performance. She continued to perform in variety, her radio fame featuring prominently in her billing. There was even a touring version of *Shipmates Ashore*, with Doris, Debroy Somers and his orchestra, and other regular contributors. For three months, beginning in late 1943, the show visited different provincial cities with Doris hosting the radio programme remotely from wherever she happened to be that week. In 1945, shortly before the end of the war, she combined her radio hosting duties with appearances six nights a week in *Sweet Yesterday*, a musical romance set in Napoleonic France just before the Battle of Trafalgar. The stars were a husband-and-wife duo, Anne Ziegler and Webster Booth, then at the height of their popularity. The plot has echoes of *The Scarlet Pimpernel* and *A Tale of Two Cities*. One provincial reviewer wrote:

> The chief comedy part – that of Sans-Gêne, Napoleon's ex-washer woman is in the hands of that exquisitely vulgar artist, Doris Hare

... an actress with a genius for the sudden quirk of ribaldry. This she produces with so much explosive enjoyment and such a rich significance that the most mediocre lines take on sparkle and the reflection is born that had Sans-Gêne been Doris Hare the course of history might have been noticeably different.[417]

After its provincial tour, *Sweet Yesterday* would have a respectable run of 196 performances at London's Adelphi Theatre despite mediocre reviews. The consensus seemed to be that the music, lyrics, and book, while pleasant enough were rather dated. In the words of the *Tatler* reviewer, 'the makers of the piece' seemed to have 'said to themselves ... yes, we remember very well how this sort of thing has always been done, and that is how we will do it.' He also found Doris's low comedy style somewhat discordant:

Miss Doris Hare has a good deal to do with the plot. She is Madame Sans-Gêne, Napoleon's witty washerwoman, but since she is not once allowed to be witty but is constantly facetious in broad music-hall style, she has the odd effect of seeming to be a cheerful parody of all the grandiosities going on around her.[418]

I have to admit that I am intrigued by the idea of Doris achieving a kind of Brechtian alienation in the context of this Baroness Orczy-like romanticism of the French Revolution.

In May 1946 she would have a starring role in 'a new farcical comedy', *Quartette in Discord*, in which she played a married women in thrall to the teachings of Freud. There was a provincial tour of the show, after which it was supposed to open in London, but, as was to become an all too familiar pattern over the next decade, *Quartette in Discord* died before reaching the West End. A brief item in a Liverpool paper when *Quartette in Discord* was playing there indicates the frenetic pace of Doris's life at this time:

Hostess-star of the Merchant Navy radio programme "Shipmates Ashore," Miss Doris Hare, is to present prizes at the Adelphi Hotel in aid of the new canteen for the Apostleship of the Sea. She will go along after her performance in "Quartette in Discord" at the Royal Court.

Fig. 33 – Lenare Studio portrait of Doris at home in 1947, with her husband, John Fraser Roberts, elder daughter, Susan, and the author. The Lenare Studio specialised in society photographs. Here we see Doris and John 'performing' middle-class marriage, with Doris giving (as she sang in Coward's 'Three White Feathers') 'a first rate reading of the part'.

In addition to the matinee and evening performance and her appearance at the dance, she will make a midnight journey to London to record this week's "Shipmates Ashore" programme the following morning and get back at 5:30 on Thursday for the evening performance at 6:30, only to leave at midnight for London again to record the special Victory Day Programme.

With similar journeys last Saturday from Leeds and next Saturday from Liverpool for programme conferences, she will have made four such journeys in eight days.[419]

Her stamina is all the more remarkable given that at this time she would have been pregnant with me. Doris came from a family in which women, like men, had a profession, and like any professional man of the time, she saw no conflict between career and marriage. Once married, she simply added the role of wife and mother to all her other roles.

On 26 March 1947, two months after I was born, Doris hosted her last *Shipmates Ashore*. Less than a month later, on 22 April, she opened at the Saville Theatre as one of the principals in *1066 and All That*. This was a revival of a successful 1935 revue by Reginald Arkell, updated to reflect its post-war moment. The show was based on W. C. Sellar and R. J. Yeatman's *1066 and All That: A Memorable History of England, comprising all the parts you can remember, including 103 Good Things, 5 Bad Kings and 2 Genuine Dates*. Reprinted more than fifty times since its original publication in 1930 (and still in print), *1066 and All That* was described by left-wing historian Raphael Samuel as 'that much underrated anti-imperialist tract', a book that 'punctured the more bombastic claims of drum-and-trumpet history'.[420] There is, for instance, its wonderful rewriting of the Magna Carta, which reads in part:

1. That no one was to be put to death save for some reason – (except the common people).
2. That everyone should be free – (except the common people)
...
6. That the Barons should not be tried except by a special jury of other Barons who would understand.[421]

To turn the book into a stage show, Arkell had introduced the characters of Everyman (played by Leslie Henson, a popular musical comedy star) and his wife (played by Doris). Everyman here, in the words of the critic W. A. Darlington, is 'the downtrodden little man, always getting the worst of the deal throughout the ages'.[422] The stage version retained the book's populist scepticism, appropriate in a Britain that had overwhelmingly voted Labour just two years earlier. As the couple and their son are shown around a waxworks museum by a pompous guide, Henson falls into a daydream in which the waxworks come to life and act out parodies of history. Doris played a number of historical figures including Nell Gwyn and Marie Lloyd. For *The Tatler's* Beaumont Kent,

To any old playgoer one of the pleasantest of the new features of the *1066 And All That*, at the Saville, is Doris Hare's impersonation of Marie Lloyd singing 'One of the ruins that Cromwell knocked abaht a bit'. She manages quite uncannily to recapture the voice and style of the great comedienne. Yet as Marie Lloyd died in 1922 it is hardly surprising to learn that Miss Hare has nothing more than a dim childhood memory of seeing her, on one occasion only, from the wings of the old Alhambra.

Fig.34 – Doris and Leslie Henson as the Common Man and his wife in *1066 and All That*, 1947. The Common Man and his wife are citizens of a country that has just won a war but is enduring the hardships of post-war austerity. Rationing had become even stricter; the show's burlesque of King John's reign included a giant ration book dated 1214-15.

Doris explained to Kent,

> If I do manage to imitate Marie successfully ... it is entirely due
> to her sister Alice (who is now seventy-two) for she coached me for
> the part. "Whatever you do," she said, "don't hurry. Take your time.
> Marie always did that and that is how she got her effect so surely."
>
> The elastic-side boots, the forlorn hat, the handbag and the coat
> which Miss Hare wears all belonged to Marie.[423]

Like *Sweet Yesterday*, *1066 And All That* had a respectable run, 188
performances, finally closing in October.

Doris continued broadcasting after she left *Shipmates*, although
more sporadically. In 1950, for three months she hosted a weekly
fifteen-minute programme, *Doris Hare's Record Choice*, and was part
of a light-hearted, all-female series, *Ladies Please*. *The Stage* provided
a preview,

> [The programme] will be presented in the form of a revue, played
> by women, about women, for women. The only exception will be
> Rae Jenkins and the variety orchestra, and a male visitor, who will
> be put on trial by the women of the company for his alleged
> "masculine failings." Leading counsel for the prosecution each
> week will be Jeanne de Casalis and Doris Hare.[424]

The Daily Mirror's Robert Cannell complained – his tongue
firmly in his cheek – that 'BBC executives, ALL men, are having
much too much to say about the details of the show', driving his
point home with italics, '*The whole point of an all-girls programme is
surely to let them alone, so that we can listen to the little dears talking to
each other.*'[425] It is noteworthy that the lead scriptwriter for this 'all-
girls' show was the male comedy writer, Godfrey Harrison. In 1950
women challenging male power was a harmless joke. Doris herself
rarely challenged the status quo. Working in a profession in which
women had long had a prominent place as actresses, she was just
determined to pursue her career as best she could.

In the decade after she left *Shipmates* this was not always easy. She
was thirty-seven when Howard Thomas asked her to host his new

programme. By the time its format was changed, and she was let go, she was forty-two and entering that problematic limbo in which so many actresses find themselves in their middle years: no longer 'young', but too young for older character parts.

A radio performer has a certain invisibility. All listeners have is the voice, they cannot see the embodied realities of age, ethnicity and the like. To her many fans she was a husky, welcoming voice that did not speak in the careful, middle-class tones usually heard on the BBC. How listeners imagined her, however, was often at odds with her actual appearance and demeanour. The *Sunday Pictorial* journalist (quoted in Chapter 8) who found that Doris in person was 'not half so rough and tough as she sounds in *Shipmates Ashore*', also noted that the slim, just over five-foot Doris was 'Less plump than she sounds'.[426] On its own, a voice often conveys little about the speaker's age. Soon after the programme ended, or maybe in its final years, she had an encounter that etched itself into her memory. It happened when she handed in a form in a post office. Despite her fame, she was often not recognised by her fans until they heard her voice or saw her name, and it was only when she read the name that the woman behind the counter realised whom she was serving. She was dumbfounded: 'You're Doris Hare? I'd never have believed it.' Doris responded light-heartedly, 'Oh, I expect you thought I was a much bigger woman?', only to receive the deflating reply: 'No, I thought you were young.' One of the most difficult periods of her career was about to begin.

The Difficult Years
In the summer of 1948, more than a year after the end of *Shipmates*, *The Stage* reported:

> With the brave and gallant spirit of a real trouper, Doris Hare comes to the rescue of colleagues in distress, by stepping into the shoes of Binnie Hale, who had to relinquish her part in "Four, Five, Six" on account of illness.

Doris's broad style, the writer felt, was a slightly awkward fit with this revue:

While Miss Hare's generosity will be applauded in that it enables this show to carry on and keep faith with the public, one feels that she would be more at home in a more boisterous atmosphere than that produced by the music and lyrics at the Duke of York's.[427]

The reality was that Doris was not being bombarded with work offers, replacing Binnie Hale provided an opportunity to return to the West End. Prior to this she had returned to touring in variety, and even featured as a guest star in 'The All-Star "New Look" Pierrot Show *The Pom-Poms*' at the Dolphin Theatre, Brighton, an echo of her much earlier performing days. A year after her stint in *Four, Five, Six*, she was back starring in the *Fol-de-Rols* Concert Party summer season at Llandudno. In 1951 she was again reduced to temporarily replacing the star of a West End show. This time it was taking over from Cicely Courtneidge (later Mum in the first series of *On the Buses*), who was taking a two-week holiday. The show was *Gay's the Word*, Ivor Novello's last musical, which opened a month before his death at fifty-eight, a death that Harold Hobson, one of the leading British theatre critics of the twentieth century, saw as marking 'the ending of the tradition of romantic flamboyance in the British theatre'.[428] But while the old pre-war theatre seemed to be dying, if not dead, the new was still struggling to be born.

Often forgotten in the accepted narrative of the theatrical desert in London before John Osborne's *Look Back in Anger* burst upon the scene in 1956, are the 'little theatres', small performance spaces specialising in limited runs of challenging new plays and translations. Set up as membership organisations, they were exempt from oversight by the Lord Chamberlain's censors and often staged plays the censor would never pass. While doing the research for this book, much to my surprise I discovered that in late 1950, Doris was in a play at one of these little theatres: a dramatization of André Gide's novella *La Symphonie Pastorale*, part of a season of translations of French plays at the New Lindsey Theatre Club. The play features the struggle between a pastor and his son over the affections of a young, blind waif the pastor has brought home and raised, 'leading', in the words of the *Daily Herald* reviewer, 'to inevitable tragedy on Ibsen lines'. The reviewer went on to express surprise that Doris had been cast in such a serious role: 'Doris Hare, of all people, [is] the depressed, over-tolerant wife [of the pastor].' [429] Nonetheless, The *Birmingham Gazette* judged that 'Doris Hare as the wife, has moved so easily from her comedy parts to tragedy in this, that she should move with the play into the West End if it is ever transplanted.'[430] But, as with most of the plays presented at these 'little theatres', this never happened, and it would be some time before she would again be cast in such serious fare.

The early 1950s were one of the lowest points in Doris's career. Memories of her *Shipmates* fame were fading, and she was cast in a succession of plays for which she had high hopes but which, like *Quartette in Discord*, died on their pre-London tour. Among these were *Touch of Love* (1951), a farce in which she starred with Douglas Byng, and that she would later refer to as 'The Kiss of Death', and *Mother is a Darling* (1953), savaged in the *Yorkshire Evening Post*:

> *Mother is a Darling*, a new play (if play is the right word) ... certainly has the benefit of Doris Hare's well gowned presence as a scatter-brained mother of three girls, but as a whole it has so little real substance, and is such a restless jumble of unconvincing motives, dartings in and out, and tedious passages of almost pointless talk, that ... it leaves unanswered the basic question, "Why?"[431]

A year later there was *A Horse! A Horse!* by the wonderfully named L. Du Garde Peach, which also never made it to the West End. While the play itself was unmemorable, this tour would turn out to be memorable for a quite different reason. But that is a story for the next chapter.

There were also the plays that made it into the West End, but rapidly succumbed. On one memorable occasion the play in question, *Lions Corner*, lasted just one night. Sitting on a bus on her way to the theatre for the second night's performance, Doris noticed newspaper sellers' placards announcing: 'West End play closes after one night.' Only when she arrived at the theatre did she discover the play was *Lions Corner*. The musical *Lucky Boy* (1953) had almost as brief a West End run, the *West London Observer* reviewer writing: 'The evening is only notable for the heroic struggle of Miss Doris Hare to make something out of precious little.'[432]

A determination to make the best of what she was offered, even if this was not of the highest quality, and never to admit defeat, was a leitmotif in Doris's life as she struggled through these difficult years. Finally, around 1955 things slowly began to improve. In that year she was cast as the middle-aged widow of a publican in A. P. Herbert and Vivian Ellis's *Water Gypsies*, a musical based on Herbert's popular, pre-war novel of life among the boatpeople of the London canals, a show that gave Dora Bryan her breakthrough role. For the most part the reviewers found it somewhat old fashioned but pleasant. The heart of the show they agreed was Bryan: 'Miss Bryan's impact on the proceedings is roughly equivalent to the introduction of a jet aircraft into an Old Tyme pastoral play.'[433] After the notices came out, the billing outside the theatre was changed to 'Dora Bryan in A. P. Herbert's *The Water Gipsies*'. Doris's was not a starring role, but the widow and her equally middle-aged suitor (played by the veteran performer Jerry Vernon) have a duet, 'Why should Spring have all the flowers?', in which they celebrate the joys of love in later life. In the words of one reviewer, the performers gave the song 'a vigorous, heart-warming airing'.[434] For Derek Granger in the *Financial Times*, 'Doris Hare is, as ever, a perfect duck'.[435] The show ran for seven months, and would have run longer if Bryan had not left after becoming pregnant.

There was also television. In the summer of 1946 the BBC TV service began broadcasting again after closing down during the war years. The earliest post-war television performance by Doris I have been able to track down once again linked her with Emlyn Williams, a 1948 production of Williams's 1940 play *The Light of Heart*, starring Donald Wolfit in his first television performance as the alcoholic, broken-down actor, Maddoc Thomas, who is cared for by his devoted, crippled daughter. Doris played Fan, the good-time neighbour and bad influence on Maddoc, the part that her sister Winnie had played when Williams had toured with the play some seven years earlier. In the second half of the fifties Doris began doing more television. In 1957 she was one of the regular celebrity panellists on *State Your Case* on ABC TV, one of the new commercial companies that began broadcasting once the BBC lost its television monopoly in 1955. In *State Your Case* a series of claimants would each make their case for why they should be awarded £100 to spend on a specific project. The celebrity panel acted as their counsel with an ABC TV counsel cross-examining them, trying to point out flaws in their argument. The audience at home was the jury, writing into the programme with their choice of who should receive the £100. Things were still tough for Doris, however. In February 1958, she again took over from Cicely Courtneidge for a couple of weeks while Courtneidge took a holiday, this time in the comedy *The Bride and the Bachelor*.

A Comedy Mentor

In the summer of 1958 Doris starred in the touring version of Walter Greenwood's *Saturday Night at the Crown*, playing the leading role of Ada that Thora Hird had played in the West End. One night a young actor came to see the show. His name was Tony Warren. A few years later he would create Britain's first working-class soap opera, *Coronation Street*, inspired in part, as he told Richard Hoggart's son Simon, by *Uses of Literacy*, which 'had shown him that it was possible to write rich and eventful drama about working-class life'.[436] In 1958, however, Warren was an aspiring and impoverished actor. In an interview my sister and I recorded with him shortly before his death in 2016, he tells the story of his first meeting with Doris:

> I was living in the Interval Club, which was a residential club in Dean Street for Roman Catholic actors. Of course I wasn't a Roman Catholic but I got in by saying I was considering conversion. A lot of them were in a terrible tatty tour, which had been cast for the most part in the Interval Club, of *Saturday Night at the Crown* playing twice nightly at Chiswick Empire. So all my mates from the Club were in it. There were some good characters, people like Ken Parry and Harry Littlewood, all those people were in it, and some right rubbish as well, but the star of the show on proper money was Doris.

So I went to see the show and I went into the dressing room afterwards and it was as though she recognised me because she said, 'what are you doing all dressed up in your new carpet slippers?' and I said, 'well, I save my shoes' and she said, 'well, what for?' and I said, 'auditions'. She said, 'my darling boy' and that was that.

They would remain fast friends until her death some forty years later. For Warren, Doris was one of two key theatrical mentors:

I learned timing from Doris. Time and again I've done things where I've had to stand up on my legs and talk for an hour and I think, I know exactly where I got that pause from and the quick look afterwards. That was from Doris and Dougie [Douglas Byng].

Warren saw Doris as so much a creature of the theatre that in his mind the theatre was her birthplace. When they were casting the pilot for *Coronation Street*, despite his determination that only actors born in the north be cast, he immediately thought of her. The casting people complained,

"Tony you're very tricky because you only want people who were born within ten miles of the studio" and I said, "well, I'd like to see Doris Hare" and they said, "Tony, Doris Hare doesn't come from round here" and I said, "Doris Hare comes from everywhere, she was born on tour." So she came and she read for Ena [Sharples], and she also read for Martha Longhurst, and Margaret Morris, who was the casting director, said to me, "which do you think?" and I said, "she's wonderful as both" and she said, "right, I'm going to offer her both." I said yes because I loved Doris and I loved her work and so she was offered both.

Doris declined both offers. I was still quite young at the time, and she was reluctant to leave London and move to Manchester.

A Recognised Character Actress
Almost immediately after the 'terrible tatty tour' of *Saturday Night at the Crown* things began to turn around for Doris. A key moment was

when she was cast in *Valmouth*, a musical based on Ronald Firbank's 1919 novel. After a short tour, *Valmouth* opened at the Lyric Hammersmith in October 1958 before transferring to the Saville Theatre. The show's book, music, and lyrics were written by Sandy Wilson, who a few years earlier had a huge success with *The Boy Friend*, an affectionate spoof of 1920s musicals that ran for more than five years in London. Its Broadway production would give a young Julie Andrews her first American triumph. *Valmouth* was a very different animal, a harbinger of change. The novel is one of a series written by Firbank in the first decades of the twentieth century, all of which embody an exquisitely witty, and profoundly camp sensibility. It deals with the complicated love-lives, and sexual shenanigans of a group of nonagenarians and centenarians – kept preternaturally young by the pure air of the spa town of Valmouth – and the town's other inhabitants. Included amongst these are the Tooke family, Firbank's parody of Thomas Hardyesque rustics. Wilson's book for *Valmouth* stuck closely to Firbank's linguistic style. The *Tatler* reviewer, probably more familiar with the novel than some other critics, noted that the adaptation 'uses as much as possible of Firbank's dialogue and sticks reasonably close (until the rather dreadful conventional musical comedy ending) to his theme, which is the seduction of innocence by experience'.[437] Like the ending, Wilson's songs are closer to conventional musical comedy than to Firbank's sophisticated irony. Nonetheless, there was enough of Firbank in the show to make it a challenge for audiences in the late 1950s. Five years before Susan Sontag published 'Notes on Camp', propelling the concept into the mainstream, *Valmouth's* camp sensibility came as something of a shock to audiences. With its themes of sexually predatory older women, procurement, religious obsession, inter-racial marriage, and homosexuality, it was a world away from the cosy Ruritania of Novello's musical comedies, and the big American musicals (*Oklahoma*, *Annie Get Your Gun*, *Carousel*) that had replaced them.

Doris played Granny Tooke, the 120-year-old matriarch of the family, determinedly clinging to life at all costs. The 'permissive, toothless Granny Tooke', Eric Shorter (former theatre critic for *The Telegraph*) wrote later was one of Doris's 'best performances in the theatre'.[438] The Black outsider with whom the permissive Granny

Fig. 35 – Doris as Granny Tooke in *Valmouth* in the original 1958 production. When *Valmouth* was revived in 1982, Doris explained to Sheridan Morley: 'People think I remove all my teeth for the role, but I can't you know, they are still all my own, so I just fold my lips over them like Moore Marriott in the Will Hay films.' (*The Times*, 19 May 1982)

Tooke forms an unlikely friendship with the masseuse and procurer, Mrs Yajnavalka, who was played at the Lyric Hammersmith by the American Bertice Reading, and at the Saville by the jazz singer Cleo Laine. Doris and Laine became good friends in real life. In 1958 the singer had little theatre experience; and in her autobiography she recalls Doris teaching her about comedy:

> The show [*Valmouth*] gathered a cult following: people came to see it over and over again ... My part, Mrs Yaj, needed experience in the art of delivering a comic line, which I didn't have, but under the

careful guidance of my good buddy, Doris, I had daily lessons on how to counteract the upstagers, how not to kill my laugh line and not to be despondent when the laugh didn't come – it happened to the best of them.[439]

Valmouth received generally positive, if not rave, reviews. Between its time at the Lyric Hammersmith and the Saville Theatre, it managed a run of 186 performances. It also became something of a cult show within the gay community, many of whom went to see it repeatedly. In later years the original cast album became a coveted item, changing hands for up to £40 (over £800 in 2022). In 1975 there was a BBC radio broadcast of *Valmouth*, interestingly on the Corporation's highbrow station, Radio 3. Doris was again Granny Tooke with her old friend Elizabeth Welch as Mrs Yajnavalka. Seven years later, the Chichester Festival Theatre revived it with several of the original cast, including Doris, Bertice Reading, and Fenella Fielding. But once again it tended to polarise audiences into a smallish band of enthusiastic devotees and a larger number whose response was more like that of the *Illustrated London News* reviewer:

> Those familiar with the peacock-feather caprices of Ronald Firbank will know that Valmouth is some distance from Falmouth. I confess I spent a proportion of the first act wondering what that gentle Cornish port might make of a lively centenarian, a coloured masseuse, a singing Cardinal, a dancing nun, an idyllic shepherd and the rest of the Firbank bunch.
>
> Sandy Wilson with a talent for likeable tunes sought bravely to shuffle these people and others into a musical play. But it seemed to me that at the Chichester premiere West Sussex was as politely baffled as Falmouth might have been. Either you love this brand of neo-Gothic extravaganza or you do not. … the piece, as a whole, is a taste I have signally failed to acquire.[440]

Nonetheless over time, according to *The Guardian's* 2014 obituary of Wilson, while *The Boy Friend* may have had the greater commercial success, *Valmouth* 'came to be widely acknowledged as

Wilson's masterpiece'.[441] For the fifty-three-year-old Doris, her performance as the 120-year Granny Tooke established her as a character actor on the far shore of the young/old dichotomy. She had finally escaped the limbo of the difficult 'middle years'.

By the late 1950s Doris was doing an increasing amount of television. In 1960 she was in all twenty episodes of *A House Called Bell Tower*, an afternoon serial that told the stories of those living in an old rambling house. Doris played the landlady. 'The avowed intention', the BBC explained, 'is to provide an easy, escape period for afternoon viewers, not stimulating, fast moving, self-contained 15-minute plays.'[442] This innocuous serial came and went without leaving much of an impression. Doris's career, however, was about to take a new and much more interesting turn. It began when in 1961 she was offered a role in Max Frisch's *The Fire Raisers* at London's Royal Court Theatre, where in 1956 George Devine's English Stage Company had staged Osborne's *Look Back in Anger*, supposedly transforming British Theatre overnight. In 1961 Devine's Royal Court seemed to many the beating heart of avant-garde theatre. For Doris, *Fire Raisers* was the opening act of a memorable five years during which she would work with some of the most interesting and highbrow directors who were busy reinventing British theatre.

CHAPTER 11

SERIOUS THEATRE
LOOKS FOR ITS ROOTS

In the unashamed coupling of 'high' and 'low'
the theatrical poet finds his most persuasive voice.

Tony Harrison[443]

Most of Doris's career was spent in the world of popular entertainment. The critics who wrote about her tended to define her comedy, and indeed her whole performance style, as 'low'. And yet in the 1960s directors such as Lindsay Anderson, Peter Hall, and Peter Brook, all intellectual heavy hitters, cast her in plays by Harold Pinter, Max Frisch, and Frederick Dürrenmatt. How was it that this comedian with 'her gift of low comedy characterization'[444] found such a welcoming home amongst the intellectuals? To understand this apparent paradox we need to remember the seismic upheaval taking place in British theatre. Doris's entry into the world of 'serious' theatre – theatre that saw itself as offering more than pure entertainment – coincided with a particularly exciting time for British theatre in the 1960s.

Embracing the 'Low'
In 1960 the venerable Shakespeare Memorial Theatre - renamed the Royal Shakespeare Company (RSC) by its charismatic new director, Peter Hall - expanded from its Stratford-upon-Avon base, taking on the lease of London's Aldwych Theatre to present more contemporary drama. Then in 1962, after more than a century of debate and wrangling, the National Theatre was finally launched. In addition to these institutional innovations, new plays were challenging the accepted norms of the West End. But what kind of challenge was this?

It is widely agreed that something changed in British theatre in the mid-1950s. For many years the moment everything changed was said to be 8 May 1956, the opening night of John Osborne's *Look Back in Anger*, the third production of the newly formed English Stage Company's inaugural season at the Royal Court Theatre. Championed by two of the most influential theatre critics, Ken Tynan in the *Observer*, and Hobson in the *Sunday Times* – at a time when newspaper critics wielded far greater power than they do today – it created a sensation. Alan Sillitoe, author of the novel *Saturday Night and Sunday Morning*, declared: 'John Osborne didn't contribute to British theatre: he set off a landmine called *Look Back in Anger* and blew most of it up. The bits have settled back into place, of course, but it can never be the same again.'[445] As with most origin stories, the truth is more complicated: Osborne's play was one event in a remarkable year. As Michael Billington wrote in his obituary of Tynan,

> a series of eruptions ... took place within an extraordinary year in British theatre from August 1955 to August 1956: the premieres of *Waiting for Godot* and *Look Back in Anger*, the flowering of Joan Littlewood's Theatre Workshop with Brendan Behan's *The Quare Fellow*, and the arrival of the Berliner Ensemble with a three-play Brecht season.[446]

It took a few years, however, for the effects to be felt. Nonetheless, by the beginning of the 1960s the pre-war theatre landscape familiar to Doris was being transformed. Central to the new theatre, elbowing its way into the cosy world of the West End establishment, was the belief that theatre should not just be about escapist entertainment. In a 1987 interview for the British Library Theatre Archive Project, Hobson explained his dissatisfaction with that earlier theatre: 'It was too frivolous, too exclusively upper middle class. It ignored the existence of nine-tenths of the world – more than nine-tenths.'[447] Lindsay Anderson, looking back on the early days of the Royal Court's English Stage Company (before he began his own directing career there) recalled, perhaps not altogether accurately, 'a blessed absence of that "desire to divert" (and particularly, of course, the desire to divert an English middle-class audience, out for an amusing evening) which had always maddened me in the West End theatre'.[448]

The seismic shifts remaking the theatrical landscape were part of wider upheavals roiling British society. Those looking for a new kind of theatre saw themselves as part of these. The English Stage Company's Artistic Director George Devine's vision was 'to bring the nation to the stage and to produce plays that examined the challenges and possibilities of the time'.[449] In his posthumously published memoir, Stuart Hall, one of the most perceptive analysts of post-war Britain, describes the sense of the ground shifting experienced by him and other left-wing intellectuals in the mid-1950s:

> We were clearly stepping into a new political conjuncture. It's the moment too of that confusing and confused phenomenon, the Angry Young Men, the birth of the Royal Court Theatre in its new dispensation, rock and roll and of the Free Cinema movement of Lindsay Anderson and Karel Reisz.[450]

Part of what was happening was that 'culture' – understood here not in the anthropological sense of a particular way of life, but as 'the works and practices of intellectual and especially artistic activity … music, literature, painting and sculpture, theatre and film'[451] – was increasingly being seen as a central to political struggle. And if there were to be plays 'that examined the challenges and possibilities of the time', they could not ignore popular culture, however low it might be. Indeed, they should celebrate it. Raymond Williams in his influential *Culture and Society* (first published in 1958) makes the point that there is a long history of popular culture transforming over time into high culture: when the novel, now enshrined in high culture, emerged in the eighteenth century alongside the rise of a new middle-class reading public, it was seen by society's arbitrators of taste as a 'vulgar phenomenon'[452]

Those searching for a new kind of theatre rejected the traditional high/low distinction. Michael Billington, the biographer of Harold Pinter – not a playwright immediately associated with popular culture – stresses how indebted his first play, *The Birthday Party*, is

to the popular culture of the rep theatres in which the aspiring playwright spent many years while developing his craft:

> [*The Birthday Party*] bears the stamp of the thrillers and comedies of
> its day; like a stick of seaside rock, it says 'rep' all the way through.
> The faintly maniacal fugitive, the interventionist authority figures,
> the cliché-toting working-class characters: these were the very stuff
> of 1950s theatre.[453]

In addition, as Billington notes, Pinter drew on the variety tradition so familiar to Doris:

> Ronald Knowles articulated a thought that had been dogging me
> for years when he suggested that the comedy double act of Jewel
> and Warriss, famous in the 1950s on music-hall and radio, was the
> prototype of Goldberg and McCann [in *The Birthday Party*]. Ben
> Warriss, Sleek and sharp-suited with patent-leather hair, was always
> the bullying straight man; Jimmy Jewel, nervously apprehensive,
> was the comic-fall guy. Their double act was a classic study in domi-
> nation and submission.[454]

Then there is Joan Littlewood, whose landmark 1963 Theatre
Workshop production, *Oh, What a Lovely War*, exposing the folly
and corruption of World War I, used the popular songs of the time,
juxtaposing their jingoism and sentimentality with the realism, and
robust humour, of the songs written by soldiers actually enduring
the horrors of trench warfare. To heighten the sense of theatricality,
Littlewood dressed the actors not in uniforms but in the Pierrot
costumes of the seaside concert parties Doris and her siblings knew
so well.

Samuel Beckett's less explicitly political *Waiting For Godot*
provides a fascinating example of high/low mixing. According to
Beckett scholar and biographer, James Knowlson:

> whatever real-life sources the dialogue [in *Waiting for Godot*] may
> have, it probably owes far more to forms and rhythms borrowed
> from the music-hall (cross-talk, recited monologues, songs and a

soliloquy) and to its philosophical sources (among which are Descartes, Geulinex, Kant, Schopenhauer, and Heidegger) than it does to any real-life conversations.[455]

Beckett's theatre-going as an undergraduate in Dublin was not limited to the serious fare to be found at the Abbey Theatre, he also frequented venues that 'put him in touch with a lighter kind of theatre that grew out of the revues and music-hall sketches of the "illegitimate" theatre or the circus'.[456] He also loved the early silent films of Buster Keaton and Charlie Chaplin - both performers whose comedy origins were in American vaudeville and British music hall.[457]

The great Beckett champion, Theodor Adorno, by contrast, condemned the mingling of high and low. For this relentless scourge of commoditised culture and the culture industry, one of the great sins of the latter is that it 'intentionally integrates its consumers from above. To the detriment of both it forces together the spheres of high and low art, separated for thousands of years.'[458] Contrast this with Tony Harrison's statement (the epigraph to this chapter): 'In the unashamed coupling of "high" and "low" the theatrical poet finds his most persuasive voice.'[459] Harrison, a renowned poet and trans-lator of Greek classical and French neoclassical drama, reminds us that low elements were always an integral part of the classics.

Shakespeare, too, intermingled comedy, often low comedy, with high tragedy, an intermingling that offended some later critics. Harrison quotes a wonderfully schoolmasterly passage, laden with distaste, written by Robert Bridges, Poet Laureate from 1913 to1930:

> Shakespeare should not be put into the hands of the young without the warning that the foolish things in his plays were written to please the foolish, the filthy for the filthy, and the brutal for the brutal; and that if out of our veneration for his genius we are led to admire or even tolerate such things, we may be thereby not conforming ourselves to him, but only degrading ourselves to the level of his audience, and learning contamination from those wretched beings who can never be forgiven their share in preventing the greatest poet and dramatist of the world from being the best artist.[460]

For Harrison, it is precisely this intermingling that explains the greatness of Shakespeare's plays, and why they, like the classic plays of the ancient world, still speak to modern audiences, but only as long as their low elements are embraced.

In 1981 the National Theatre, now under the direction of Peter Hall, commissioned Harrison to provide a new translation of Aeschylus' *Oresteia* for the large, open stage of the Olivier Theatre. Harrison sought a non-naturalistic theatricality. He recounts a dream he had while working on the project which embodies his conviction that the 'low' belongs in serious drama. It ends with the sentence I used as the epigraph to Chapter 5, and it is worth quoting at length.

Once I had agreed to work with Peter Hall on the *Oresteia*, I had a vivid dream ... I dreamed that there was in my hallway in Newcastle a large, rather ornately bound visitors' book, but its engraved cover read '*Oresteia*', or, to be precise, 'ΟΡΕΣΤΕΙΑ', as it was embossed in Greek script. I think it was meant as a kind of audition roster for the chorus of Aeschylus' trilogy. In my garden ... there was assembled a long queue of men, all old men. They all wrote their names in the book and left without a word. Each of them seemed to have no trouble with the Greek script on the cover, and they each ran a finger over the gilded Greek and then opened the book, ran the same finger down the list of previous signatories and then signed themselves, then closed it again for the man behind to read and trail his finger on the ancient Greek. Strangely, though it was a repeated action, each signatory brought to the occasion his own definite individual style. When the last one had left, I picked up the book and read the names. They were all the names of the comedians I had seen in panto as the dame or a solo act, at the Leeds Empire or Grand Theatre: Norman Evans, Frank Randall, Nat Jackley, Robb Wilton, Arthur Lucan ('Old Mother Riley', but for some reason without Kitty), Jewell and Warriss, etc. ... the list went on for pages. The kind of theatricality that they had, though still definitely alive in the last days of vaudeville, had more or less disappeared from so-called 'serious' theatre, and I carried their presences with me as a sometimes grinning and gurning, but always supportive, chorus, paradoxically, into the quest for an Aeschylean *gravitas*. One of the secrets of that theatricality, still preserved in the popular forms, is that the audience is there to be addressed, not to be eavesdroppers on some private happening.[461]

The theatricality that Harrison is committed to incorporating is the theatricality that helped shape Doris as a performer. Interestingly, the dream list of this classics scholar and champion of the low does not include any women. Low women performers, like Marie Lloyd, were prominent in the glory days of music hall, but as music hall turned into variety, the 'vulgar' woman comic became increasingly marginalised. Nonetheless, Harrison would have seen women on his outings to the theatre as a child. And one of them might well have been Doris, who was still performing in variety in the 1940s and 50s. The BBC recognised her long history in variety in *Old Boys Network*, a 1981 BBC2 series that gave each of six veteran comedians an hour to reminisce and tell stories. There was just one woman: Doris. Also included was Nat Jackley, one of the old men in Harrison's dream.

Fig. 36 – BBC2's *Old Boys Network* line-up, 1981. From left to right: Richard Murdoch, Chesney Allen, Percy Edwards, Doris, Leslie Sarony, Nat Jackley. All the 'old boys' were over seventy but still working. At seventy-six, Doris was the third eldest.

A crucial element of classical drama, Harrison argues, is the satyr play, a quintessential embodiment of low comedy: 'Though most are missing or have been air-brushed out of classical literature, all the great tragedians wrote satyr plays. After the trilogy of tragedies on came the chorus of dancing satyrs, half men, half goat, with enormous phalluses.'[462] They may have lacked the 'enormous phalluses', but 'half men, half goat' seems a rather accurate description of the middle-aged Stan Butler and his bus conductor mate Jack, forever in lustful pursuit of nubile women.

'A wide variety of acting traditions and backgrounds'

It was Lindsay Anderson, the man 'maddened' by 'the desire to divert an English middle-class audience', who cast Doris in *The Fire Raisers*. He would go on to direct *This Sporting Life* (1963), one of the greatest of the British social realist films, and in 1968, *If...*, a sharp-eyed attack on the hidebound hierarchies and hypocrisies of British society. Anderson's fiercely left-wing politics, like those of many with whom Doris worked during her time in the serious theatre, were not hers, but this was never a problem. She was careful to keep her enthusiasm for the Conservative Party and her professional life in separate boxes.

A year before *The Fire Raisers*, Anderson had directed the original stage production of Keith Waterhouse's *Billy Liar*, starring a still-unknown Albert Finney. He had offered Doris the part of the senile old grandmother. Newly confident after her success in *Valmouth*, she had turned it down, feared that taking on another geriatric would get her typecast as aged crones. Still in her early fifties, she felt it was a bit too soon for that. The middle-aged housewife in *Fire Raisers* was a far more attractive proposition and she was happy to accept.

Leaving aside her brief appearances in Molière (1938) and Gide (1950), *The Fire Raisers* marked Doris's entry into the 'legitimate' theatre. The distinction between popular and legitimate theatre goes back to the eighteenth-century struggles of the patent theatres, Covent Garden, Drury Lane and the Haymarket – the only three theatres allowed to perform spoken drama – to prevent the many minor, or 'illegitimate' theatres from encroaching on their Rights. Even if it may not have always been strictly enforced, repeal of the law had to wait until the 1843 Theatres Act, the same Act that led to the emergence of the portable theatres. And while the old legal distinction may be long gone, its ghost has continued to haunt British theatre.

In his 1961 production of *The Fire Raisers*, Anderson deliberately brought together actors from high and popular culture. The play, by the Swiss playwright and novelist, Max Frisch, is a darkly comic parable of the dangers of appeasement. It tells the story of a town suffering from an epidemic of arson attacks. Biederman, a complacent, prosperous businessman, allows two strangers to move into his attic. As they bring in more and more drums of petrol and other incendiary devices, it becomes ever more obvious that his 'guests' are arsonists, but Biederman and his wife refuse to face the truth. Alfred Marks played Biederman, Doris his wife. Anderson had determined to assemble a group of actors from what he saw as the most dynamic sectors of British theatre, noting in the Programme, 'A wide variety of acting traditions and backgrounds are represented in our cast – many of whom are appearing at the Royal Court for the first time.'[463] Like Doris, Marks came from the world of popular comedy. The arsonists were played by James Booth and Colin Blakely, and the Biederman's maid by Ann Beach. Both Booth and Beach had worked with Joan Littlewood's Theatre Workshop, while Blakely's background was in more conventional straight theatre: the Royal Court and the RSC. The music for the play – there was a chorus of singing firemen – was provided by Dudley Moore, fresh from his success with *Beyond the Fringe*.

In general the reviews for *The Fire Raisers* were good. Hobson was particularly laudatory of the acting, which he compared favourably with the RSC's production of *The Cherry Orchard* a week earlier: 'The performance by Alfred Marks, Ann Beach, Colin Blakely, Doris Hare, and the rest of the company has the flow, the consistency, the unbroken surface we had hoped for in last week's *Cherry Orchard*.'[464] Anderson, it seems, had successfully melded the different acting traditions. A further inclusion of the popular, however, left the critics bemused: the once popular, one-act Victorian farce *Box and Cox* as a curtain raiser. 'I cannot imagine', *The Stage*'s R. B. Marriott wrote, 'why this most unsuitable old thing was dragged up.'[465]

Written by John Maddison Morton, the farce – taken, like so many British plays, from a French original – features a landlady, Mrs Bouncer (played by Doris) who, unbeknownst to them, lets the same room to two lodgers, Box, who works nights as a printer, and Cox who works days as a hatter. The play, which was likely one of the 'laughable farces' that ended the entertainment offered by Doris's parents' portable theatre, pokes fun at the conventions of melodrama, as in this exchange in the culminating moments of the piece:

> Box: Cox! You'll excuse the apparent insanity of the remark, but the more I gaze on your features, the more I'm convinced that you're my long lost brother.
> Cox: The very observation I was going to make to you!
> Box: Ah—tell me—in mercy tell me—have you such a thing as a strawberry mark on your left arm?
> Cox: No!
> Box: Then it is he![466]

Whereupon they immediately rush into each other's arms.

Although I have no evidence for this, my guess is that Anderson included *Box and Cox* because he wanted the evening's entertainment to begin with a challenge to what Harrison described as 'the clichés of naturalistic drama'.[467] The acting in *Fire Raisers* was more naturalistic than the stylised farce of *Box and Cox*, but the play has something of the heightened realism of a Brechtian parable.

That Doris was unafraid of new ways of staging plays was demonstrated by her next venture, a production in March 1962 at the recently opened Pembroke Theatre, Croydon. The Pembroke claimed to be Britain's first 'theatre in the round', and was attracting some headline performers, such as Fay Compton and Margaret Rutherford. The play, a farce entitled *The Prince of Portobello*, was, however, not one of its triumphs. The *Stage* reviewer found it 'agreeable, but not especially inventive', one problem being that 'farce seems least suited to presentations in the round'. Doris's charlady character, however, was judged 'a small masterpiece in timing and characterisation'.[468]

Associate Artist with the RSC

In July 1962 Anthony Page, Anderson's assistant at the Royal Court, was asked to direct Thomas Middleton's *Women Beware Women*, a play from the early seventeenth century. It would be the fourth production of the RSC's experimental season at the New Arts Theatre, the theatre where in August 1955 Peter Hall had directed the English language premiere of Beckett's *Waiting for Godot*. Giving long neglected classics stage productions was part of the mission Peter Hall had defined for the RSC. *Women Beware Women*, not performed for more than three centuries, certainly qualified, and Page's production was much praised. The budgets for the productions at the tiny Arts Theatre were far from lavish, but Page's stripped-down production made a virtue of the limited funds. In his review, R. B. Marriott noted, 'Mr Page made striking use of the small stage in his imaginative and tautly moving production' and that 'there is a study to be remembered by Doris Hare, as the mother of Leantio.'[469] Leantio was played by Nicol Williamson. There is a scene in which the innocent old woman plays, and loses, a chess game with Pauline Jameson's silkily manipulative Livia, as unbeknownst to her, her daughter-in-law, Bianca, is being seduced by the Duke of Florence. Some years later, when Page took a training course in directing for television, he remembered Doris's performance, staging the scene when the naive old mother visits the Duke's Palace as his test piece. Doris remembered him filming her as she walked wonderingly along an endless corridor lined with ancestral portraits. Her performance also made an impression on Peter Hall, who asked her to join to RSC as an Associate Artist for the 1963 season. She would stay with the Company for the next two years.

According to RSC historian Sally Beauman, while the Arts Theatre's experimental season was not a financial success, 'it was both memorable and exciting and included some exceptionally good productions.'[470] Along with Page's *Women Beware Women*, one of these was David Rudkin's *Afore Night Come*, a dark play that exposes 'the violence beneath the crust of everyday life',[471] as Michael Billington wrote in a review of the 2001 revival, Doris would take over the sole female role when the play transferred to the Aldwych in 1964.

Fig. 37 – Doris and Patrick Magee in the Royal Shakespeare Company's 1964 production of David Rudkin's *Afore Night Come*. Doris was the only woman in this dark play of atavistic violence which in 1962 had won Rudkin the *Evening Standard* Drama Award for most promising playwright.

The years when Doris was a member of the RSC marked a high-point of Hall's directorship. The productions included Hall and John Barton's landmark *The Wars of the Roses*, which presented Shakespeare's cycle of history plays from *King Richard II* to *King Richard III*, bringing back the three early *King Henry VI* plays, long considered virtually unplayable. *The Wars of the Roses*, for Beauman, marked the beginning of 'one of those extraordinary periods that can happen to theatres when they suddenly make a breakthrough, and everything they touch turns to gold'.[472] In 1962 Peter Brook, together with Michel Saint-Denis, joined Hall at the RSC as part of a triumvirate of artistic directors.

In her first season with the RSC Doris had a small part in Brook's production of *The Physicists* by the Swiss playwright Frederick Dürrenmatt. The play, by turns darkly comic and deadly serious, explores the horrendous consequences of scientific knowledge with the potential to destroy mankind, and the reality that once known, scientific knowledge cannot be unknown. Irene Worth, Goneril in Brook's celebrated *King Lear* with Paul Scofield, played the hunchbacked director of an asylum for the insane. Despite being apparent opposites professionally – Worth, an actor in the words of her *Guardian* obituary, 'happiest in the avant-garde',[473] Doris, a product of variety and the commercial theatre – the two of them got on famously and became good friends. Doris shared a dressing room with a young Diana Rigg (a member of the RSC for several years before her ascent to television cultdom in *The Avengers*), who had a small part in *The Physicists*. The future Emma Peel remembered that time fondly in a tribute she wrote for Doris's Ninetieth Birthday book: 'a true test of a person is to share a small, squalid dressing-room with them for several months, and in later years to recollect the experience with love and happiness.' Another member of the cast of *The Physicists* was Cyril Cusack, a child actor with Doris all those years ago when she and her mother Kate had been part of his father's (Breffni O'Rourke's) fit-up company in Ireland.

Doris was always a team player. She even agreed to a walk-on part with one line in Hall's revival of his 1959 Stratford production of *A Midsummer Night's Dream*, which transferred to the Aldwych as part of the 1963 season. Doris's role was that of Matron Fairy, played in the Stratford production by the future novelist, Margaret Drabble. Doris also played Mrs Peachum in Peter Wood's not very well received production of *The Beggar's Opera*. Although it was praised for the acting and Sean Kenny's creative sets, the reviewers balked at this ballad opera being performed by actors who could sing but did not have trained operatic voices.

She would have a tiny role in Clifford Williams's brilliant production of Christopher Marlowe's *The Jew of Malta*, played as a dark comedy. Before agreeing Doris had a request: she had always wanted to wear a proper Shakespearean cape on stage. If the RSC would come up with a cape, she would do it. Vastly amused, Hall said that he thought they could find a suitable cape in the wardrobe, and Doris played the part. Clifford Williams's production was judged a triumph by the critics. For *The Stage's* R. B. Marriott it was 'brilliant'. Williams, he wrote, had allowed *The Jew of Malta* 'to make light of itself wittily, imaginatively, freely. Yet the wonders of the play still emerge powerfully.'[474]

'A classic study in domination and submission'

In 1964 Doris played Meg in the RSC's production of Harold Pinter's first play, *The Birthday Party*, directed by its author, the first major London revival. Doris remembered the production as a highlight of her time with the RSC.

The original production of *The Birthday Party* opened at the Lyric Hammersmith in May 1958. Savaged by the critics, it was taken off after less than a week. By 1964, however, Pinter was recognised as one of Britain's most interesting young playwrights, and audiences were more open to plays that did not conform to the standard conventions of the 'well-made play'. Although not, perhaps predictably, the *Daily Mirror* reviewer: 'To me the play, if it can be called that, remains a piece of arty-crafty nonsense – beautifully acted nonsense last night by Brewster Mason, Doris Hare and Patrick Magee.'[475]

This was not the first time Doris had worked with Pinter. During the difficult years after her wartime fame had faded, one of the many plays that were supposed to come into the West End, but died en route, was L. Du Garde Peach's farce *A Horse! A Horse!*, mentioned in the previous chapter. Hugh Wakefield and Doris played the leading roles of the Duke and Duchess of Wistburgh. *The Stage's* review of the play's Eastbourne premiere in July 1954 was damning, but probably fair:

> The comedy is not strong, and a brave cast works hard to get laughs out of material that has as its highlights a string of poor puns. Hugh Wakefield struggles with the part of the slightly mental Duke, and breezy Doris Hare also does her best to keep the comedy going.[476]

The play's plot revolves around the impoverished aristocrat's ownership of a talking horse . Working the horse's head was a twenty-four-year-old Harold Pinter, at that time an aspiring actor using the name David Baron, finding jobs mainly in different repertory companies, while working at his writing on the side. In hindsight the idea of the man who would become one of Britain's leading intellectual playwrights, manipulating a horse's ears in a sub-standard farce seems bizarre, but, according to Billington, this was not wasted time. The 'weird double life' Pinter was leading, 'a poetic intellectual on the regional roundabout, rather as if Kafka had been obliged to appear in *Charley's Aunt*', also provided valuable experience: 'he was learning every day about the practical mechanics of theatre: of what works and what doesn't, of how to pick up or lose a laugh, of how to create an effect through the surprise entrance or a well-timed "curtain".'[477]

In addition to whatever he may have learnt about the 'practical mechanics of theatre', the tour of *A Horse! A Horse!* gave Pinter the seed that would later develop into *The Birthday Party*. 'As so often with Pinter', Billington notes, 'the play derived from an image that took obstinate root in his memory.'[478] And this memory dated from his stay in Eastbourne. For struggling actors on tour, finding an affordable place to stay was often a problem. Not yet having found digs in Eastbourne, he was having a drink in a pub when he met a 'strange laconic man', who told him he could stay in his digs if he wanted. Having no alternative, he accepted. In time the laconic lodger, the landlady who never left him alone, and her quiescent husband would become *The Birthday Party*'s Stanley, Meg and Petey.

Like all Pinter's plays, *The Birthday Party* is a play about power that can be interpreted in many ways. For Billington,

> *The Birthday Party* is not simply a play about a truculent recluse whose will is broken by two authority figures. It is a much more complex work about a defiant rebel who exposes the insecurity upon which adherence to orthodoxy and tradition actually rests.[479]

Doris tended not to reflect too deeply on the ultimate meaning of plays in which she acted. Her concern was rather with understanding her role, its relation to the other characters, and the all-important

Fig. 38 – *A Horse! A Horse!* (1954) with Doris, Cyril Smith, Hugh Wakefield, and (working the horse's head) Harold Pinter. It was a shame, Doris felt, that such a handsome young man should be hidden away inside a horse's head.

Fig. 39 – Doris and Bryan Pringle in the Royal Shakespeare Company's production of Harold Pinter's *The Birthday Party*, 1964. This production was one of Doris's most cherished memories of her time with the Royal Shakespeare Company.

matter of getting laughs. I am reminded of the approach of one of Beckett's favourite actors Billie Whitelaw (with whom Doris would later act at the Chichester Festival Theatre), who according to Beckett's biographer, 'never asked him about the meaning of his lines, simply how to deliver them'.[480] 'Pinter's faithful reproduction of the repetitions, hesitations and lacunae of everyday speech, alongside the exuberance of street argot' is for Billington, 'his single most important contribution to British drama.'[481] Doris also recognised that Pinter's apparently highly stylised language did indeed reflect ordinary speech. After beginning to rehearse the play, as she told me, she realised that she had just had almost the same conversation at breakfast with my father that Meg has with Petey as she serves him breakfast. However, the absolute fidelity to the text, insisted on by Pinter, was something new for her. I remember her remarking on how he corrected her quite sharply when she added a sigh that was not in the script. But even though she had always prized her ability to improvise, she recognised that this text was something different, and was happy to accept this new discipline. As a veteran of comedy, when they started playing to an audience, she was struck by how predictable the laughs were. Normally, as she told the young Cleo Laine when they appeared together in *Valmouth*, you have to expect that sometimes for inexplicable reasons a laugh just does not come. In *The Birthday Party* the laughs came in the same places at each performance. And despite its grim subject matter, there were plenty of laughs in the play - a few too many for some of the critics, who felt the production played up the comedy a little too much.

Despite having directed the play himself, Pinter was not entirely happy with the production. While Peter Wood's first disastrous production had veered towards the grotesque, his production, as he told Billington, '"pushed" it back, probably too far, towards naturalism. But I had to do the play with resident RSC actors - apart from Patrick Magee, who as McCann, was the strongest member of the cast and whom I introduced to the company.'[482] Nonetheless, Eric Shorter, the former theatre critic of *The Telegraph*, would later write of Doris's performance: 'Characters who might in other hands have been rated obscure or wearisome - the sluttish half-wit Meg for example in Pinter's *Birthday Party* in 1964 - became in Hare's distinctive and funny.'[483] She also received a warm note from John Gielgud.

Dear Doris Hare,

I must congratulate you on your really lovely acting in The Birthday Party – so true and touching as well as funny. The critics have not begun to do you justice - they are only interested in justifying their own lack of perception in not realising the cleverness of the play when it was first put on. I should think it is fun to act in – and you gave me so much pleasure I had to write. But please don't dream of troubling to answer.

Most sincerely,
John Gielgud[484]

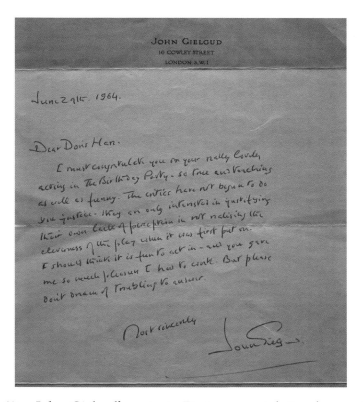

Fig. 40 – John Gielgud's note to Doris congratulating her on her performance in *The Birthday Party*, 29 June 1964. One of the twentieth century's greatest classical actors, Gielgud was born a few months before Doris (14 April 1904), and died a few days before her (21 May 2000).

One memory from *The Birthday Party* that remained with Doris was the night Janet Suzman, who played the flirtatious upstairs neighbour Lulu, was ill, and her understudy took over. The understudy (shortly before her triumph in Peter Brook's celebrated production of Peter Weiss's the *Marat/Sade*) was Glenda Jackson. When she made her entrance, Doris told me, it was as if a blazing comet had burst through the door.

Midsummer Night's Dream was not Doris's only venture into Shakespeare with the RSC. She also played Mistress Quickly in a less well-received production of *The Merry Wives of Windsor* directed by John Blatchley, better known as a director of opera. It starred Clive Swift (Margaret Drabble's first husband), rather miscast, as Falstaff, Brenda Bruce and Patsy Byrne as the merry wives, and Ian Richardson and Timothy West as their suspicious husbands. The sets and costumes were highly stylised and the director's aim, as quoted in *The Stage*, was 'to produce a real English old-style Lyceum pantomime, with Fred Karno routines and the ripeness of Victorian music hall'.[485] West remembered it as 'a not very fortunate production ... in which none of us were particularly happy'.[486]

In 1965 Doris was asked by Laurence Olivier to join the National Theatre's third and final summer season at the Chichester Festival Theatre. She was happy to accept, and rapidly fell in love with the theatre and the city of Chichester. At the end of the season she bought a house there, first as a weekend cottage, moving there full-time after her divorce in 1975. She would return to the Festival Theatre in 1967, 1982 and 1984.

In her history of the RSC, Beauman judges 1965-6 to have been a 'golden' period for Olivier's National, similar to Hall's RSC years when everything they touched turned to gold.[487] In 1965 Doris joined an impressive line-up of actors at Chichester: Albert Finney, Derek Jacobi, Maggie Smith, Billie Whitelaw, and a young Ian McKellen, among others. Finney and Smith starred in Strindberg's *Miss Julie*, which was played as a double bill with the premiere of Peter Shaffer's farce *Black Comedy*, in which Doris played a repressed spinster who slowly becomes more and more inebriated until she erupts in an incoherent rant against modern society. She also played a theatrical landlady in Pinero's *Trelawny of the Wells*, first produced in 1898.

Black Comedy makes considerable demands on its actors. The action takes place in the flat of a sculptor, played by Derek Jacobi, and in addition to the normal fast-paced business of farce, the characters are supposed to be in the dark unable to see each other, except for the first few minutes when the stage is in darkness. The premise is that at the end of those first few minutes a fuse is blown and the flat is plunged into darkness, although now the stage is fully lit. The conceit is borrowed from a celebrated routine in Noh drama where two warriors fight, supposedly in the dark although the stage is fully lit. Despite having limited rehearsal time, during which Shaffer was putting the final touches to the play, it was a resounding success. This was in large part thanks to the skill of its actors, who also included Finney and Smith. After lauding Smith and Finney as 'gloriously funny', the *Tatler* reviewer described Doris's performance 'as the slightly squiffy old lady', as 'memorably good'.[488] Both *Black Comedy* and *Trelawny of the Wells* transferred to the Old Vic, the London home of the National before it moved to its own theatre on the South Bank.

A Decent, Plodding Director

While Doris established herself as a significant presence in live theatre, radio and television, this was not true of film. Although she made a fair number of films, for the most part she was confined to small character cameo roles, or as in the *Buses* and *Confessions* series, stereotypical portrayals of a cockney Mum. *A Place to Go*, a drama directed by Basil Dearden, made during her years with the RSC and the National, was the one exception. But if Doris moved into serious theatre at something like a golden time in British theatre, and worked with some of the most interesting directors of the day, she was not so lucky with *A Place to Go*.

Basil Dearden (1911-1971), a veteran of Ealing Studios, was known for his versatility and workmanlike professionalism rather than for any great creative genius. David Thomson's judgement is particularly harsh: 'Dearden's versatility was with essentially inert subjects and his proficiency was at the expense of inventiveness or artistic personality. ... His films are decent, empty and plodding.'[489] Shot in 1963 and released in 1964, *A Place To Go* came at the end of a period during which a series of powerful working-class dramas (including Jack Clayton's *Room at the Top* [1959], Karel Reisz's *Saturday Night and Sunday Morning* [1960], Tony Richardson's *Taste of Honey* [1961] and *Loneliness of the Long Distance Runner* [1962], and Lindsay Anderson's *This Sporting Life* [1963]) seemed to revitalise British film. *A Place to Go* is set in a working-class milieu, London's Bethnal Green, on the cusp of social change, but it cannot be said to be up to the standard of Clayton, Reisz or Richardson. It starred Rita Tushingham and Mike Sarne, a singer who had recently had a brief burst of fame with a novelty hit, 'Come Outside'. Doris and Bernard Lee played Sarne's parents, Matt and Lil Flint. Although Doris was once again playing a cockney matriarch, Lil Flint is a character with more depth, who struggles to come to terms with Matt's firing from his job as a docker and her sense that he has failed in his proper role as male breadwinner. A major problem with the film is that it seems unsure of whether it is a thriller or a social realist drama, a problem that had more to do with Dearden and the script than the performers. The *Daily Mirror's* review is typical: 'Bernard Lee and Doris Hare lend their experienced knowhow to the competent but uninspired plot.'[490] Far more experienced as a stage than a film performer, Doris credited the veteran film actor Lee with helping her understand acting for the camera; an indication of her willingness, even in her late fifties, to learn from other performers. 'In film, Doris,' she remembered him telling her, as he opened his hand, thumb and fingers a few inches apart, and drew it across his eyes, 'it's all here'.

Workmanlike and plodding he may have been, but a couple of years before *A Place to Go*, Dearden had made a successful caper movie with a far stronger script, *The League of Gentlemen*, in which Doris had a cameo role. The film features an embittered ex-army officer, played by Jack Hawkins, who recruits a band of ex-servicemen – all dishonourably discharged – for a bank heist. It begins with a series of brief scenes, each of which portrays the dismal circumstances of one of Hawkins's little band prior to his recruitment by Hawkins. These circumstances primarily involve problematic women, one of whom is played by Doris. I had almost forgotten the film when ten years after her death I was sitting in an art gallery in New York watching Christian Marclay's extraordinary art installation, *The Clock,* a montage of 12,000 moments from different films, each including a shot of a timepiece with a specific time, that lasts 24 hours, the time shown on the screen exactly the same as the actual time when the film is projected. This might sound mind-numbingly boring, but thanks to Marclay's editing genius, the film is mesmerising. And one of Marclay's little snippets is a scene from *The League of Gentlemen*. In a shabby suburban room a woman is serving dinner to her husband and Daddy, her senile father, each seated at a different table. The camera roams over the room with its clock on the mantlepiece. Daddy giggles inanely at the television, the husband is silent, ignoring his wife's relentless, cheerful, banal monologue that never ceases for an instant. The message is clear, here is a man entrapped in a domestic hell. After several hours of viewing I was in a trance-like state, lost in a reverie about the way Marclay's ever shifting montage lays bare the ways in which films construct narratives, when my reverie was interrupted. Just as in Sarajevo, I heard my mother's voice. Even before recognising her on the screen, I recognised her voice. But almost before I had time to register that it was indeed her, Marclay had shifted to another narrative.

An Open Mind

During the years Doris was with the RSC and the National I was a teenager living at home and she and I saw many memorable productions. She never saw 'serious' theatre as superior to more popular fare; she simply appreciated good theatre, and good acting, wherever she found it. In 1964 we saw a production of *Waiting for Godot* at the Royal Court, directed by Anthony Page (assisted by Beckett). Vladimir was played by Nicol Williamson. The production was one that met with Beckett's approval: 'You know there's a touch of genius in that man [Nicol Williamson] somewhere. ... It was a wonderful production.'[491] Doris certainly agreed. Like many people, she did not know what exactly the play was about, but this did not bother her. She responded to its humour and the powerful performances by Williamson, Alfred Lynch (Estragon), Jack McGowan (Lucky), and Paul Curran (Pozzo). A few years later

Doris and I would attend the first night of another Beckett directed by Page with the assistance of Beckett, *Not I* at the Royal Court with Beckett's favourite, Billie Whitelaw. Again, while she would have been hard put to explain the play, she was bowled over by the sheer power of this scream of anguish, and by Whitelaw's performance.

Doris was open to all theatre. In the summer of 1967 we went to a performance by a Japanese Noh company, part of Peter Daubeny's annual World Theatre Season at the Aldwych. An actor to her bones, she recognised the power of this minimalist form of theatre. In later years she often talked about the effect this performance had on her. Her response to new kinds of theatre, so different from the commercial theatre with which she had grown up, was diametrically opposed to the condemnation of her beloved mentor Noël Coward, who 'pronounced Beckett's *Waiting for Godot* "pretentious rubbish without any claim to importance whatsoever".[492]

Across the Cultural Spectrum

To her disappointment Olivier did not renew Doris's contract with the National after the first year, although she accepted this rebuff with good grace. She had lived with the ups and downs of an actor's career her whole life. For the remaining more than two decades of her career she would move between the 'legitimate' and the 'low'. The question of which was superior, the repertory of the RSC and the National, or the low comedy of *Buses*, did not concern her. Each had their audience; the ability to appeal to that audience was what mattered. From her earliest days as Little Doris Hare, Doris was an extraordinarily versatile performer. She sang, she danced, she made people laugh. As an actress (with apologies to Shakespeare), Pinter was not too heavy, nor *Buses* too light. Through all the shifts in British popular culture, Doris always seemed able to adapt, continually reinventing herself. She left the National a well-established character actress, and for the next twenty years she was rarely out of work, appearing in a wide range of genres across the high/low spectrum.

She continued to be cast in more serious roles, often it seems as nurses. In 1967, a year after leaving the National, she had happily returned to the Chichester Festival Theatre, then under the artistic direction of John Clements, playing Nurse Guinness in Bernard

Shaw's Chekhovian *Heartbreak House*, a role she would play twice more: in 1978 on a British-Council-sponsored tour of Latin America, and in London in 1983 in a production with Rex Harrison and Diana Rigg, with whom she had shared a dressing room in their RSC days. In 1977 she played the Nurse in Peter Coe's touring production of *Romeo and Juliet* with Michele Dotrice and Clive Francis as the young lovers. 'Doris Hare', one reviewer noted, 'stands out as a rich warm earth mother, fortunately not too much the clown.'[493]

A record of another of her more serious performances still survives in the BFI archive, and was even uploaded to YouTube in 2020. The play by the Marxist David Mercer was *Shooting the Chandelier*, broadcast in the BBC series Play of the Week in 1977. The play, described by the *New York Times* as 'very special and strangely haunting television',[494] is set in Czechoslovakia in the immediate aftermath of World War II. It explores the confrontation between a Stalinist officer, played by Edward Fox, and his one-time professor, now sunk in alcoholic despair, played by Denholm Elliot. The Russians are about to commandeer a war-damaged aristocratic manor for a future interrogation centre. Living in the house, whose owners were murdered by the Nazis, is their traumatised daughter hovering on the brink of insanity. Doris played Milena, her old nurse trying to protect her. 'Doris Hare's nurse and companion', *The Stage's* reviewer wrote, 'was a self-effacing contribution to a memorable production, a combination of dignity and protectiveness that created a whole person in a few brief appearances and establishes Miss Hare as a much-underrated serious actress.'[495]

Doris was also cast in two plays by Alan Bennett. The 1978 British Council tour paired *Heartbreak House* with Bennett's *Habeas Corpus* with Doris playing Mrs Swabb; in 1984 she played Miss Nisbitt in a revival of *Forty Years On*, Bennett's first play after the success of *Beyond the Fringe*. Bennett is difficult to place on the high/low continuum; he seems to inhabit his own unique niche. 'Greatly undervalued as a political figure', as Fintan O'Toole notes, Bennett is excluded from the tradition of English radical literature by Marxist critics such as Terry Eagleton.[496] As Bennett writes ruefully in his *Diaries* (quoted by O'Toole), 'I am in the pigeon-hole marked "no threat" and did I stab Judi Dench with a pitchfork I

Fig. 41 – Doris the serious actress, 1977. Doris in character as Milena, the nurse and protector of the traumatised sole surviving member of an aristocratic Czechoslovakian family in David Mercer's 1977 television play for BBC2, *Shooting the Chandelier.*

should still be a teddy bear.' Perhaps Bennett's sin in the eyes of intellectuals such as Eagleton, has a lot to do with his plays and other writings being considered too accessible and too popular.

Forty Years On features a school play put on at a failing public school, and includes parodies of icons of British literary culture, such as Oscar Wilde, Virginia Woolf and the Bloomsbury set, and T. E. Lawrence (whom the headmaster confuses with D. H. Lawrence). But although it is light-hearted, described by its author in 1984 as 'as much a revue as a play'[497] – a genre in which Doris was very much at home – there are some serious reflections on twentieth-century British history underlying all the jokes. The revival opened in 1984 at Chichester, before transferring to the West End. Also in this production was a young actor, Stephen Fry. Fry's background could not have been more different than Doris's. A contemporary of Hugh Laurie and Emma Thompson, he was one of the wits of Cambridge University's Footlights club. Together with Laurie and Thompson, he had written and acted in the 1981 Footlights revue, *The Cellar Tapes*, winner of the inaugural Perrier Award. *Forty Years On* was his professional debut. When I began working on this book, he shared his memories of Doris with me.

> I was the youngest member of the cast (aside from the boys who played the pupils of the school in the play) and Doris the oldest. As such we seemed inexorably drawn together. Even when the play opened in Chichester she wanted to be out every night after the performance at a dinner, while the rest of the cast all seemed ready for bed.

Like Bennett, both Fry and Doris understood and appreciated comedy in all its forms. Doris's first venture after leaving Olivier's Old Vic took her back to the low end of the spectrum: a tour in 1966 of *Victorian Music-Hall*, a show devised and directed by John Moffat, described in his *Guardian* obituary as 'a devastatingly clinical and classical stage actor of irreproachable taste and valour',[498] but who also had a passion for traditional music hall. Recreations of music hall were popularised by the long-running BBC series *The Good Old Days* that ran from 1953 to 1983. In truth, this nostalgic programme, with its audience and performers dressed in period costumes, bore little resemblance to actual music halls. As the *Stage* reviewer wrote when Moffat's show was revived a couple of years later, 'Let's face it, the modern version of the Victorian music-hall bears about the same relationship to the original as does the drawing-room version of a joke to its bar-room crudity.' The performer 'who comes nearest to the spirit of the old halls' he felt was Doris. 'Brash, bold, bawdy soubrette, she holds any audience whether it is on a tender, drunken tour of London pubs or, in bulging tights and tunic, "Soldiers of the Queen". '[499]

As a child, Doris had witnessed the dying days of music hall, and she, too, was sceptical of its recreations' claims to authenticity. She was very fond of Moffat, however, and delighted to have an opportunity to sing Marie Lloyd's 'One of the ruins that Cromwell knocked about a bit' and other classics. Draped in veils suspended on long rods she devised a parody of Loie Fuller's famous serpentine dance, reminiscent of the burlesque dances she had done with Henry de Bray at the start of her career. In its review of the original production *The Stage* called for more of 'Doris Hare in ludicrous clothes doing ludicrous acts'.[500]

A few years later she would embody the matriarch of the Butler family in the definitively low *On the Buses*. When the series ended most of the regular cast remained trapped in their *Buses* characters. Reg Varney would complain to his future obituary writer, 'Whatever I did after *On The Buses*, nobody wanted to know about it.'[501] This was not true for Doris, perhaps because she was already well established as a character actor. In 1981, for instance, she was cast as a matriarch from the opposite end of the social scale in the television series, *Diamonds*, a thirteen-part saga about a scheming and fractious diamond merchant family in which Doris played the patriarch's widow.

Comedy and Truth

In 1975, after more than thirty years of marriage, Doris and John divorced. As with any marriage, the reasons for the failure are complex with different narratives depending on who is telling the story. Whatever the reasons, it hit Doris hard and remained a source of sadness for her, but she refused to allow it to affect her work. At the time she was appearing in the farce, *No Sex Please, We're British*, as Eleanor Hunter, a role originally played by her old friend Evelyn Laye, with whom Doris had played such a memorable wartime concert at Scapa Flow. Opening in 1971, and almost uniformly panned by the critics, *No Sex Please* ended up running in London for a record-breaking sixteen years. The evening after her divorce was granted, Doris played her role as usual. She refused to take any medication to cope with the stress; she had tried some once and found it deadened her performance.

Ten years later, soon after the run of *Forty Years On* ended in January 1985, Doris decided to sell her house in Chichester and move to Wales, where my sister Sue was living. Her career began to wind down, but she kept working. In 1988 she even made a brief foray into the new 1980s world of British alternative comedy when Alexei Sayle, a central figure in the alternative comedy movement, cast her as Dolly Goddess of Bleach in his BBC2 show, *Alexei Sayle's Stuff*. And in 1990 she had a cameo as a drinking, gambling nun in a comedy film *Nuns on the Run*, starring Eric Idle and Robbie Coltrane as crooks on the run, hiding out in a convent disguised as nuns.

Her last stage performance was in the farce, *Runs in the Family*, at London's Playhouse Theatre in 1992. *The Stage* wrote of the eighty-seven-year-old Doris's 'delightful' cameo as an aged but 'sprightly mother'.[502] Written by Britain's most prolific author of farces, Ray Cooney, *Runs in the Family* exemplifies the underlying truth of the genre as defined by another of its acknowledged masters, Michael Frayn:

I think farce does capture in a very stylized way something of the difficulty that human beings have in imposing their intentions and plans on the world. People have always got grand ideas about what they are going to do and how the world should be, and inevitably life trips them up and changes everything, and farce is a stylization of that.[503]

My sister and I asked Cooney about his memories of Doris. He told us she fulfilled his need for 'actors who are real and truthful, but who appreciate how to deal with the pauses and things like that'.[504] One performance from earlier in her career stays with me as exemplifying her ability to create, in Cooney's words, 'real and truthful' comic characters: her rendition of the Scottish comedian Will Fyffe's iconic song 'I belong to Glasgow'. She sang it in a one-woman show she devised in 1977 in which she sang some of her old songs, including 'Three White Feathers' and other Coward numbers, and reminisced about her life. Her reminiscences included funny, self-deprecating stories from her time as the child actress Little Doris Hare through all the many ups and down of her long career. At the suggestion of Emlyn Williams, Doris called the show *Hare!*. I saw it when it was part of Cleo Laine and John Dankworth's Wavendon Festival.

There is a family connection to Fyffe. In Chapter 1 I told the story of how Doris's parents found refuge with a portable theatre in Scotland when, just as they were about to open their own portable theatre, the 1898 mine owners' lockout shut down the Welsh coalfields and they had to put their plans on hold. The Scottish portable was run by Will Fyffe's father, John. Will, then aged about thirteen, was a member of the company, and he retained a lifelong affection for the Hare family. Thanks to this long-standing relationship, Doris was granted the rare privilege of incorporating some of his comedy patter when she sang his famous song.

Doris's comedy personas were usually female, but not always. When she was fifteen, she had placed an ad in *The Stage* inviting offers for 'Flappers or Boys',[505] and later, urchins, including the reluctant wartime evacuee in *Lights Up!* (see Fig. 26), would be part of her roster of characters. For 'I belong to Glasgow' she conjured up another male character, adult this time – while wearing an evening dress.

The song, written by Fyffe sometime in the 1920s, is sung by a good-natured drunk, who accepts that he is one of life's foot soldiers, looked down on by the more prosperous, but is far from ground down. He sings:

> I belong to Glasgow, dear old Glasgow town,
> But something's the matter with Glasgow,
> For it's going round and round!
> I'm only a common old workin' lad,
> As anyone here can see,
> But when I get a couple of drinks on a Saturday,
> Glasgow belongs to me![506]

Doris incorporated a little of Fyffe's patter, and some skilful physical comedy: the drunk explains 'I went home by rail', not a train but the railing he uses to support himself as he stumbles along the street. As I watched her, I saw the humour and irrepressible spirit of 'a common old workin' lad' who accepts his lot in a harsh, industrial city but whose spirit and sense of humour are irrepressible as he asserts his right to a bit of fun.

In 1995, after living with my sister for ten years, Doris moved to Denville Hall, a retirement home for actors. She lived there until her death in 2000. During those five years she continued to make the occasional professional appearance. One of her many fund-raising initiatives when she was hosting *Shipmates Ashore* had been for a cinema at Springbok, a retraining centre for men leaving the Merchant Navy. After the war Springbok became a retirement home providing care to seamen, many badly injured in the war. The cinema was later converted into another retirement unit, but a plaque honouring Charles Jarman of the Seamen's union – a great supporter of Doris – had been saved, and was to be reinstalled on the building. Even after half a century, Doris was remembered by many elderly

Fig. 42 – Doris opening the cinema at Springbok Training Centre for Merchant Seamen in 1949. Doris is looking at the plaque honouring Charles Jarman (always her great supporter), the General Secretary of the National Union of Seamen, who had died in 1947.

merchant seamen and she was invited to attend a lunch to mark its installation. She accepted immediately. My sister drove her down. Dressed in one of the many outfits she had for such occasions – her 'opening and shutting outfits' she called them – at ninety-three she still looked every inch the elegant star. A pianist played some of her old songs and she sang them to a hugely appreciative audience.

Within the profession Denville Hall is seen as a place for those who have worked in straight theatre. There is an even older retirement home for variety performers, Brinsworth House, founded in 1911, that describes itself on its website as the 'Old Pros' Paradise'.[507] It is telling that even in retirement the old distinction between the 'legitimate theatre' and popular entertainment persisted. Doris may have spent much of her life in variety and popular entertainment; nonetheless it is fitting that she ended her days in Denville Hall. Its founder, Alfred Denville, was born into a portable theatre family; according to him, his mother was 'one of the smartest and cleverest singing chambermaids of the day'.[508] Indeed, he must be one of the few children who rather than running away to join the theatre, ran away from the theatre, albeit for only a few weeks. In later years he would become a wealthy impresario, running numerous touring companies. He began his career with the portables, however, and as a young man he was one of the founders of the Travelling Theatre Managers' Association of which Doris's parents Bert (shortly before his untimely death) and Kate were original members. In 1947 Doris and Kate attended Denville Hall's celebrity-studded, twenty-first anniversary celebration.[509] Thirty years earlier its founder had been one of the recommenders listed on Bertie's Actors' Orphanage application.

The year before she moved to Denville Hall, at the age of eighty-nine, Doris gave her final performance, playing a tiny role in *Second Best*, a film directed by Chris Menges. The film starred William Hurt as a lonely, unmarried, Welsh village postmaster, who decides to adopt a child. Doris is one of his elderly customers. Shot in the small Welsh town of Knighton, close to the mining communities in which her parents' portable had played a century earlier, and less than seventy miles from Bargoed, the town where she was born, it seems an appropriate end to her career.

ENDNOTES

CHAPTER 1: A FAMILY BUSINESS

[1] Jones, 1895: 11.

[2] Price, 1984: 19. For an account of the portables that relies heavily on the reminiscences of the nineteenth-century portable theatre proprietor Sam Wild (1815-1883), see Josephine Harrop (1989). Ann Featherstone has written about some of the women who ran portable theatres (Featherstone, 2018).

[3] My information on Bargoed's history comes from *Bargoed and Gilfach: A Local History* (Gelligaer Historical Society, 2011).

[4] Orwell, 1989: 83.

[5] http://www.nationalarchives.gov.uk/pathways/census/living/food/beer.htm, accessed 30 April 2020.

[6] Haggar, 1953: 15.

[7] *The Era*, 6 September 1874.

[8] *The Era*, 11 February 1905.

[9] *The Era*, 30 December 1905.

[10] *The Era*, 14 October 1905.

[11] *The Stage*, 14 December 1888.

[12] *Yorkshire Gazette*, 27 February 1892.

[13] *The Stage*, 11 March 1948.

[14] *The Era*, 24 November 1894.

[15] *The Stage*, 28 March 1895.

[16] *The Stage*, 17 January 1895.

[17] *The Stage*, 7 January 1897.

[18] Haggar, 1953: 19.

[19] *The Stage*, 1 April 1897.

[20] *Monmouthshire Beacon*, June, July and August 1905.

[21] *Cardiff Times*, 26 November 1898.

[22] Yorke, 2007: 29.
[23] *The Tredegar, Bargoed and Caerphilly Journal*, 14 November 1907.
[24] *The Stage*, 7 November 1907. A Brins cylinder was part of a limelight burner.
[25] *The Stage*, 16 April 1908.
[26] See Ann Featherstone 2018: 10.

CHAPTER 2: THE WORLD OF THE PORTABLES
[27] Quoted in Price, 1955: 84
[28] Dickens, 1901b: 89.
[29] Quoted in Price, 1955: 66.
[30] Price, 1984: 18.
[31] Price, 1955: 65.
[32] LAC/106/E/29 – 'Rules to be observed by the members of Mrs Latimer's Mammoth Theatre', undated, Theatre Collection, Richard Burton Archives, Swansea University.
[33] Quoted in Price, 1955: 87.
[34] Chekhov, 2004: 96.
[35] Slater, 2009: 31.
[36] Dickens, 1901a: 243.
[37] Price, 1955: 92.
[38] Haggar, 1953: 10.
[39] Quoted in Davis, 2004: 42.
[40] Barnes, 1976: 9.
[41] Yorke, 2007: 30.
[42] Featherstone, 2021.
[43] 'Rules and Regulations with Regard to Theatres', found loose in Monmouthshire County Council Register of Theatrical Licences, 1914-1920, Gwent Archives C/GP/B/66.
[44] Price, 1955: 90.
[45] *Western Mail*, 13 December 1900.
[46] Price, 1955: 87.
[47] Quoted in Price, 1955: 87-88, emphasis in original.
[48] 'A Colliery Manager's Opinion', *South Wales Daily News*, 2 December 1897.
[49] Prosecution of Strolling Players at Brentford', *The Era* 20 November 1870.
[50] *The Era*, 21 July 1894.
[51] *Monmouthshire Beacon*, 14 July 1905.
[52] Price, 1955: 87.
[53] *Monmouthshire Beacon*, 13 August 1909.

54 *Monmouthshire Beacon*, 23 July 1909.

55 Haggar, 1953: 15.

56 *Monmouthshire Beacon*, 30 July 1909.

57 Quoted in Baker, 1978: 40.

58 Melford, 1913: 26-27.

59 *The Era*, 8 September 1888.

60 *The Stage*, 14 September 1905.

61 The basis for the legal decision is cited in letter to *The Stage*, 30 November 1905.

62 *The Stage*, 30 April 1908.

63 *The Stage*, 29 June 1916.

64 LAC/106/E/8-10 – *The Portable Times* (monthly journal published by the Travelling Theatres Managers' Association), 1 June, 10 August and 10 September 1909, Theatre Collection, Richard Burton Archives, Swansea University.

65 *New Tredegar, Bargoed and Caerphilly Journal*, 23 November 1911.

CHAPTER 3: DORIS, THE CHILD ACTRESS

66 Quoted in Auerbach, 1989: 30.

67 Fisch, 2004: 101.

68 Advert published in the *Monmouthshire Beacon* and quoted in Yorke, 2007: 125-6.

69 Quoted in Yorke, 2007: 125.

70 *Monmouthshire Beacon*, 6 August 1909.

71 Fowler, 1937: 176.

72 Gill, 1938: 21.

73 *The Stage*, 3 October 1912; *The Era*, 29 January 1913; *The Era*, 29 March 1913; *The Era*, 24 September 1913.

74 *Tamworth Herald*, 2 May 1914.

75 Powell, Orlando; Harrington, John P.; and Starmer, "Looking For The Love-Light In Your Eyes" (1908). *Vocal Popular Sheet Music Collection.* Score 1027. (https://digitalcommons.library.umaine.edu/mmb-vp/1027.)

76 *The Stage*, 24 December 1914.

77 *The Stage*, 16 December 1915.

78 *The Stage*, 10 June 1915.

79 Cochran, 1945: 121-122.

80 *The Stage*, 10 June 1915.

81 *Arbroath Herald and Advertiser*, 16 July 1915.

82 *The Era*, 14 October 1914.

83 *The Stage*, 9 August 1951.

[84] Williams, 1961: 145.

[85] Williams, 1961: 146.

[86] See for instance, *The Stage*, 6 February 1919.

[87] *The Stage*, 16 January 1919. Buck and Wing is a form of tap dance. What Buck and Schott dance is remains a mystery but I assume it is some kind of tap dance.

[88] Morley, 2016: 17.

[89] Greene, 1937.

[90] Robert Ashby has written a history of the Actors Orphanage (https://actorschildren.org/about-act/our-history/, accessed 13 October 2021).

[91] The Actors' Children's Trust, 1916 Minutes Book of the Actors' Orphanage.

[92] The Actors' Children's Trust, 1916 Minutes Book of the Actors' Orphanage.

[93] *Uxbridge and West Drayton Gazette*, 9 January 1925.

[94] *Coventry Herald*, 7 July 1917.

[95] *Just a Little Pair of Shoes*, British Library Lord Chamberlain's Play Collection LCP 1916/22.

[96] *The Era*, 18 October 1916.

[97] *Gloucester Journal*, 23 December 1916.

[98] 'Don't Put Your Daughter on the Stage, Mrs Worthington': © 1947 (Renewed) Warner/Chappell Music, Ltd., used by permission of Alfred Music.

[99] Morley, 2016: 16.

[100] Morley, 2016: 19.

[101] Quoted in *The Stage*, 25 October 1917. As I noted (p. 12), the family used both Breamer and Breamar.

[102] Quoted in Herr, 1991: 18.

[103] Abbey Theatre website, https://www.abbeytheatre.ie/about/history/, accessed 29 May 2022.

[104] *Irish Independent*, 18 September 1919.

[105] Advert for Keatings Insect Powder, quoted in Higgs, 2014: 32.

[106] Cusack,1972: 24.

[107] Cusack, 1972: 28.

[108] Jerome, 1890: 71.

[109] *The Stage*, 16 December 1920.

CHAPTER 4: OF MELODRAMA AND PERFORMANCE

[110] Mayer, 2004: 146, Mayer's emphasis.

[111] Thompson, 1968: 13.

[112] Quoted in Perry, 2010: 19.

[113] Brooks, 1995: 20.

[114] Brooks, 1995: 89.

[115] Dickens, 1901a: 250.

[116] Booth, 1965: 49.

[117] Morton, Charles, Agency. Collection of American Popular Drama, [Box 28, Folder 9], Special Collections Research Center, University of Chicago Library.

[118] Mayer, 2004: 149.

[119] Brooks, 1995: 20.

[120] Fawkes, 1979: xvi.

[121] Coyne, 1872.

[122] Ascherson, 2021: 5

[123] Brooks, 1995: 20.

[124] Gill, 1938: 13.

[125] Gill, 1938: 40.

[126] Jerome, 2016: 25.

[127] Gill, 1938: 37-38.

[128] Haggar, 1953: 11.

[129] Haggar, 1953: 19.

[130] Gill, 1938: 44.

[131] Melford, 1913: 27-29.

[132] *The Stage*, 2 October 1919.

[133] Quoted in Booth, 1965: 209.

[134] LAC/106/E/8-10 – *The Portable Times* (monthly journal published by the Travelling Theatres Managers' Association), 1 June, 10 August and 10 September 1909, Theatre Collection, Richard Burton Archives, Swansea University. 10 August issue.

[135] Booth, 1991: 126.

[136] The trick, known as 'the seize', is described in Featherstone, 2017.

[137] Brooks, 1995: 47.

[138] Dickens, 1964a: 249-250.

[139] Dickens, 1964b: 324.

[140] Dickens, 1901a: 321.

[141] Dickens, 1901a: 278.

[142] Booth, 1965: 199.

[143] Gill, 1938: 73.

[144] *The Stage*, 2 October 1919.

[145] Quoted in Newey, 2005: 163.

[146] Hoggart, 2009: 5.

[147] Harrison, 2017b: 244-245.

[148] Craig, 1987.

CHAPTER 5: FROM CONCERT PARTY TO CABERET AND REVUE

[149] Harrison, 2017a: 333.

[150] *The Stage*, 27 January 1921.

[151] *The Stage*, 8 March, 1923.

[152] *The Stage*, 26 July 1923.

[153] *The Stage*, 3 June 1926.

[154] Rowntree and Lavers, 1951: 261.

[155] East, 1977: 46.

[156] *The Stage*, 19 April 1917.

[157] *Hull Daily Mail*, 18 June 1918.

[158] *Folkestone, Hythe, Sandgate and Cheriton Herald*, 16 August 1919.

[159] *Birmingham Mail*, 23 January 1917.

[160] *The Stage*, 22 February 1917.

[161] *The Stage*, 30 August 1917.

[162] *The Stage*, 6 January 1921.

[163] *The Stage*, 10 February 1921.

[164] *Derby Daily Telegraph*, 6 December 1921.

[165] Orwell, 2000b: 200-201.

[166] Orwell, 1940.

[167] 18 February 1922.

[168] *Kent and Sussex Courier*, 14 July 1922.

[169] Wilmut, 1985: 17.

[170] *Hampshire Telegraph*, 9 March1923.

[171] Pentelow, 2013, 7.

[172] Quoted in Godbolt, 1984: 32-33.

[173] Rye, 2014: 36.

[174] Parsonage, 2005: 183.

[175] Quoted in Parsonage, 2005: 167.

[176] Quoted in Parsonage, 2005: 168.

[177] Parsonage, 2005: 187.

[178] *The Sportsman*, 6 June 1924.

[179] *The Bystander*, 9 July 1924.

[180] Quoted in MacKenzie, 1986: 8.

[181] *Sunday Post*, 15 June 1924.

[182] *The Era*, 1 October 1924.

[183] All quotes in this paragraph, *The Era*, 1 October 1924.

[184] Orwell, 2000a: 204, 212.

[185] See Said, 1987.

[186] Quoted in Williams, 2002: 411.

[187] Kipling, 2002: 3.

[188] *The Stage*, 9 September 1926.

[189] Press cutting in one of Doris's scrapbooks, newspaper unidentified, nd.

[190] *Nottingham Journal*, 21 December 1926.

[191] *The Stage*, 28 June 1928.

[192] Press cutting in one of Doris's scrapbooks, *Rand Daily Mail*, nd.

[193] *The Stage*, 3 November 1929.

[194] *The Era*, 4 December 1929.

[195] Wilmut, 1985: 123.

[196] *The Tatler*, 26 June 1929.

[197] *The Bystander*, 12 June 1929.

[198] *The Era*, 25 June 1930.

[199] Press cutting in one of Doris's scrapbook, newspaper unidentified, nd.

[200] *Todmorden and District News,* 20 February 1931.

[201] *Brighton and Hove Herald*, 8 November 1930.

[202] *The Tatler*, 26 June 1929.

[203] *The Era*, 21 January 1931.

CHAPTER 6: INTO THE WEST END

[204] From a review of *Hi Diddle Diddle* by Play Bill in the *Illustrated Sporting and Dramatic News*, 12 October 1934.

[205] Mills, 2001: 81.

[206] Mills, 2001: 96.

[207] Mills, 2001: 112.

[208] Mills, 2001:112.

[209] Mills, 2001: 114.

[210] Morley, 2016: 165-166.

[211] Morley, 2016: 167.

[212] *The Bystander*, 28 September 1932.

[213] Quoted in Morley, 2016: 167.

[214] *Brighton and Hove Illustrated Weekly News*, 21 October 1932.

[215] Quoted in Lahr, 1982: 138.

[216] Lahr, 1982: 3.

[217] *The People,*18 September 1932.

[218] Noel Coward Society http://www.noelcowardmusic.com/ncmi/m.html, accessed 25 May 2022.

219 Day, 1998: 157.
220 'Mad About the Boy': © 1932 (Renewed) Warner/Chappell Music, Ltd., used by permission of Alfred Music.
221 'Three White Feathers': © 1939 (Renewed) Warner/Chappell Music, Ltd., used by permission of Alfred Music.
222 *The Era*, 31 August 1932.
223 *The Tatler*, 5 October 1932.
224 *The Era*, 31 August 1932.
225 *Perthshire Advertiser*, 12 August 1933.
226 Quoted in Moore, 2005: 126.
227 *The Bystander*, 17 October 1933.
228 *Illustrated Sporting and Dramatic News*, 12 October1934; *The Sphere*, 13 October 1934.
229 *The Sketch*, 17 October 1934.
230 Morley, 1986: 58.
231 *Birmingham Gazette*, 27 April 1935.
232 *Yorkshire Post*, 27 April 1935.
233 *The Era*, 25 September 1935.
234 *The Era*, 4 May 1932.
235 *The Bystander*, 23 October 1935.
236 *The Era*, 18 May 1932.
237 *The Era*, 17 August 1932.
238 *The Bystander*, 9 October 1935.
239 *The Tatler*, 9 October 1935.
240 Wilmut, 1985: 128.
241 *The Era*, 1 July 1936.
242 Quoted in Day, 1998: 145.
243 'Twentieth Century Blues': © 1931 (Renewed)Warner/Chappell Music, Ltd., used by permission of Alfred Music.
244 Williams, 1973: 266.
245 *Birmingham Gazette*, 25 August 1936.
246 *Evening Dispatch*, 25 August 1936.
247 Harding, 1993: 97.
248 *New York Evening Journal*, 29 September 1936.
249 At that time, the social world of London nightclubs included high society, rich business people, people from the world of show business, members of the underworld, etc. At the same time it was relatively small, so everybody knew everybody else. Tilly Marks (in Doris's telling) was very much a party girl, but she was no beauty. There is a famous family story of a party in New York with a Texas

millionaire Tilly had her eye on and everyone was warned to steer clear. Despite this Betty and millionaire disappeared, Betty surfacing several days later still in the same, although by now slightly soiled, evening dress. Apparently, Tilly did not hold this episode against Betty or the other Hares.

[250] *Daily Express*, 21 July 1937.
[251] Quoted in Day, 1998: 175.
[252] Typewritten memo from scrapbook, 2 March 1937.
[253] Quoted in Laffey, 1989: 62.
[254] *NBC Artists Service Memo*, March 1937.
[255] Scrapbook, unknown publication, 24 March 1937.
[256] Scrapbook, unknown publication, nd.
[257] Quoted in Morley, 1986: 235.
[258] Payn, 1994: 230.
[259] Day, 1998: 195.
[260] 'I Went to a Marvellous Party': © 1938 (Renewed)Warner/Chappell Music, Ltd., used by permission of Alfred Music.
[261] Morley, 2016: 200.
[262] *Dundee Evening News*, 21 July 1937.
[263] *The Stage*, 11 November 1937.
[264] *The Era*, 10 March 1938.
[265] Mills, 2001: 198.
[266] *The Bystander*, 18 May 1938.
[267] Mills, 2001: 199.
[268] Quoted in Mills, 2001: 199.
[269] *The Sketch*, 23 November 1938.
[270] *The Sphere*, 26 November 1938.
[271] *Illustrated London News*, 26 November 1938.
[272] Fawkes, 1979: xiv.
[273] *Liverpool Evening Express*, 17 March 1939.
[274] *Yorkshire Post*, 21 March 1939.

CHAPTER 7: HARE PRODUCTIONS

[275] Dunn, 1998: 62–63.
[276] *Gloucester Citizen*, 8 November, 1927.
[277] *The Stage*, 31 May 1928.
[278] *The Stage*, 26 June 1930.
[279] Rowell and Jackson, 1984: 21.
[280] Gardener, 2004: 74.
[281] Rowell and Jackson, 1984: 73.

[282] Rowell and Jackson, 1984: 176.

[283] Ustinov, 1977: 119.

[284] Dunn, 1998: 8.

[285] Quoted in Lyn Gardener's Theatre Blog in *The Guardian*, https://www.theguardian.com/stage/theatreblog/2012/nov/20/repertory-theatre-ian-mckellen, accessed 23 August 2019.

[286] Quoted in Dunn, 1998: 203–204.

[287] Quoted in Dunn, 1998: 200.

[288] Quoted in Dunn, 1998: 62.

[289] Billington, 2007: 45.

[290] Quoted in Dunn, 1998: 206–207.

[291] Quoted in Dunn, 1998: 192.

[292] Quoted in Dunn, 1998: 207.

[293] *Bucks Herald*, 10 February 1939.

[294] Dunn, 1998: 8.

[295] Dunn, 1998: 178.

[296] *Bucks Herald*, 14 April 1939.

[297] Ustinov, 1977: 119.

[298] *Bucks Herald*, 28 April 1939.

[299] Quoted in Lahr, 1982: 87.

[300] *Bucks Herald*, 5 May 1939.

[301] *Bucks Herald*, 9 February 1940.

[302] *Bucks Herald*, 23 June 1939.

[303] *Bucks Herald*, 14 July 1939.

[304] *Bucks Herald*, 31 March 1939.

CHAPTER 8: RADIO HOSTESS OF THE RED ENSIGN

[305] George Orwell, 2000c: 241.

[306] *Sunday Times*, 9 February 1940.

[307] *The Stage*, 30 November 1939.

[308] Laye, 1958: 147.

[309] Laye, 1958: 148.

[310] Quoted in McIntyre, 1993: 159.

[311] *Lancashire Evening Post*, 11 July 1931.

[312] Quoted in Moore, 2005: 130.

[313] Quoted in Moore, 2005: 130.

[314] *Middlesbrough Daily Gazette*, 5 February 1934.

[315] Stourton, 2017: 52.

[316] *Birmingham Daily Gazette*, 21 May and 18 June 1937.

[317] *Sunderland Daily Echo,* 16 August 1937.

318 *Daily Mail*, 8 May 1936.
319 Curran and Seaton, 2003: 126.
320 Thomas, 1977: 49.
321 Thomas, 1977: 50.
322 Quoted in Crissell, 2002: 59.
323 Williams, 1961: 374.
324 Hobsbawm, 1994: 196.
325 Stourton, 1917: 3.
326 Nicholls, 1996: 74.
327 Quoted in Nicholas, 1996: 75, emphasis in original.
328 Quoted in Baade, 2012: 139.
329 Doris scrapbooks, cutting labelled *The Star*, 1934.
330 *Radio Times*, 24 January 1941: 3.
331 Thomas, 1977: 17.
332 Thomas, 1977: 20.
333 Quoted in Stourton, 2017: 258.
334 Quoted in Thomas, 1977: 95.
335 Thomas, 1977: 100.
336 Thomas, 1977: 100.
337 Thomas, 1977: 101.
338 Thomas, 1977: 107.
339 Thomas, 1977: 102.
340 Lane, 1995: 70.
341 Thomas, 1977: 102.
342 Thomas, 1977: 102-103, my emphasis.
343 Calder, 1992: back cover.
344 Thomas, 1977: 103.
345 Thomas, 1977: 103.
346 Thomas, 1977: 102.
347 Thomas, 1977: 103.
348 Thomas, 1977: 103–104.
349 Lane, 1990: 61.
350 Lane, 1990: 136.
351 *Sunday Pictorial*, 7 January 1945.
352 BBC Written Archives R30/3, 048/2 Outside Broadcasts 'Shipmates Ashore' 1943.
353 BBC Written Archives R30/3, 048/2 Outside Broadcasts 'Shipmates Ashore' 1943.
354 Personal communication, 13 December 2021.
355 Hancock, 1946: 102–103.

[356] Thomas, 1977: 109.

[357] Thomas, 1977: 107.

[358] Interview with Anna Karen, 25 October 2017.

[359] BBC WAC R30/3, 048/1 OBS Shipmates Ashore 1941/1942.

[360] Thomas, *Reynolds Illustrated News*, 13 February 1944.

CHAPTER 9: A WORKING-CLASS MATRIARCH

[361] Hoggart, 2009a: 87.

[362] https://www.radiotimes.com/film/wxmx/holiday-on-the-buses/, accessed 11 October 2019.

[363] Coady, 1970, Coady's emphasis.

[364] Hoggart, 2009b: 353.

[365] Hoggart, 2009b: 349.

[366] Orwell, 2000b: 194.

[367] Orwell, 2000b: 200.

[368] Orwell, 2000b: 194.

[369] Orwell, 2000b: 203.

[370] Hunt, 1998: 126.

[371] *The Guardian*, 24 May 2011.

[372] Bean, 2011: 67.

[373] Orwell, 1940, my emphasis.

[374] Hoggart, 2009a: 117.

[375] *Sunday Pictorial*, 18 August 1940.

[376] *Western Morning News*, 29 August 1940.

[377] Theatre World, Sep 1940.

[378] *The Stage*, 30 November 1939.

[379] Walker, 2009: ix.

[380] Brook, 1972: 78.

[381] Hoggart, 2009a: 115.

[382] *On the Buses*, 'Going Steady', Series 3, Episode 11.

[383] Wolfe, 2003: 62.

[384] Wolfe, 2003: 62.

[385] See, for instance, Hoggart, 2009a: 29.

[386] Orwell, 2009b: 196.

[387] Walker, 2009: 131.

[388] *On the Buses*, 'Going Steady', Series 3, Episode 11.

[389] Orwell, 2009b: 196.

[390] *On the Buses*, 'Aunt Maud', Series 2, Episode 4.

[391] Hunt, 1998: 42.

[392] Quoted in Wilmut, 1985: 121-122, emphasis in original.

[393] Dixon, 2013.

[394] Dixon, 2013.

[395] Quoted in Wilmut, 1985: 123, emphasis in original.

[396] Dixon, 2013, emphasis in original.

[397] *On the Buses,* 'The Inspector's Niece', Series 3, Episode 3.

[398] Enright, 2019: 52.

[399] Orwell, 2009a: 193–194.

[400] Interview with Anna Karen, 25 October 2017.

[401] Wright, 2009: 2.

[402] *Daily Mirror*, 16 December 1972.

[403] Roberts, 2011.

[404] Sheridan, 2011: 20.

[405] Hunt, 1998: 32.

[406] Orwell, 1989: 108

[407] Sheridan, 2011: 125.

[408] Sheridan, 2011: 164–165.

[409] Sheridan, 2011: 181.

[410] *Daily Mirror*, 8 August 1975.

[411] Sheridan, 2011: 125.

[412] Quoted in Hunt, 1998: 115.

CHAPTER 10: THE YEARS OF TRANSITION

[413] Pattie, 2012: 37-38.

[414] David Pattie commenting on W. Somerset Maugham's outraged review of John Osborne's *Look Back in Anger*, Pattie, 2012: 2.

[415] Pattie, 2012: 29.

[416] Quoted in Pattie, 2012: 69.

[417] Alan Bendle, *Manchester Evening News*, 17 April 1945.

[418] The Tatler, 11 July 1945.

[419] *Liverpool Echo*, 21 May 1946.

[420] Samuel, 1998: 82.

[421] Sellar and Yeatman, 1930: 26.

[422] *The Telegraph*, 25 April 1947.

[423] *The Tatler*, 4 June 1947.

[424] *The Stage*, 27 April 1950.

[425] *Daily Mirror*, 8 May 1950.

[426] *Sunday Pictorial*, 7 January 1945.

[427] *The Stage*, 26 August 1948.

[428] Hobson, 1984: 147.

[429] *Daily Herald*, 17 November 1950.

[430] *Birmingham Daily Gazette*, 18 November 1950.

[431] *Yorkshire Evening Post*, 17 July 1953.

[432] *West London Observer*, 25 September 1953.

[433] *The Stage*, 8 September 1955.

[434] Press cutting in one of Doris's scrapbooks, newspaper not identified, undated.

[435] Press cutting in one of Doris's scrapbooks, undated.

[436] See Simon Hoggart's forward to the 2009 edition of *Uses of Literacy* (Hoggart, 2009: vi).

[437] *The Tatler*, 15 October 1958.

[438] Obituary of Doris, *The Guardian*, 31 May 2000.

[439] Laine, 1994: 164.

[440] *Illustrated London News*, 1 July 1982.

[441] *The Guardian*, 27 August 2014.

[442] Quoted in the *Coventry Evening Telegraph*, 1 January 1960.

CHAPTER 11: SERIOUS THEATRE LOOKS FOR ITS ROOTS

[443] Harrison, 2017a: 334.

[444] *The Stage,* 30 November 1939.

[445] Quoted in Thompson, 2016.

[446] Billington, 2001.

[447] https://sounds.bl.uk/related-content/TRANSCRIPTS/024T-1CDR0025456X-ZZZZA0.pdf, accessed 28 November 2019.

[448] Anderson, 2004: 78-79.

[449] Royal Court Theatre website, https://royalcourttheatre.com/about/history/, accessed 29 November 2019.

[450] Hall, 2017: 252.

[451] Williams, 1983: 90.

[452] Williams, 1963: 295.

[453] Billington, 2007: 76.

[454] Billington, 2007: 77.

[455] Knowlson, 1996: 343.

[456] Knowlson, 1996: 71.

[457] Knowlson, 1996: 108.

[458] Adorno, 2000: 231.

[459] Harrison, 2017a: 334.

[460] Quoted in Harrison, 2017c: 209.

[461] Harrison, 2017a: 332-333.

[462] Harrison, 20017d: 494.

[463] Royal Court Theatre Programme for *The Fire Raisers*, University of

Bristol Theatre Collection MM/2/TH/LO/RYC/44.

[464] *Sunday Times*, 24 December 1961.

[465] *The Stage*, 28 December 1961.

[466] http://www.gutenberg.org/files/42523/42523-h/42523-h.htm, accessed 10 June 2020.

[467] Harrison, 2017a: 332.

[468] *The Stage*, 22 March, 1962.

[469] *The Stage*, 12 July 1962.

[470] Beauman, 1982: 249.

[471] *The Guardian*, 26 September 2001.

[472] Beauman, 1982: 271.

[473] *The Guardian*, 12 March, 2002.

[474] *The Stage*, 8 October 1964.

[475] *The Daily Mirror*, 19 June 1964.

[476] *The Stage*, 29 July 1954.

[477] Billington, 2007: 49.

[478] Billington, 2007: 75.

[479] Billington, 2007: 80.

[480] Knowlson, 1996: 529.

[481] Billington, 2007: 391.

[482] Quoted in Billington, 2007: 156.

[483] *The Guardian*, 31 May 2000.

[484] Letter dated June 29th, 1964, author's private collection, reproduced by permission of the trustees of the Sir John Gielgud Charitable Trust.

[485] *The Stage*, 22 October 1964.

[486] West's tribute to Doris in her Ninetieth Birthday Book.

[487] Beauman, 1982: 271.

[488] *The Tatler*, 18 August 1965.

[489] Thomson, 2002: 213.

[490] *Daily Mirror*, 17 April 1964.

[491] Quoted in Knowlson, 1996: 468.

[492] Quoted in Lahr, 1982: 139.

[493] Press cutting from one of Doris's scrapbooks, newspaper unidentified, undated.

[494] *New York Times*, 10 May 1978.

[495] *The Stage*, 3 November 1977.

[496] Fintan O'Toole, 2018: 50.

[497] Bennett: 1984.

[498] *The Guardian*, 16 September 2012.

[499] *The Stage*, 25 April 1968.

500 *The Stage*, 16 June 1966.

501 Anthony Hayward, 'Reg Varney Obituary', *The Independent*, 18 November 2008.

502 *The Stage*, 8 October 1992.

503 Frayn in conversation with Michael Berkeley on BBC Radio 3's *Private Passions*, 1 July 2018.

504 Interview with Ray Cooney (19 September 2017)

505 *The Stage*, 17 February 1921.

506 Will Fyffe can be heard singing 'I belong to Glasgow' with some of the accompanying patter on Youtube (https://www.youtube.com/watch?v=Oww8HXLsxDw, accessed 25 April 2020).

507 http://www.royalvarietycharity.org/brinsworth-house, accessed 8 April 2020.

508 Ashby, 2010:1.

509 *Harrow Observer and Gazette*, 22 May 1947.

BIBLIOGRAPHY

Adorno, Theodor. 2000. *The Adorno Reader* edited by Brian O'Connor. Oxford: Blackwell Publishers Ltd.

Anderson, Lindsay. 2004. 'The Court Style' in *Never Apologise: The Collected Writings Lindsay Anderson* edited by Paul Ryan. London: Plexus, pp. 78-82

Ascherson, Neal. 2021. 'Imperial Narcotic'. *London Review of Books*, Vol. 43, No. 22, 18 November, p. 5

Ashby, Robert. 2010. 'Alfred Denville: Actor, impresario, MP for Newcastle upon Tyne, and founder of Denville Hall'. TACT (The Actors' Children's Trust), June

Auerbach, Nina. 1989. *Ellen Terry: A Player in Her Time*. New York: W. W. Norton and Co.

Baade, Christina L. 2012. *Victory Through Harmony: The BBC and Popular Music in World War II*. Oxford: Oxford University Press

Baker, Michael. 1978. *The Rise of the Victorian Actor* London: Croom Helm

Barnes, John. 1976. *The Beginnings of the Cinema in England*, London: David and Charles

Bean, Richard. 2011. *One Man, Two Guvnors* (Based on *The Servant of Two Masters* by Carlo Goldoni). London: Oberon Books

Beauman, Sally. 1982. *The Royal Shakespeare Company: A History of Ten Decades*. Oxford: Oxford University Press

Bennett, Alan. 1984. 'Lost Jokes', *London Review of Books*, Vol. 6, No. 14, 2 August

Billington, Michael. 2007. *Harold Pinter*. London: Faber and Faber

— 2001. 'Tynan's gift was to make criticism glamorous and sexy', *The Guardian*, 24 September

Booth Michael R. 1965. *English Melodrama*, London: Herbert Jenkins Ltd.

— 1991. *Theatre in the Victorian Age*, Cambridge: Cambridge University Press

Brook, Peter. 1972. *The Empty Space*. Harmondsworth: Pelican Books

Brooks, Peter. 1995 [1976]. *The Melodramatic Imagination: Balzac, Henry James, Melodrama, and the Mode of Excess.* New Haven and London: Yale University Press

Calder, Angus. 1992. *The Myth of the Blitz*. London: Pimlico

Chekhov, Anton. 2004. *Anton Chekhov: A Life in Letters*. Edited by Rosamund Bartlett. Translated by Rosamund Bartlett and Anthony Phillips. London: Penguin Books

Coady, Matthew. 1970. 'TV Matthew Coady's view'. *Daily Mirror*, 28 March

Cochran, Charles B. 1945. *A Showman Looks On*. London: J. M. Dent and Sons

Coyne, J. Stirling. 1872. *The Woman in Red*. London: Thomas Hailes Lacy

Craig, Mike. 1987. *It's a Funny Business says Doris Hare*. BBC Radio 2, 28 October. BBC Sound Archives, B4866/1

Crissell, Andrew. 2002 [2nd Edition]. *An Introductory History of British Broadcast*, London: Routledge

Curran, James, and Jean Seaton. 2003 [6th Edition]. *Power Without Responsibility: The Press, Broadcasting, And New Media In Britain*, London: Routledge

Cusack, Cyril. 1972. 'Every Week a Different School' in *A Paler Shade of Green* by Des Hickey and Gus Smith. London: Leslie Frewin Publishers Ltd, pp. 23-35

Davis, Tracy C. 2004. 'The Show Business Economy and its Discontents' in the *Cambridge Companion to Victorian and Edwardian Theatre*. Edited by Kerry Powell. Cambridge: Cambridge University Press, pp. 36-51

Day, Barry. 1998. *Noël Coward: the Complete Lyrics*, edited and annotated by Barry Day. Woodstock, New York: The Overlook Press

Dickens, Charles. 1901a. *The Life and Adventures of Nickolas Nickleby*. The Authentic Edition. *The Works of Charles Dickens in Twenty-one Volumes*, Vol. V. London: Chapman and Hall

— 1901b. *Sketches by Boz: Illustrative of Every-Day Life and Every-Day People*. The Authentic Edition. *The Works of Charles Dickens in Twenty-one Volumes*, Vol. XVI. London: Chapman and Hall

— 1964a. 'Joe Whelks and the Drama' in *The Dickens Theatrical Reader* edited by Edgar and Eleanor Johnson, Boston and Toronto: Little, Brown and Company, pp. 237-250

— 1964b. 'A Cheap Theatre' in *The Dickens Theatrical Reader* edited by Edgar and Eleanor Johnson, Boston and Toronto: Little, Brown and Company, pp. 320-325

Dixon, Stephen. 2013 'Billy Russell' (http://voices-of-variety.com/billy-russell/ accessed 3 September, 2019)

Dunn, Kate. 1998. *Exit Through the Fireplace: The Great Days of Rep*. London: John Murray

East, John M. 1977. *Max Miller: the Cheeky Chappie*. London: W. H. Allen & Co.

Enright, Anne. 2019. 'Diary'. *London Review of Books*, Vol. 41, No. 20, 24 October, pp. 52-53

Fawkes, Richard. 1979. *Dion Boucicault*, London: Quartet Books Ltd.

Featherstone, Ann. 1917. 'Dickens and the Dog-Drama: the Walworth Dog meets the Uncommercial Traveller' (https://dickenssociety.org/archives/1589, accessed 16 October 2021)

2018. 'A Good Woman of Business: The Female Manager in the Portable Theatre'. *Nineteenth-Century Theatre and Film*, Vol. 45 (1), pp. 9-26

2021. 'Portable theatres and the law' TS. [typescript] Author's private collection

Fisch Audrey. 2004. 'Uncle Tom and Harriet Beecher Stowe in England', *the Cambridge Companion to Harriet Beecher Stowe*. Edited by Cindy Weinstein, pp. 96-112

Fitzpatrick, Percy. 2012 [1907]. *Jock of the Bushveld*. Scotts Valley, California: Createspace Independent Publishing Platform

Fowler, H. W. 1937 [1926]. *A Dictionary of Modern English Usage*. Oxford: The Clarendon Press

Gardner, Viv. 2004. 'Provincial stages, 1900-1934: touring and early repertory theatre' in *The Cambridge History of British Theatre* Vol 3, edited by Baz Kershaw, Cambridge: Cambridge University Press, pp. 60-85

Gelligaer Historical Society. 2011. *Bargoed and Gilfach: A Local History*, Gelligaer Publishing

Gill, Maud. 1938. *See the Players*, Birmingham: George Ronald

Godbolt, Jim. 1985. *A History of Jazz in Britain 1919-1950*, London: Quartet Books

Greene, Graham. 1937. 'Wee Willie Winkie', in *Night and Day*, 28 October

Haggar, Walter. 1953. 'Recollections: Early Days of Show Business with A Portable Theatre in South Wales', *Dock Leaves*, pp. 8-22

Hall, Stuart, with Bill Schwartz. 2017. *Familiar Stranger: A Life Between Two Islands*, Durham and London: Duke University Press

Hancock, H. E. 1946. 'Shipmates Ashore', *Sea Breezes* (New Series) Vol. 1 January – June

Harding, James. 1993. *Emlyn Williams: A Life*. London: Weidenfeld and Nicolson

Harrison, Tony. 2017a. 'Egil and Eagle-Bark' [2001] in Tony Harrison *The Inky Digit of Defiance: Selected Prose 1966-2016*. London: Faber and Faber, pp. 331-372

— 2017b. 'Honorary Doctorate, Athens: Acceptance Speech' [1998] in Tony Harrison *The Inky Digit of Defiance: Selected Prose 1966-2016*. London: Faber and Faber, pp. 241-245

— 2017c. 'The Trackers of Oxyrhynchus' [1989] in Tony Harrison *The Inky Digit of Defiance: Selected Prose 1966-2016*. London: Faber and Faber, pp. 201-222

— 2017d. 'The David Cohen Prize for Literature 2015' in Tony Harrison *The Inky Digit of Defiance: Selected Prose 1966-2016*. London: Faber and Faber, pp. 491-499

Harrop, Josephine. 1989. *Victorian Portable Theatres*. London: Society for Theatre Research

Herr, Cheryl. 1991. *For the Land They Loved: Irish Political Melodramas, 1890-1925*. Syracuse NY: Syracuse University Press

Higgs, Michelle. 2014. *A Visitor's Guide to Victorian England*. Barnsley: Pen and Sword Books Ltd

Hobsbawm, Eric. 1994 *The Age of Extremes: A History of the World 1914-1991*. New York: Pantheon Books

Hobson, Harold. 1984. *Theatre in Britain 1920-1983: A Personal View*. Oxford: Phaidon

Hoggart, Richard. 2009a [1957]. *The Uses of Literacy: Aspects of Working-Class Life*. London: Penguin Books.

— 2009b [1991]. 'Studying Culture: Reflections and Assessments' [originally published in *Media,Culture and Society*, Vol. 13] included in *The Uses of Literacy: Aspects of Working-Class Life*, 2009 edition. London: Penguin Books, pp. 346-364

Jerome, Jerome K. 2016 [1885]. *On the Stage - and Off: the Brief Career of a Would-be Actor*. Lavergne, Tn: Createspace Independent Publishing Platform, 2016 [1885 edition, London: Field and Tuer]

— 1890. *Stage-Land: Curious Habits and Customs of Its Inhabitants*. London: New York: Henry Holt

Jones, Henry Arthur. 1895. *The Renascence of the English Drama: Essays, Lectures, and Fragments Relating to the Modern English Stage, Written and Delivered in the Years 1883-1894*. London: Macmillan and Co. [Reprinted by Leopold Classic Library, nd]

Kipling, Rudyard. 2002 [1901]. *Kim*. Norton critical edition, edited by Zohreh T. Sullivan. New York and London: W. W. Norton & Company

Knowlson, James. 1996. *Damned to Fame: The Life of Samuel Beckett*. New York: Grove Press

Laffey, Bruce. 1989. *Beatrice Lillie: The Funniest Woman in the World*. New York: Wynwood Press

Lahr, John. 1982. *Coward the Playwright*, London: Methuen

Laine, Cleo. 1994. *Cleo*, New York: Simon and Schuster

Lane, Tony. 1990. *The Merchant Seamen's War*, Liverpool: the Bluecoat Press

— 1995. 'The " People's War " At Sea: Class Bureaucracy, Work Discipline And British Merchant Seamen, 1939-1945', *Scottish Labour History* [Journal Of The Scottish Labour History Society], No. 30, pp. 61-86

Laye, Evelyn. 1958. *Boo, to My Friends*. London: Hurst and Blackett

Mayer, Davis. 2004. 'Encountering Melodrama'. *The Cambridge Companion to Victorian and Edwardian Theatre*, edited by Kerry Powell. Cambridge: Cambridge University Press, pp. 145-163

McIntyre, Ian. 1993. *The Expense of Glory: A Life of John Reith*. London: Harper Colllins

Melford, Mark. 1913. *Life in A Booth and Something Else*, London: Hendersons

Mills, John. 2001. *Up in the Clouds, Gentlemen Please*. London: Orion Books Ltd

Moore James Ross. 2005. *André Charlot: The Genius of Intimate Revue*. Jefferson, North Carolina, and London: MacFarland & Company Inc.

Morley, Sheridan. 1986. *The Great Stage Stars: Distinguished Theatrical Careers of the Past and Present*. New York: Facts on File Inc.

2016 [1969]. *A Talent to Amuse: A Life of Noël Coward*. London: Dean Street Press

Newey, Katherine. 2005. *Women's Theatre Writing in Victorian Britain*. London: Macmillan Palgrave

Nicholas, Siân. 1996. *The Echo of War: Home Front Propaganda and the Wartime BBC, 1939-45*, Manchester University Press

Orwell, George. 1940. 'Review of *Applesauce*, Holborn Empire'. *Time and Tide*, September

— 1989 [1937]. *The Road to Wigan Pier*. London: Penguin

— 2000a [1942]. 'Rudyard Kipling' in *George Orwell: Essays*. London: Penguin Books (published in association with Martin Secker and Warburg), pp. 203 – 215

— 2000b [1941]. 'The Art of Donald McGill' in *George Orwell: Essays*. London: Penguin Books (published in association with Martin Secker and Warburg), pp. 193–203

— 2000c [1945]. 'Poetry and the Microphone' in *George Orwell: Essays*. London: Penguin Books (published in association with Martin Secker and Warburg), pp. 239 – 246

O' Toole, Fintan. 2018. 'Backing into the Spotlight', *New York Review of Books*, Vol. 65, No.1, January 18, pp. 50-52

Parsonage, Catherine. 2005. *The Evolution of Jazz in Britain 1880-1935*. Farnham, Surrey: Ashgate Publishing Limited

Pattie, David. 2012. *Modern British Playwriting: the 1950s: Voices, Documents, New Interpretations*. London: Methuen Drama

Payn, Graham with Barry Day. 1994. *My Life with Noël Coward*. New York and London: Applause

Pentelow, Mike. 2013. 'Dancing with Dukes and Dope Dealers', *Fitzrovia News* 128, Spring, p. 7.

Perry, Seamus. 2010. 'Look on the Bright Side' *London Review of Books*, Vol. 32 No. 4, 24 February, pp. 19-22

Price, Cecil. 1955. 'Portable Theatres in Wales, 1843-1914'. *National Library of Wales Journal* ix, pp. 65-92

— 1984. *Professional Theatre in Wales*. University College of Swansea, Printed by Gomer Press, Llandysul, Dyfed

Roberts, Andrew. 2011. 'On the Buses: just like a Ken Loach film'. *The Guardian*, 23 June

Rowell, George and Anthony Jackson. 1984. *The Repertory Movement: A History of Regional Theatre in Britain*. Cambridge: Cambridge University Press

Rowntree, B. and G. R. Lavers. 1951. *English Life and Leisure: A Social Study*, London: Longman, Green and Co.

Rye, Howard. 2014. 'Towards A Black British Jazz: Studies in Acculturation 1860-1935' in *Black British Jazz: Routes, Ownership and Performance*. Edited by Jason Toynbee, Catherine Tackley and Mark Doffman, Farnham, Surrey: Ashgate Publishing Limited, pp. 23-42

Said, Edward. 1987. 'Introduction' to *Kim* by Rudyard Kipling. London and New York: Penguin Classics, pp. 7-46

Samuel, Raphael. 1998. *Island Stories: Unravelling Britain. Theatres of Memory, Vol. II*. Edited by Alison Light with Sally Alexander and Gareth Stedman Jones. London: Verso

Sellar, W. C. and R. J. Yeatman. 1930. *1066 and All That: A Memorable History of England, comprising all the parts you can remember, including 103 Good Things, 5 Bad Kings and 2 Genuine Dates*. London: Methuen and Co. Ltd.

Sheridan, Simon. 2011. *Keeping the British End Up: Four Decades of Saucy Cinema*. London: Titan Books

Slater, Michael. 2009. *Charles Dickens*. New Haven: Yale University Press

Stourton, Edward. 2017. *Auntie's War: The BBC During the Second World War*. London: Doubleday

Thomas, Howard. 1944. 'The BBC Must Come to YOU for Talent'. *Reynolds Illustrated News*, 13 February

— 1977. *With an Independent Air: Encounters during a Lifetime of Broadcasting*. London: Weidenfeld and Nicolson

Thompson, E. P. 1968. *The Making of the English Working Class*. Harmondsworth: Penguin Books

Thompson, Isobel. 2016. '60 years of the Royal Court'. *Vanity Fair*, 20 June

Thomson, David. 2002. *The New Biographical Dictionary of Film*. New York: Alfred A. Knopf

Ustinov, Peter. 1977 *Dear Me*. Boston and Toronto: Little, Brown and Company, Atlantic Monthly Press

Walker, Craig. 2009. *On the Buses: The Complete Story*. Clacton on Sea, Essex: Apex Publishing

Williams, Emlyn. 1961. *George: An Early Autobiography*, London: Hamish Hamilton

— 1973. *Emlyn: An Early Autobiography* 1927-1935 London: The Bodley Head.

Williams, Patrick. 2002. '*Kim* and Orientalism' in Rudyard Kipling 2002 [1901] *Kim*. Norton critical edition, edited by Zohreh T. Sullivan. New York and London: W. W. Norton & Company, pp. 410-425

Williams, Raymond. 1963 [1958]. *Culture and Society 1780-1950*. London: Penguin Books

1983. *Keywords: A Vocabulary of Culture and Society*. London: Fontana Paperbacks.

Wilmut, Roger. 1985. *Kindly Leave the Stage! The Story of Variety 1919-1960*. London: Methuen

Wolfe, Ronald. 2003 [original edition 1992]. *Writing Comedy: A Guide to Scriptwriting for TV, Radio, Film and Stage*. London: Robert Hale

Yorke, Peter. 2007. *William Haggar Fairground Film Maker: Biography of A Pioneer of the Cinema*, Bedlinog: Accent Press

INDEX

(by Paula Clarke Bain)

Note: Index page numbers in italic denote images.
Page numbers in the form 260n103 indicate endnotes.
DH is Doris Hare.